P9-AOJ-472

MORE LIVES THAN ONE

By the same author

THE FORGOTTEN PENINSULA

HUMAN NATURE AND THE HUMAN CONDITION

GRAND CANYON

THE GREAT CHAIN OF LIFE

THE VOICE OF THE DESERT

MEASURE OF MAN

THE DESERT YEAR

MODERNISM IN MODERN DRAMA:
A Definition and an Estimate

THE BEST OF TWO WORLDS

THE TWELVE SEASONS

HENRY DAVID THOREAU

SAMUEL JOHNSON

AMERICAN DRAMA SINCE 1918:
An Informal History

WAS EUROPE A SUCCESS?

EXPERIENCE AND ART:
Some Aspects of the Esthetics of Literature

FIVE MASTERS:
A Study in the Mutation of the Novel

MODERN TEMPER:
A Study and a Confession

EDGAR ALLAN POE:
A Study in Genius

MORE LIVES THAN ONE

Joseph Wood Krutch

1962

William Sloane Associates

NEW YORK

Grateful acknowledgment is made to the writers for permission to quote from letters from James Burnham, Bertrand Russell, and Aldous Huxley. Acknowledgment is made to Ellery Sedgwick, Jr., for permission to quote from a letter from Ellery Sedgwick; to Carlotta Monterey O'Neill for permission to quote from letters from Eugene O'Neill; to John Evans for permission to quote from a letter from Mabel Dodge Luhan; and to the Mercantile-Safe Deposit and Trust Company, Baltimore, Maryland, for permission to quote from a letter from H. L. Mencken.

Acknowledgment is made also to McGraw-Hill Book Company, Inc., for permission to quote briefly from *The Boswell Papers;* to Harcourt, Brace & World, Inc., for permission to quote from *The Modern Temper;* to Houghton Mifflin Company for permission to quote from *The Great Chain of Life;* to *The American Scholar, The Nation,* and *The Saturday Review of Literature* for permission to quote from the writings of Mr. Krutch first published in those periodicals; and to Blanche A. Corin for permission to quote from Mr. Krutch's article, "Defense of the Professional Reviewer," first published in *Theatre Annual, 1943.*

The lyrics of the song, *Heaven Will Protect the Working Girl,* are quoted by special permission of the copyright owner, Jerry Vogel Music Company, Inc., 112 West 44th Street, New York 36, New York.

Published simultaneously in the Dominion of Canada
by George J. McLeod Limited, Toronto.
Manufactured in the United States of America by H. Wolff, New York.
Designed by Marshall Lee.
Library of Congress Catalog Card Number 62-15765

Second printing, October 1962

For Marcelle

Part One

1

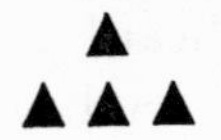

I was born in what was then the quiet little town of Knoxville, Tennessee. I went to its public schools, and afterward until I was twenty-one to the State University whose campus was ten minutes from our home. I then migrated to the graduate school at Columbia University, taught for a while in a small Brooklyn college, did a good deal of journalism, returned to teach at Columbia, and wrote a number of books, some of which enjoyed a modest success.

Does this give me an excuse for writing an autobiography? Certainly not if biographies are an impertinence unless they concern someone whose brave deeds, spectacular misconduct, or profound influence has aroused a curiosity it is a duty to satisfy. On the other hand, novels are often found whose accounts of equally unimportant lives have a certain interest if the telling is honest and the author can fulfill what Thoreau said he required of every writer: namely, "a simple and sincere account of his own life, and not merely what he has heard of other men's lives; some such account as he would send to his kindred in a distant land; for if he has lived sincerely, it must have been in a distant land to me.

At least the prospective reader has now been warned. My life has been interesting only in the sense that most of the time it was interesting to me. And to quote Thoreau again: "I should not talk so much about myself if there were anybody else whom I knew as well." I have lived long enough to remember ways of life which are now history and once well-known persons who are either history also, or nearly forgotten. The automobile, the phonograph, the moving picture, and the radio were all invented within my time and I can remember when I first became aware of them. I have also lived through one of the most rapid revolutions history has ever known in the accepted standards of decency. In my youth women had "bosoms" but not breasts, and "legs" was a dirty word. When they went swimming they wore stockings and men wore shirts with half sleeves. To borrow Franklin P. Adams' fine phrase: "I can remember when an ankle was way uptown."

My birth certificate (of which I once had to get a copy) is dated November 25, 1893, and reads: "White, legitimate, born alive." It is hardly worth noting that the last of these officially certified facts has by now been obvious for so long that it is no longer important, but it is of some significance that the first two, also, are at least less significant than they were in a day when indiscretions of a certain kind were less easily forgiven either the perpetrators or the by-products, and when not to be white was frankly admitted to rightfully entail some pretty severe penalties.

I dare say that though I was probably adolescent before I knew what "legitimate" meant, the fact that the difference between white and black was as fundamental as, well, as the difference between white and black, was one of the very first of the things which I took for granted. Though I can't be sure, I rather think I had graduated from college before it ever occurred to me that separate schools for whites and Negroes was not as much a matter of simple decency as separate toilets for boys and girls. Knoxville was not a community much given to questioning things as they were.

Since I left it in 1915 when I was twenty-one years old I have visited it many times, but for shorter and shorter periods at greater and greater intervals. Each time that I go I see less that I recognize, fewer and fewer people I know. Spiritually as well as physically it seems very little like the town that was once my world, and the last time I was there I met only one person on the street who recognized me.

No doubt most former inhabitants of most towns have had a similar experience, but Knoxville has undergone the effect not only of the forces which have transformed most towns but of some very special ones as well. As the administrative seat of the TVA it grew by leaps and bounds both in population and in the awareness of the world. Then, about fifty miles away, the mysterious community of Oak Ridge sprang into being to become in effect a suburb.

My Knoxville was, on the contrary, a town of only a little more than thirty thousand and carried on with Chattanooga the inevitable running quarrel concerning which was the larger and the more progressive. But only toward the end of my stay there did the new race of Rotarians and "boosters" begin to develop the new techniques of local chauvinism. Such importance as the town had it owed chiefly to the fact that it was the county seat and the home of the University, and, as such, quite superior to less sophisticated towns, especially to Maryville to which visiting comic actors always made dutiful, slighting reference under instruction from the local stage manager.

The farmers of the surrounding country drove their wagons in at night, slept in them in the public square, and were ready the next morning individually to offer for sale a few bushels of green beans, a few pounds of homemade butter, a few dressed chickens, and a dishpan of lye hominy covered with a piece of cheesecloth to keep it moist. I can still see my father moving from wagon to wagon, snapping the beans to discover which were freshest, bending the breastbones of the chickens to find the youngest.

Many terms, the very origin of which had probably been forgotten, were still universally used. The train which was ultimately to carry me away to New York was always referred to as "the Vestibule"—a survival, I suppose, from the days when only the most important trains had their rear platforms enclosed. A short line over which a sort of donkey engine pulled a few cars to a community some five miles away was "the dummy" and the subject of what may well have been, after Mother Goose, the first specimen of the poetic art I ever learned by heart. I supposed at the time that it had been composed by a local bard but it was actually, I believe, widely current and merely adapted to each local scene by a change of the two proper names:

Some folks say that the Dummy won't run
But I done seen what the Dummy's done done.
It left Fountain City at half-past one
And got into Knoxville at the settin' of the sun.

7

Probably few still living inhabitants of Knoxville now remember the odd terminology which was once taken for granted, but in the hills not far away so many Seventeenth Century words still linger that a local physician repeated to me only a few years ago the reply given by a patient who was asked the origin of a badly swollen ankle: "Well, Doc, I just hunkered down, it creeled, and then it poned up 'til I thought hit was agoin' to beal." All but one of the strange words is, I believe, to be found in large dictionaries. Translation: "I squatted on my heel, it twisted, and swelled up so much I thought it might ulcerate."

Social distinctions in Knoxville were real enough and already based rather more on wealth than on family, but at least everyone knew, and spoke to, nearly everyone else. Very few boys were sent away to preparatory schools and only comparatively few from the richest or most pretentious families attended either the one private school for boys or the corresponding one for girls. The latter was called with fine Victorian effect, "The East Tennessee Female Institute." Most of us went to the public schools where the chief distinction between the more and the less respectable group was that by the middle of May members of the less respectable began to appear barefooted in the classroom. We others waited until we could ceremoniously remove our shoes and stockings immediately on returning home after the last day of classes. None except the children of self-consciously superior parents put shoes on again except for dress-up occasions, especially Sundays.

Another odd social distinction, then probably valid in most communities and, for all I know, still prevalent, concerned the acceptable ways in which a boy might earn money. Only ragamuffins sold newspapers in the center of town. But to have a "route" along which papers were delivered daily was more than permissible. It was, indeed, something to be proud of. If all of this suggests a Norman Rockwell magazine cover the fact is that these so popular works of art do actually represent the United States of half a century ago more truly than they do even country or small-town life today.

My mother was born in Brooklyn, the daughter of a Joseph Wood who had come from England as a young man, married in this country a Grey of Scotch descent, and moved to Tennessee primarily, I have always suspected, that he might employ slave labor in the tannery he established in Knoxville. I remember him only very dimly as a rather stern patriarch with a long white beard who had begot twelve children of whom a surprising number lived to a very advanced age. He was well known as "a Southern sympathizer" and for that I know he paid a considerable penalty. East Tennessee was predominately Union in its sympathies and he chose the wrong side. One of my childhood memories is of a large portfolio containing many thousands of dollars in Confederate currency—which was, alas, no longer current. I still have a gold-headed cane presented to him on his golden wedding and a silver medal awarded at the Columbian Exposition for the excellence of his leather. My mother lived to be past ninety-two and one of her brothers held on until he was only a few months short of one hundred.

My father was the son of a North German musician—his real name was Krützsch—who came to this country at the time of the great Forty-eight migration, bringing with him a sixteen-year-old bride. He was dead long before I was born and his widow, who lived until I was in college, was the only one of my grandparents who had any influence upon me. That influence was, I think, very considerable.

Throughout my childhood and adolescence I was aware

of her chiefly as what could be called a typical German grandmother, and I suspect that it was her example which taught me the interest in animals and plants which was later to become a major concern. She raised canaries, pampered a parrot and a pug dog, and assiduously tended a small greenhouse in the yard of her modest home overlooking a magnificent bend in the Tennessee River. A Sunday afternoon visit to Grossmother was an excursion into an atmosphere quite different from that of my own more conventional home.

As I came gradually to realize when I grew older, she was much more than merely a German grandmother. She was also an intelligent, strong-minded woman of independent convictions who had brought into the provincial atmosphere of Knoxville and had managed to maintain, even in the reduced circumstances of a widow without financial resources, something of the sophisticated and aristocratic disregard of convention acquired from the world into which she had been born. Grossmother, whose maiden name was Von Wiersing, was the daughter of the younger son of a minor noble family attached to the provincial court of Saxe-Coburg, which enjoyed rather more importance than it would have otherwise from the fact that it gave to Victorian England its Prince Albert. She could have remembered all this only dimly as something of another world and another life, but it helped mold a character which made her respected in a community to whose conventions she never completely conformed.

My father, born in 1856 (the same year as Bernard Shaw!), was the youngest of her three sons and one daughter. For some reason he was the responsible head of the family when it was threatened with real poverty in the days after the Civil War. Perhaps because this burden fell upon him while he was still an adolescent he was the most conventional of the family and one whose interests hardly extended beyond his business (at which he was only moderately successful), his home, and his children.

By the time I was old enough to understand such things I realized that his position was in the very middle of the middle class and (a little later) that his mother, two brothers, and sister were anomalies in that they were among the few Knoxville members of the classless class of artists and mild Bohemians who were accepted and even respected by those financially and socially above them. My own mother was the first to comment to me on the remarkable fact that so conventional a community as Knoxville regarded Grossmother with entire respect although she had been twice divorced and had been heard to say, "If I were a man there is not a woman alive I would marry."

Since it is probable that, to a certain extent, my early nonconformist interests, opinions, and habits were influenced and developed by Grossmother and her children, some account of these relatives is essential.

All were what was called "artistic" when such an aberration was not common, but only one actually achieved even a small reputation other than local. Uncle Oskar, the only one to leave Knoxville, was a teacher of the piano in Washington, D.C., and just competent enough as a performer to have been invited to play at the White House.

Aunt Lou, also a "music teacher," was for many years the most popular in a city certainly not conspicuously musical. Neither she nor either of her two "artistic" brothers married, and her real distinction was a certain independence of character not usual in small-town music teachers. For one thing she was a resolute camper in an age when ladies were still supposed to be timid. For another, her Bohemianism included a fine scorn for the conventions of dress, and it was characteristic of her attitude that she rather liked to hear a more affluent friend, whom she had once accompanied to France, tell what had happened when the two of them stopped at the Bon Marché to get a straw hat for some expedition into the country. Aunt Lou snatched one marked "three francs" from an outside table but, seeing another for only two, threw down the first and rushed off with the other on her head. A block away she was caught up with by a frantic salesman who pointed to two holes in the crown of the hat and exclaimed, "But, Madame, that one is for a horse!"

Uncle Charlie I save for the last because, though he was the mildest man I ever knew, he was also the most original of the three relatives and the only one who had what might be called a secret life. By profession he was the town's best known portrait photographer though he was so unaggressive he usually worked for someone else. By avocation he was organist in the less fashionable of the two Episcopal churches and a painter of watercolors who devoted himself exclusively to landscapes of the Great Smoky Mountains. No one ever knew what he really thought about anything for he agreed pleasantly with what anybody said on any subject whatsoever. Though he lived into his eighties, the only occasion on which he was ever known to put his foot down was the time he won a raging battle with Knoxville's most respected violinist who outraged his sense of propriety by insisting that she would "render" a solo version of the Intermezzo from *Cavalleria Rusticana* in the course of a church service.

What his religious faith was or, indeed, whether or not he actually had any, no one will ever know, but he was deeply "churchy" and always a guest at the annual mid-day dinner where the Bishop was overfed. The fact that this dignitary was, during most of my boyhood, the moderately eminent Episcopalian Bishop Gailor whose round rosy countenance was less suggestive of spirituality than of some medieval caricature of the too-well fed ecclesiastic did not interfere with the awe with which Uncle Charlie regarded the official representative of what was, I suspect, the only institution he respected. Invariably Uncle Charlie came to our house for Sunday night supper and I never forgot the evening when, after a long and thoughtful pause, he said: "I sat next to the Bishop at noon. He said that he was feeling slightly bilious and thought he would take a dose of calomel." After another pause he added: "You know it had somehow never occurred to me that a *bishop* would take calomel."

So far as I know, no one in Knoxville had ever seen Uncle Charlie take a drink but everyone knew that during at least the last twenty or thirty years of his life he was never quite sober. Every summer he disappeared for a month or more into the Smokies where he lived with a family of mountaineers in one of the isolated valleys far beyond the reach of the logging train which alone connected what is now the Appalachian National Park with the outside world. There he shared his hosts' beans and bacon and, I have no doubt, partook moderately of their moonshine. From these expeditions he returned with sketches to be elaborated into the vistas of peaks and clouds of which he must have painted a hundred or more. His technique was limited and his reputation never got beyond East Tennessee but he did have a feeling for his subject and there was hardly a Knoxville family with any pretentions to smartness which did not own at least one of his productions. Many of them, I am sure, still hold places of honor in "the best homes," as one does also in the University library.

Uncle Charlie and Aunt Lou lived with Grossmother

until she died and they continued to occupy her house as long as they lived. It was Aunt Lou herself who, late in life, finally revealed the existence of her brother's secret. Every Thursday morning for at least twenty years he had said just before leaving the house, "Oh, by the way, Lou, I won't be home for dinner tonight." Never did he hint what his engagement was or even that the formula had been repeated once a week without fail year after year. I should like to think that this so inoffensive a man enjoyed a secret sin, or at least had his mild little fling on schedule. But I am very much afraid that Thursday nights were as innocent as all the others. Probably he merely had a standing engagement with some very humble family and did not want to risk so much as an inaudible sniff from his sister who might be Bohemian but would also make a distinction between Bohemianism and lower middle-class dullness.

Lacking the example of such mild independence of behavior as that furnished by my grandmother and three of her children, I might have been even more molded than I was into the uneventful pattern of Knoxville existence, where conformity was not the conscious thing it has since become but merely taken for granted as the almost inevitable effect of a slow-moving community where no one thought of radical change, desirable or undesirable, because it was assumed that things would go on much as they always had. Members of the new generation would grow up to marry neighbors, follow in their father's footsteps, and quite probably go on living in the houses where they had been born.

Of the influence of my remarkably understanding, sympathetic, loving, and sensibly indulgent parents and of my two brothers I shall have to speak presently, but at the moment I cannot help stressing the extent to which my parents fitted the pattern. They were well enough educated by the modest standards of the community but "intellectual ferment" was hardly part of its prevailing atmosphere. The whole of Europe and America was living in the afterglow of Nineteenth Century complacency and awareness of such preliminary stirrings of doubt, dissatisfaction, and anxieties as affected intellectual centers had hardly reached Knoxville despite the presence of the quietly traditional state university. Those who read current books read Harold McGrath, George Barr McCutcheon, Owen Wister, John Fox, Jr., and perhaps, if they were unusually intellectual, the novelist Winston Churchill. But it was only by accident and after I had got into college that I so much as heard of H. G. Wells and Bernard Shaw.

Few if any Knoxville children were ever "overstimulated." The public school system (and I believe the two private schools also) were so traditional that they had all but forgotten what the tradition was supposed to be about. We did learn to read and write, as many present-day pupils do not, and we were exposed to those "classics" which had somehow become entrenched in the schools: Two plays of Shakespeare, Milton's *Minor Poems, Sir Roger de Coverley,* and *Silas Marner*. I thought they all were unmitigated bores as did, I suspect, my teacher. Yet I did voluntarily learn by heart a few lines of Milton and I well remember that the first impulse I ever had to write anything was in imitation of the Sir Roger de Coverley papers. In fact, I think it would not be stretching a point to say that the character of the Spectator, who had embraced observation and reporting as his role in life, first made that seem to me an attractive one, and I may have been at that moment first encouraged towards the "detachment," rather than the "commitment," for which I have often been blamed in our own more stirring times.

Except that we were exposed—though no more than exposed—to a few enduring works of literature instead of being allowed, as in some modern schools, to write "reports" on whatever trash we happened to favor, the school system was about as bad as possible. In these pre-Deweyian days no one had ever heard of "progressive methods," and it was only about the time when I went to college that Professors of Education began to appear there. One of the principal functions of the school system was to provide a livelihood for worthy spinsters and widows who might otherwise have become a charge upon the community. They got their jobs exclusively on the basis of need and respectability, and they were assigned to whatever grade in the elementary school or to whatever subject in the high school happened to offer a vacancy at the moment.

The result was not always happy either for teacher or pupil. The former were often nervous wrecks as a result of their brave struggle to do something for which they had neither gift nor preparation. The latter often got a rather odd idea of the nature of learning. Under my high school teacher of history I memorized a textbook, paragraph by paragraph, each of which I promptly forgot when, for the next day, I memorized the succeeding paragraphs. I was taught physics by an elderly spinster who had not the faintest idea what a scientific principle was and who, to my great delight but also perhaps to the detriment of my modesty, used to call upon me to explain Archimedes' Law or to perform one of the experiments which, in her hands, never came off, partly because she didn't know what they were supposed to demonstrate. The Latin teacher, a rather pathetic spinster, was the only member of the high school faculty who had a genuine interest, however slight, in her subject and she was just sufficiently concerned with its declining popularity to say to me when I announced that I was dropping it in my senior year: "Et tu, Brute!" Yet she taught Latin not as a language, however dead, but as a sort of cryptogram we were expected to solve with the aid of the vocabulary at the back of the book and the useful footnotes explaining the more unusual constructions.

Looking back I can see that even as a child I was very mildly maverick and dimly aware of the fact. I was "a good student" only by the unexacting standards of the schools, but I was more interested in various hobbies than in games; solitary rather than gregarious and with standards of value not quite those most current. Still, I was certainly no prodigy and only occasionally read books of either literature or instruction slightly above the level of my fellows.

It was the influence of my home, my parents, and of the younger of my brothers rather than grammar or high school which encouraged my growth in the direction it was to take. Yet the family atmosphere was unusual only in that it was peaceful, secure, and sympathetically tolerant. My parents were intelligent but neither especially intellectual or artistic. Nor had they ever heard of "tender loving care" or of the necessity for "giving their children love." Nevertheless, they were loving and indulgent without fuss or sentimentality. I doubt that they would have been resolutely "permissive" had there been occasion to be so, but I was tractable and so anxious to please that "discipline" was not called for.

I cannot remember ever having been formally "punished," either corporally or otherwise, except on the one and only occasion when a hairbrush was mildly applied to my rear after I had been discovered in the basement at about age six conducting an anatomical investigation upon the person of a co-operative young girl. My mother was conventional enough to regard this as quite serious and it provoked from her the inevitable question which no child ever answers: "Whatever possessed you?" I might have replied, "Why, Nature and a healthy curiosity," but of course I didn't.

Neither at home nor in school did I receive any "sex instruction" though I learned some of the more obvious facts in the place which one of Havelock Ellis's correspondents called the best, namely, "in the gutter." I am not aware that this did me any harm and I have always suspected that though formal "sex education" may be conducive to "a satisfactory sexual adjustment" in later life it is not a very useful preparation for either passion or love.

Such fears, anxieties, doubts, and obsessions as I suffered from (and they were not a few), as well as such intellectual curiosities as awoke in me, were nearly all, so far as I am aware, spontaneous growths. That is probably one of the reasons why I have always been inclined to doubt the great importance now commonly ascribed to infant and child "conditionings," good or bad, and why I believe that the direction in which the twig is bent counts for less than its native tendency to incline one way or another.

St. Augustine and Freud both noted the fact that babies are cast howling upon the shores of this world. One thought it was because they bring with them the sin of Adam; the other because they resent being born at all. According to Freud, birth is the first "trauma," and our subsequent psychic history is largely a matter of the successive traumas we suffer. Things—wounding things—happen *to* us; and to these wounds we "react."

Many of the biographies and autobiographies written

during the last three decades show how generally this view is accepted, even by those not consciously Freudian. Usually we are not told how a light suddenly broke on the way to some Damascus, but how the hero's personality began to take shape when he was beaten by a cruel parent, mistreated at school, seduced by a playmate, fired from his first job, or sent to reform school by authorities who didn't understand that he was "just mixed-up."

Perhaps Rousseau started the fashion when he described the delicious pleasure discovered in that fateful spanking on his bare behind which made him, he thought, what he was ever after to be. Even intellectuals seem frequently to go on the assumption that the biographer or autobiographer in search of a clue or a key should look not for an idea or a thought, but for the traumatic experience of which the thought (if any) was a by-product. The frank teller of his own story does not say that while listening to the barefoot friars singing in the Forum he was suddenly inspired to write the story of the Decline and Fall. He is more likely to tell us how the bully around the corner knocked off his cap or stole his lollipop, and how, in that moment, was born his lifelong interest in juvenile delinquency.

How much of all this, I wonder, is mere convention? How many of us if left to ourselves would conclude from self-examination that the most significant moments in our lives were not those when we suffered some trauma but those when some idea, some conviction, or some ambition came to us either out of the blue or only tangentially related to any external event?

Possibly, if I were determined to follow fashion, I could make more than should be made of certain minor happenings in my own life, though admittedly they cannot be wholly insignificant if I still remember them. I do, for instance, still remember from my first year in elementary school the vivid sense of injustice generated when a bad-tempered teacher ran angrily through the whole class getting a wrong answer to the same question and then, when she finally got to me, was so exasperated that she did not even listen to the right one. Did this really make me self-righteous, cocksure, and convinced that the world was doing me wrong? If I actually am all this, did I become so at that moment, or do I remember the moment because I was already self-righteous and convinced that the world was not doing me justice?

I can also remember—as who cannot?—early glimpses into the forbidden world of sex in addition to that provided by the incident already mentioned. Did I not once teach another neighborhood girl of my own age an obscene and witless limerick? Did she not, after receiving it favorably, then repeat it to her mother, thus giving me a first demonstration of female treachery which might have led me to distrust all women forever after? Had I turned into a misogynist or a sex maniac some of my traumas might be cited as causative factors, but I doubt that they were to me, or to most children, more serious than the physical scratches and bruises no child escapes.

When I ask myself in what significant ways I can remember a child really father to the man, most memories turn out to be connected with thoughts I found myself thinking or attitudes I found myself taking rather than with "traumatic incidents." No external event of my pre-adolescent years is more vivid than a remark I remember making on the way home from executing some commission for my mother. Somewhere, probably at the Sunday School I still attended because it was expected of me, I had heard a reference to the time when the lion and the lamb would lie down together and I said to myself, or rather to some imaginary antagonist, "If the lion ever tries it he will starve to death." This was not, I fear, a very polished epigram, but I have never forgotten the moment when it seemed as significant as any remark which could possibly be made and it furnished the starting point for an essential part of all the thoughts about the universe I have ever had since.

No one who had grasped firmly what it implied was likely to succumb to any form of utopianism. It was years later that I first met the phrase "a contingent universe," but when I did meet it I knew at once what it meant and hardly needed to digest it. I was already sure that certain characteristics of the cosmos in which we live are inherent in it; that we are part of "a world we never made"—and cannot entirely remake.

When first I heard of Darwin and his theories they seemed to me only a wonderfully rich elaboration of my fable of the lion and the lamb. I took my stand with Science against Religion, because Science seemed to be describing the contingencies while Religion shut its foolish eyes upon them. It was much much later before the fact that I disliked some of these contingencies, the very fact that a child of this universe *can* dislike them, struck me as no less significant than the contingencies themselves.

But neither the contingency of the universe nor a certain concept of original sin that the two implied did more to make me whatever I am than another idea which burst upon me on the day when I first really *saw* a Royal Baking Powder can—or rather, to be perfectly exact, the picture of such a can which used to appear regularly in a colored advertisement on the back cover of the old *Cosmopolitan.* A little later I was to read Shaw's *Androcles and the Lion* in *Everybody's Magazine,* and that was important too. But not so important as the baking powder can.

Perhaps I should be ashamed to mention it had not diligent inquiry convinced me that many others had the same experience and that the effect of that particular advertisement may have done more than *McGuffey's Readers* to mold the American intellectual. Some, to be sure, missed the baking powder and were stopped in their tracks by Quaker Oats instead. But the difference is unimportant, and I have sometimes met ready comprehension when I asked without preliminaries: "Were you a Baking Powder man or a Quaker Oats man?"

For the benefit of those who were blind to these advertisements, I had better explain.

The can and the package were both adorned with pictures of the container itself. Therefore, the advertisements included a picture of a picture. And that picture must of necessity include a picture, of a picture, of a picture. In practice, of course, the series finally ended with a dot. But it shouldn't have. And thus I became simultaneously aware of two stupendous facts. Infinity can be neither represented nor imagined, but logically it must exist. The brain reels, and it is a painful experience. But here at least is a trauma which must be suffered before any human being can become fully human. Perhaps if I were psychoanalyzed it would be discovered that some forgotten triviality had a greater effect upon my life. But I doubt it.

Twig-bending has always seemed to me a process of which the results are far from certain, not only because twigs have their own stubborn directions but also because human twigs, at least, often reveal a perverse tendency to insist upon growing in the direction opposite to that to which they have been forcibly inclined. In my own case I well remember one of the few occasions during which I responded to being preached at and it was an occasion when the result was the exact opposite of what the preacher hoped for.

When I was about twelve I was taken to hear the Bishop—the same who most inappropriately took calomel—during his annual visitation. His subject was Herbert Spencer, of whom I had never heard, but of whom the Bishop disapproved so eloquently that I sought Spencer's *Synthetic Philosophy* at the library the very next day. I don't think I ever got all the way through even the first volume, but I was so impressed by the introductory discourse on "The Knowable and the Unknowable" that on this basis alone I was for some years, say from twelve to sixteen, a devout Spencerian. It was not until quite a bit later that I began to be aware of a catch: Much of the Unknowable is so much more important than most of the Knowable that even guesses about it are more interesting and more fateful than positive knowledge about the rest. What, for instance, one finds oneself believing about the nature of the beautiful and the good does more to determine conduct, as well as the whole tenor and color of existence, than all one can know about the stage history of *Hamlet* or the function of hormones.

To this day I am more sympathetic toward those who recognize the two realms, the Knowable and the Unknowable, than to those who maintain that by hook or by crook—by induction or deduction, science or metaphysics, logic or revelation—everything is knowable. And I suppose it is because I did continue to accept the distinction without renouncing my interest in either category that I became a minor man of letters instead of the scientist I was for some time resolved to be. After all, it is with the Unknowable, not the Knowable, that literature is principally concerned—at least what is left of literature when one has subtracted the physiology, sociology, psychology, et cetera, with which it has increasingly got itself involved. Its conclusions about life may carry conviction, but they are never demonstrably true.

I have no nostalgia for my childhood and I do not idealize the kind of lives Knoxvillians lived in my day. Adults and children alike were unadventurous both physically and intellectually. Their world was thoroughly provincial and lacked stimulation as well as excitement. But I cannot help remembering at the same time how relatively free it was from both the public and the private pressures, tensions, and anxieties of today. Civilization did not seem to be threatened, and the pattern of individual lives was more firmly established. We are now accustomed to see our world as a concatenation of "problems"; few living before World War I took any such view of it. Most people were less anxious to keep up with the Joneses and had no installment payments to meet. They "entertained" seldom, spent much more time alone at home with their own families and, except for the professional theater, had few public amusements. But there were also many fewer demands on their time.

Children were expected to amuse themselves and did not have to be provided with "something to do." Since they walked to school their mothers did not spend hours a day transporting them to classes or to the scene of extracurricular activities. Neither was it expected that they would attend meetings of the P.T.A. or the League of Women Voters. I don't think I ever heard this or that required as "a civic duty," and "being a good citizen" was little more than a matter of obeying the law.

For all these reasons middle-class people had more leisure, or at least lived in a more leisurely fashion, than they do today. But there was also another, perhaps even more important, reason why they could do so, and it has to be faced. Though they had comparatively few of what we call "labor-saving devices" they had the greatest labor-saving device of all, namely servants—almost invariably black.

During my childhood only a few of the wealthiest "kept a carriage." But because domestic servants were paid so little—a few dollars a week—everyone not actually poverty-stricken had at least one as a matter of course. My own family never dreamed of aspiring to a carriage but I had a colored nurse and my mother took "someone in the kitchen" for granted. Today it is precisely the other way around. A family must be poor indeed if it does not own an automobile while many who belong definitely to the class called "rich" run their houses with no more than part-time servants.

It is often remarked that the Good Life of the Athenian citizen had slavery as its necessary condition. Similarly, the merely comfortable life of my Knoxville was based upon a less harsh version of the same institution. Tennessee was not the deep south, but neither I nor anyone else ever thought of "a Negro problem" or supposed that the modus vivendi which seemed accepted without reservation by both groups need ever be disturbed. If any lynchings occurred or if, indeed, any overt acts of violence disturbed the peace of "race relations" I do not remember them. Whether or not the Negroes actually believed themselves to be natural inferiors I do not know, but they accepted with apparent cheerfulness and often with humor the assumption that they were.

What is now called "Uncle Tomism" was very nearly

universal. Somehow I have always remembered as typical a little incident which occurred when, as an adolescent, I stopped near the market square to have my shoes shined by a peripatetic Negro youth. A policeman passed by and the boy, perhaps my own age, looked up with a cheery, "Mornin', Captain." Then after the policeman had passed he said to me with a conspiratorial grin: "He's only a lieutenant but I always ups 'em one."

In those days "white supremacy" worked, for the most part, smoothly, however wrong it may have been. And when I read today the hysterical protests against Negro jokes, Jewish jokes, and other "stereotypes" as it is fashionable to call them, I am reminded of a curious cultural phenomenon characteristic of Knoxville in my day and very revealing of the attitude of the Negroes themselves.

In the one legitimate theater Negroes were admitted only to the third or "peanut gallery" which was usually empty or nearly so. But every September the theatrical season was opened by Al G. Field's Minstrels, a company of white performers who blacked their faces to sing, dance, and crack jokes, all in terms of a "stereotype." On that night the peanut gallery was always full of Negroes howling with delight. Far from considering the performance an insult, they regarded it as a compliment. This was the one day of the year when they and their culture were given formal recognition. And though it may be true, as many will no doubt insist, that the fact merely demonstrates the completeness of the degradation which they had accepted, they certainly did not themselves see it that way. In 1962 Al G. Field's Minstrels would probably seem naïve to the whites, offensive to the colored people.

Like the white citizens of today's Knoxville, the children of these Negroes have lost something as well as gained something. For them, too, life has now become a series of problems. They have exchanged a possibly degrading acceptance of things as they are for anxiety, anger and a corroding sense of wrong. Because of them tomorrow may be better; today is, in some ways, worse.

2

▲
▲▲▲

If any of my contemporaries had liked school they would not have dared to admit it. I doubt that any of them did, and I certainly hated it from the first day I quitted the shelter of home for what seemed to me the terrifying irascibility of the first-grade teacher at the Bell House—so called because the older building which had once stood on the same site had boasted a school bell.

The dislike of school was, I think, completely unqualified until I began to take a certain interest in some high school courses. In the second or third grade I was required to learn Longfellow's verses about the youth who carried a banner with a strange device and when I was asked at home if I knew what "Excelsior" meant I replied with perfect assurance: "Of course. It's that stuff you pack things with." At that age I would no doubt have found it easier than I sometimes do now to accept the intentional irrelevancies of some modern poems with their similitudes where there is no similarity. Could it be that Longfellow was anticipating the more recent cult of ambiguity and was slyly suggesting that idealism is mere stuffing?

Such intellectual interests as I slowly developed and such reading as I did had no connection with any school work. My mother remembers that before I had learned to read I used to follow her about the house, and that as soon as she happened to sit down I would thrust into her hands some such book as *The Water-babies* or Hans Christian Andersen, my special favorites. Since I was later to become a somewhat iconoclastic intellectual I should perhaps be ashamed to admit that I have a copy of Andersen inscribed by the teacher of the Infant Class at St. John's Episcopal Church, "For Lessons and Good Behavior; Christmas 1899." Many many years later I read with profound approval Thoreau's statement "If I repent of anything it is very likely to be of my good behavior. What demon possessed me that I behaved so well?" But I am afraid that I really was a very well-behaved child, though Sunday School bored me at least as much as day school, and church services as performed by the ancient white-bearded priest aroused in me nothing except a vague alarm.

Some of Andersen's stories made a mark that I still remember, especially the savage folk tale of Little Klaus and Big Klaus, the chilling cautionary story of the proud young beauty who desecrated a loaf of bread by attempting to use it as a stepping stone across a puddle, and finally, by way of relief, the ultimate triumph of the Ugly Duckling. As for *The Water-babies* I remember almost nothing except that it worried me profoundly and I rather think that if I were ever to be psychoanalyzed the process should start by a rereading of this masterpiece to call up from my unconscious what is, perhaps, still troubling me there. Were these traumatic experiences? Perhaps. But I still think that either of those books is better food for babes than the pap certified as harmless by child psychologists.

Reading was never discouraged nor especially encouraged by my parents. Most of the books came to me by chance and I was certainly not a great reader, except perhaps by the very low standards of my contemporaries. A small volume called *Sea Side and Wayside* was the first, I think, to arouse a mild interest in animals—other than cats to which I was always almost pathologically devoted—and I pored over an extremely old textbook called *A Fourteen Weeks' Course in Natural Philosophy* so long that I knew at eight or ten more about the elementary principles of physics than did the ludicrously incompetent high school teacher who was delivered into my hands rather than I into hers.

So far as concerns belles lettres, if the term is not too exalted, I read Poe, Conan Doyle, Gaboriau, Ernest Seton-Thompson, and several volumes of an interminable series by Captain Mayne Reid which came as a premium with the *Youth's Companion.* My taste must have been pretty low for I read a great many of the Alger books, probably the thinnest fare ever fed to children, and for a time even "Nick Carter," "Old King Brady," etc., in the five-cent serials which, until the invention of the comic book, represented the lowest point to which "literature" could fall. I must have had also that tolerance of moralizing which seems characteristic of children for I was much taken by Ruskin's *King of the Golden River* and vividly remember it though I have not seen it again for more than fifty years.

As a writer I have sometimes been blamed for attempting to enter too many different fields, and, if the charge is just, the defect of mind responsible for it was perhaps announced early by the fact that as a child I was more a hobbyist than a student, changing rapidly from one preoccupation to another though the reign of the moment's supreme interest was absolute. Physics carried me hardly farther than the usual boyish experiments with doorbells, electric motors, induction coils, and such. At another time I was interested only in stamp collecting and at still another in the study of pond water under a good microscope lent me by a physician.

Knoxville's free library building (not a Carnegie) had burned down before I was old enough to use it and in my time the library was housed in an old frame building. The rather forbidding spinster librarian did not look upon me or any other children with much favor, but somehow I got the privilege of the stacks. That I spent a good deal of time in a back room poring over bound volumes of the *Scientific American* is a significant indication that I then considered myself definitely scientific rather than literary in my tastes. And it was the *Scientific American* which was indirectly responsible for the only bold adventure of which I was ever the hero.

The back numbers, which I began to read about 1905, were full of accounts of the early, unsuccessful attempts to get a flying machine into the air. Lilienthal, martyr to his experiments with gliders, and Santos-Dumont, who made rather ridiculous jumps into the air aboard elaborate, kite-like contraptions, were my heroes. Then, while this interest was still at its height, came news of the Wrights' incredible feats at Kitty Hawk.

In 1910 I wrote the term paper for my third high school year on "Flight." Next year it was announced that one of

Knoxville's newspapers would bring into town two intrepid birdmen who would give a demonstration at the old race track. Moreover—and this sent a chill down my back—it would launch a "popularity contest." The man and the woman who got the highest number of "votes" (*i.e.,* who could present the largest number of coupons cut from successive issues of the paper) would each be entitled to a ride. This, be it remembered, was in 1911, just three years after the Wrights had given their first public demonstration, and when very few people had ever seen an airplane, much less flown in one. It is true that the Wrights had flown in 1903, but the flights were secret and the rumors not generally credited.

I was a shy and unaggressive adolescent who definitely avoided contact with strangers. Yet, because what modern educationists call "adequate motivation" can do wonders, I found myself to my own amazement starting out every afternoon as soon as school was dismissed to ring the doorbells of strangers of whom I begged the coupons from their papers. I don't think I really expected to win but the remote chance was not to be missed. And as it turned out the winners were myself and a young lady some years older whose name I have forgotten and of whose subsequent history I am entirely ignorant.

Not long afterwards the flyers and their machine arrived. The former made a somewhat oddly assorted pair, one being a rather rough customer named Lincoln Beachey who became a well-known stunt flyer and killed himself a few years later, the other a quiet, cultivated Canadian named McCurdy who, only a year or two ago, repeated one of the historic cross-country flights made not long after he came to Knoxville. Their machine was a Curtiss biplane, a flimsy contraption made out of bamboo, piano wire, and oiled silk.

When I presented myself to them at the race track they informed me that they had known nothing of the newspaper's contest until they arrived, that it was completely unauthorized, and that they most certainly could not take either me or the young lady for a ride. Their machine had only one seat and would, as a matter of fact, be quite incapable of getting off the ground with a passenger.

Quite uncharacteristically I became adamant and even truculent. I had entered the contest in good faith; I had devoted much time to winning it; I was now being put in a humiliating position and if I did not get the promised reward I would see to it that the newspaper found itself in as much difficulty as I, with the help of a lawyer, could contrive. McCurdy was tight-lipped, Beachey openly furious and profane. After a consultation they suggested that a hundred dollars might be adequate compensation for my disappointment. I replied that it certainly would not.

"O.K.," said Beachey at last. "We'll strap a chair seat on the wing alongside the engine and see if we can get you in the air."

After a considerable delay the chair seat was finally affixed and I climbed onto this precarious perch. I rather doubt that Beachey, who then took the controls, really tried to leave the ground, but he ran the plane as fast as it would go all the way across the bumpy center field of the race track and stopped just short of the fence. I was too excited and too disappointed to be frightened. "See," he said, "it won't go up. Are you satisfied?" "Certainly not," I replied, "I want to fly." He glared and then paid me the only compliment I ever got on physical courage. "I gotta admit," he said, "that you don't scare easy."

There was another consultation. Finally McCurdy said he would take the airplane up and look about to see if he could locate any field which looked as though it might be long enough to get two people into the air. Later he reported that there did seem to be such a field on an island in the Tennessee River about five miles above Knoxville. He would fly the airplane there and if the young lady and I would come up next day he might be able to take us up.

The climax of the adventure can best be told in the words of two front-page stories in the sponsoring newspaper which were dug out for me a few months ago in the same library where I had pored over the *Scientific American*. The issue for Friday, April 14, 1911, reads:

> A practical demonstration was given Thursday afternoon by Aviator Beachey of the inadequacy of Johnson's Race Track for airplane passenger flights, by his efforts to make an ascent inside the restricted space of the enclosure, carrying a passenger, this attempt resulting in failure.
>
> The aviators expect to make good on the passenger carrying agreement, however, and Aviator McCurdy and a Journal and Tribune representative spent yesterday morning driving over the country looking for a suitable place and after looking over several fields, one was found which Aviator McCurdy said would do. He first located it on his highest flight of Wednesday afternoon.

Next day the story read in part:

> Knoxville has been placed indelibly on the aviation map, for under the auspices of the Journal and Tribune, the first passenger carrying airplane flights ever made in Tennessee were made Saturday afternoon from Vance's Island a short distance from the city.
>
> To Miss Mellie Cole, of Lutrell Street, belongs the distinction of being the first person carried in an airplane flight in this state, while the other passengers, flying in the order named, were Joseph W. Krutch and Wilson Coile, young Knoxvillians. Miss Cole and Mr. Krutch were the winners

of the popularity contest conducted through the Journal and Tribune, and Mr. Coile captured the balloon which carried a ticket entitling the holder to a ride in an airship . . .

A variety of means of transportation was tried by the three passengers Saturday afternoon, ranging from the most primitive, a rude hack drawn by mules, to the most modern, an airplane driven by powerful motors. Miss Cole and the young men came to the office of the Journal and Tribune by streetcars. Automobiles carried them to within a short distance of the Holston River, when the roads became too rough for the "buzz wagons." There the passengers were transferred to a rough hack, with mules for motors and plain boards for seats, and taken from the banks of the river to the island where a small ferry boat was waiting to receive them. They were "poled" across the river to the island in a boat, which was by no means of the most modern construction, as it was forced across the stream by a man with a strong hickory pole. Across the river the young folks did the pedestrian stunt to the place where the Curtiss biplane was awaiting them. Aviator McCurdy having flown to the island Friday afternoon from the race track . . .

After a preliminary flight in which he rose to a height of about 500 feet and circled the island two or three times, McCurdy brought the machine to the ground and announced that he was ready for the first passenger carrying flight.

I don't suppose the flight lasted more than five or ten minutes or that we were ever more than two or three hundred feet above the ground, but after all most flights in 1911 were hardly more ambitious. Nowadays when anyone boasts of his exploits in the air I can always say, "I flew first in 1911," and I have never yet met anyone who could top that. It was nearly fifteen years later that I was again in an airplane when I flew one of the early German commercial lines in Europe. Since then I have flown, always as a mere passenger, in pretty much everything from a Piper Cub to a Jet, but never with the sense of adventure or achievement such as I felt when I climbed down off that Curtiss biplane. No, I have no desire to be invited onto a space ship. We pioneers cannot be expected to pioneer more than once. A flying saucer just isn't my dish.

Mr. McCurdy—now the Honorable John Alexander Douglas McCurdy—was only twenty-five when he conferred upon me my passive position in the history of aviation and he went on to a distinguished career. During the same year when he was my unwilling host he made the longest overwater flight which had yet been made—the 90 miles from Key West to Havana—and in the same year broke the record for duration in the air. During the First World War he became Canada's Director of Aircraft Production, later entered politics, was appointed Lieutenant Governor of Nova Scotia (1947 to 1952) and, so I am informed, now lives in Halifax. I say "so I am informed" because I received no reply to the letter I wrote him a few months ago asking if he remembered the Knoxville affair. He was pretty mad in 1911 and I am afraid he still is.

About two years before I accompanied Mr. McCurdy as he made these first faltering steps into the air age, I had said good-by to an important part of the old world. One night I suddenly realized that I no longer believed what I had been told in Sunday School and church. For a week or two I was terrified as I have seldom been since because, paradoxically, I feared that what I did not believe might nevertheless be true and that my lack of faith might have the most appalling consequences. I told no one of my agony and in a matter of no more than the two or three weeks, it faded away to leave me for years more firm in my assured, rather narrow rationalism than I now am.

Obviously I was ready for college; and it had long been assumed that I would enter the University of Tennessee to which young middle-class Knoxvillians went as a matter of course, taking engineering or law if they intended to practice either of these professions, and Liberal Arts if, as was very commonly the case, they were not interested in any form of intellectuality and considered the university as only a sort of finishing school for males.

Neither of my two brothers had preceded me there. Fred, the eldest, had not gone because as early as the first year of high school he refused to do any studying whatsoever and was already headed toward the alcoholism and other forms of irresponsibility which were to lead him through sixty years of what must have been a very unhappy life. Charles, my other brother, began in late adolescence to suffer the ill health which continues to dog him now that he has reached his seventies, and he was compelled to withdraw from school. Despite this handicap Charles was to become far more successful financially than any other member of my immediate family and he has always been an ideal big brother. During my youth he hovered over me to protect, comfort, and encourage, sharing or promoting my hobbies, praising me when I needed praise, and helping whenever he could. Since I left Knoxvill forty years ago we have been together only for visits but he has always been ready to sympathize or to help.

Looking back I now realize, probably better than I did then, how much he was responsible for such enterprise as I exhibited in all my more unconventional activities. I don't think he actually collected coupons during the hectic days of the "popularity contest" but he certainly encouraged me, and it was he who led the way in our enthusiasm for the theater which reached a sort of climax during the end of my high school days and my early college years. Since I was regularly to review plays for the New York *Nation* from 1924 to 1952, this must have had a considerable influence on my life.

Like most provincial towns, Knoxville had in those days a legitimate theater where touring companies played one-night stands and which was open on an average of once a week during the season. This was perhaps the only respect in which "cultural opportunities" were richer then than they now are in towns of the same size, but it was an important one. The fare was varied since it included the typical repertory of what was then known as "the ten-twent'-thirt' " as well as competent companies performing the best recent Broadway plays, often with the original New York cast.

I well remember my first visit to the theater when I was five years old, for a matinee of a rural melodrama entitled *Si Plunket.* George Jean Nathan is the only one of the many I have since questioned to admit that he had ever heard of this masterpiece. I can vividly recall at least one thing in connection with it. The catastrophe occurred when, near the end, the villain fell, or perhaps was pushed, into a thrashing machine and was thus effectively disposed of. For days before the performance I contemplated the colored posters on which this incident was vividly pictured and I still remember my disappointment when I saw in the actual performance that, though fragments of the villain were discharged from the exit end of the machine, it was not belching the black smoke which the poster promised. Perhaps this early disappointment had something to do with the fact that, despite all my intense interest in the drama, I was never much interested in the theatrical as opposed to the dramatic.

From the age of five on I was a regular theatergoer and though devoted, I think not equally, to *Sis Hopkins,*

The James Boys in Missouri, Tempest and Sunshine, At the Mercy of Tiberius, etc., I preferred, for example, Maude Adams in *The Little Minister.* One week it might be *The Knobs of Tennessee,* the next John Drew and Laura Hope Crews in *The Tyranny of Tears.* We also got *Ben Hur* with real horses pounding for a few frantic minutes on a treadmill, and James O'Neill (father of Eugene) as Monte Cristo, isolated on a rock in a stormy sea but waving a sword over his head and proclaiming, "The World is Mine!"

It was my brother Charlie who discovered how the strain on the pocketbook which constant attendance entailed might be completely removed. In those days the leading theatrical weekly, *The Dramatic Mirror,* had an unpaid "correspondent" in every principal town whose duty it was to report for publication a sort of running comment on attendance, popular reaction, etc. His compensation was that to him, as to members of the police and fire departments, the traveling manager who ordinarily stationed himself alongside the ticket taker to make sure there were not too many deadheads was expected "to extend the usual courtesies."

This was so agreeable an arrangement that I soon got myself appointed to a similar position on a feeble publication called *The Footlight* which originated in Atlanta, Georgia. There was only one catch. The whole business was not much more than a racket and while most traveling managers accepted it for what it was, a few took a dim view of it and might even refuse us admission. This created no real difficulty. My brother and I were on very good terms with the local ticket taker and when we entered the lobby he would shake his head if he thought the manager was ill disposed to such as we. In that case we would simply go around to the stage door and pass from backstage into the auditorium through the door which led into one of the stage boxes.

This method had actual advantages since it enabled us, if so inclined, to pause and observe anything of interest which might be going on behind the curtain—including, for instance, various members of the less prosperous companies who would one by one apply an anxious eye to a peep hole through which they might estimate the size of the audience. I remember especially the night when Pavlova stood in one spot doing her limbering-up exercises and was apparently completely oblivious to the stage hands who examined her at a distance of only a few inches as though she were some sort of mechanical doll.

Towards the end of this period Knoxville boasted a resident stock company and Charlie became its unpaid press representative while I attached myself to him as unofficial assistant. Between us we wrote both news and "feature stories" for the two local newspapers. We became quite intimate with members of the company, and on a few occasions some of them had dinner at our house, despite the fact that, as I have previously hinted, middle-class families seldom gave dinner parties as distinguished from mere family gatherings. The young and pretty leading lady, Sue MacNamany, married the leading man and later appeared briefly on Broadway. What became of her after that I never knew. The juvenile, James Duffy, who later became the owner of a chain of stock company houses on the West Coast, was then married to a rather unimportant member of the troupe from whom, I believe, he was shortly after divorced. From a worldly point of view this was probably something of a mistake, since her name was Anna Nichols and she became, not very many years later, internationally famous and no doubt extremely wealthy as the author of the perennial *Abie's Irish Rose* which broke all existing records for length of run on Broadway. Since it was already in mid-career when I became dramatic critic of *The Nation,* and since I was then something of a highbrow, I never saw it performed in English. Later in the twenties I did see it in Budapest where the audience seemed to find it very funny indeed.

During these years when my brother and I were something more than merely passive observers of theatrical affairs the movies were emerging as a minor competition. Few supposed that they would end in depriving Knoxville of its only "legitimate theater" (it does not have one even now), and we took active interest in "the flickers" as they were then irreverently called.

I must have ben a very small child when I saw my first moving picture but the first I actually remember was shown in one of the tents of a street carnival sometime about 1904. It made so deep an impression that when, many many years later, the Museum of Modern Art announced as part of its historical series *A Trip to the Moon* made by the French pioneer George Melies, I said to myself, "That must be the film I saw at the street fair." Naturally I took the opportunity to relive the distant past and I discovered that as the shaky images succeeded one another I not only remembered them but sometimes anticipated the next scene.

I think it is not generally realized how slow was the early progress of the film in catching the attention of the public whose imaginative life it was presently to dominate. Edison's coin-operated peep shows came first, but the first public demonstration of projection on a large screen before a large audience was made before the end of the Nineteenth Century—I believe at New York's famous waxworks, the Eden Musée, where rather primitive films remained for a number of years a minor side attraction. In the larger cities they soon became a regular feature of continuous-performance vaudeville houses where they were regarded by managers as what were known in the trade as "chasers"—*i.e.*, something boring enough to discourage patrons who might be tempted to stay on through the next regular performance.

In towns like Knoxville which had no vaudeville theater, Shepherd's Moving Pictures were booked annually as a road show, offering an evening or matinee of miscellaneous films mostly produced in France by Pathé and regarded by the public as primarily an entertainment for children. The general esteem in which all such entertainment was held was so low that "*Not* a Moving Picture" was the assurance often given outside various catch-penny exhibitions and it was not until the invention itself had been familiar for almost a decade that "Nickelodeons" suddenly sprang up all over the United States and a popularity which few had anticipated grew by leaps and bounds.

By the time I entered college, Knoxville was already supporting four such theaters of which one had dared raise its admission price to ten cents. All over the country a standard pattern had been established. The program, changed daily, was approximately one hour long, and consisted of four separate "reels" of comedy, drama, and occasionally a "documentary" which was not yet so called and usually presented some such uninspiring subject as "Canning Tuna Fish in California." The best dramatic pictures were produced by one or another of the companies "licensed" by the General Film Company which claimed to hold patents giving it the exclusive right to make or project moving pictures. Inferior films were made by "independents" engaged in a continuous legal battle with the monopolists who refused to rent their reels to any theater which dared show any others. This situation continued until the General Film Monopoly was legally broken by the courts just before the First World War.

For a year or two I attended one or another of the picture theaters almost daily, and if my brother was somewhat less assiduous he again led the way to a sort of unofficial participation somewhat like the one we enjoyed in theatrical affairs. We knew the managers of all four theaters and two of them discussed their business very freely with us. We read the trade papers, and I am afraid I shall have to confess that we were early members of a group which now, alas, seems to include at least a majority of the entire population of the United States—the group whose most vivid interest, outside the affairs of business and family, is in moving pictures and those who perform in them. The first time my name ever appeared in a national magazine it was signed to a letter to *The Dramatic Mirror*. The subject was movie censorship, already vigorously advocated, and I was thrilled to find that the editor called particular attention to my letter. I have completely forgotten what I said except that, as a budding liberal, I was against it.

The stars were just emerging—Mary Pickford was the very first, though for several years she was known only as "the Biograph Girl" because the Biograph company, one of the licensed group, did not want to advertise the name of a performer who might be hired away from it. There were others who soon emerged though now almost totally forgotten.

The great migration to Hollywood had not yet taken place and when my brother took me with him to New York on one of his trips the great events were visits which a certain useful connection enabled us to make to the rather closely guarded studios of the Vitagraph Company in Flatbush and of the Edison Company in the Bronx. There we saw among others—and, incredible as it seemed to us, "in the flesh"—the obese comedian, John Bunny, and the rising star, Norma Talmadge. Years afterwards when I met some of the performers of a slightly later period—Dorothy Gish, for example—I was amazed to discover that when they seemed to me creatures of a world light years away they were actually about my own age. Mary Pickford, who was worshiped from afar by millions when I was an unsophisticated teenager, had been born the same year as I.

We were on such intimate terms with one of the Knoxville managers and were such familiar figures around his theater that when he suddenly disappeared on an unannounced vacation (presumably alcoholic) we stepped in, took charge, and managed operations for a week, checking receipts against the numbered tickets and depositing the day's take in the bank. When the manager again put in his appearance he did not, I think, thank us, but neither did he question our operations or our accounts.

For some reason or other my brother's interest and mine faded as the moving picture entered its maturity, if that is the right word, and hence, though I have some firsthand knowledge of what might be called the prehistory of the art of the film, I know almost nothing about its later developments. I suspect that there are few people in the United States who have seen fewer movies since 1915 than I have.

Most of what I have written so far will, I think, suggest that when I entered the University I was prepared to take the work there seriously as I had, indeed, taken my high school studies, but that my interests were in what can only be called a succession of hobbies rather than in matters academic, scholastic, literary, or even, except in a dilettantish way, scientific. Nor was the atmosphere of the University as a whole likely to be intellectually heady.

Since my time, this University has shared the growth in size and seriousness which has transformed many of the state universities. Its faculty now includes men of national reputation in their fields and it participates in the interests and activities of the great world of which it has become a part. But in 1911 when I entered the freshman class it was for the most part sleepily conventional. Students—pupils would be a more accurate word—seldom read anything not required. The bookstore stocked absolutely nothing except textbooks and I can remember only one of my fellows who ever bought a book of any other kind. That fellow, by the way, passed out of my life so completely that I forgot even his name until, forty years later, I met him at the dinner for Queen Mother Elizabeth given in connection with Columbia University's Bicentenary. He was Frank Hyneman Knight, a very distinguished economist at the University of Chicago. The book he owned, by the way, and which I thought a bit pretentious at the time, was Kant's *Critique* in German. He said he did not remember me, as I did not remember him, but when I mentioned the German edition of Kant he admitted somewhat sheepishly that he had indeed owned one.

"Students," such as nearly all those enrolled in Liberal Arts, did not encourage the professors to attempt more than routine instruction in the classroom. These professors were about evenly divided betwen old fogies not too different from my high school teachers and genuine scholars with knowledge and interests which they had long given up hope of sharing with any young people.

To two of the latter I am still grateful. They were Professor Buchanan (later of the University of Louisiana), who taught me calculus so well that I was for a time deluded into the belief that I might become a mathematician, and Dr. James Douglas Bruce, brother of the once well-known Senator Cabell Bruce and himself a Berlin-trained philologist. A bachelor, and perhaps a bit of a misogynist, he spent every summer in England engaged in research for his life work, a general summary of the scholarship bearing on Arthurian Romance which was published only a few years before he died and is still to be found in bibliographies of its subject. Gruff and somewhat irascible, he was very ready to respond to any flicker of interest on the part of a student, but he had so long ago given up hope of finding any member of the class who regarded a course in English Literature as more than a conventional routine which it was necessary to go through that he used to announce before examination time: "When I ask you a question I want you to tell me exactly what I have told you. I am not interested in your opinions because I do not think they are of any value."

Nevertheless, we did have our noses rubbed into a small but respectable portion of the best of English Literature, and I hasten to add that, given the circumstances, I think his pedagogical method more sensible than that which accedes to a now prevalent tendency to encourage and respect opinions based upon ignorance and offered as a substitute for either knowledge or thought. Despite his somewhat scornful attitude, Dr. Bruce commanded the unwilling respect of both the University and the community and he was forgiven such outspoken reactions as his reply to a rather pretentious lady who one day stopped him on the street to ask if he could tell her the author of some verses which she repeated. "I am glad to say that I cannot. They are very bad." And I am sure they were.

None of this is to be taken to mean that one could not get an education at the University of Tennessee if one insisted upon it. I myself learned at least something, though I worked at it only moderately harder than most of my fellows. When I entered, I thought I was interested almost exclusively in the sciences and if I did not go into the school of engineering it was because I already sensed that my interests were not so much in applied as in theoretical matters. I already assumed that I would probably be a teacher of something or other because I did not know how else one with my lack of interest in the practical applications of anything could make a living.

In my freshman year I took math and botany, because they were almost the only scientific subjects offered to entering students, and I took freshman English because it was required. The teacher of this last was one Charles Bell Burke, a rather fierce little man with a mustache waxed in military fashion and by temperament both frantically respectable and a martinet. He required us to memorize, paragraph by paragraph and almost word for word, Genung's *Principles of Rhetoric,* much as my high school teacher of history had required me to memorize Meyer's *General History*. And I must again remark that, though this, like the method employed by Dr. Bruce, is not the best kind of teaching, it at least requires effort on the part of the student; and even though it may be true, as modern education theory is inclined to insist, that there is no such thing as memory training, I believe that I learned something from Genung's rigidly formal and once so-hated textbook.

Dr. Burke was also old-fashioned enough to demand that on Fridays each member of the class should stand at the front of the room and recite some verses he had himself chosen to learn by heart. Evidently I had already developed that desire to shock which is, I suppose, quite usual with those in whom intellectual interests have begun to stir, and I remember well that I usually chose something which I knew would be highly disapproved of by this rigidly orthodox and respectable man. One Friday, for instance, I chose some quatrains of Omar including:

Oh Thou, who didst with pitfall and with gin
Beset the Road I was to wander in,
Thou wilt not with predestined Evil round
Enmesh, and then impute my Fall to Sin!

Oh Thou, who man of baser Earth didst make
And Ev'n with Paradise devised the Snake;
For all the Sin wherewith the Face of Man
Is blacken'd Man's Forgiveness give and take.

On another Friday I chose Whitman's passage beginning:

From this hour I ordain myself loose of limits and imaginary lines,
Going where I list, my own master total and absolute,
Listening to others, considering well what they say,
Pausing, searching, receiving, contemplating,
Gently but with undeniable will divesting myself of the holds that would hold me.

This second selection I thought should be particularly embarrassing since Dr. Burke had done his thesis on Whitman whom, most inconsistently, he professed to admire. But even this special challenge Dr. Burke refused to meet. At the end of each of my recitations he said merely "Hum" and then called on the next student. To the credit of his tolerance I must say that he gave me an "A."

▲

By the time I had reached my junior year I was "majoring in Math" and assuming that after I had graduated I would go to the University of Chicago, where my teacher had taken his degree, for graduate study. Two things, one negative and the other positive, provoked the sudden decision taken in the middle of my senior year to study literature at Columbia instead.

Mathematics had fascinated me. In fact, trying to solve some mathematical problem was almost the only form of mental effort which ever absorbed me so completely that I was unaware of the passage of time. Often I discovered that it was two A.M. instead of the ten-thirty I would have guessed. It was true, also, that I had done well in the conventional series of courses which, as was then the fashion, took up the "branches" one after another. But competition was not very keen and I was coming to realize that my gift for mathematics was not actually very impressive. Struggling during the first term of my senior year as one of the three who were "taking" Differential Equations, I had sense enough to say to myself something like this: "If out of a class of three in a small college I am not outstandingly the best, if indeed at least one of these three seems to have an edge on me, it is not likely that I will ever distinguish myself in this field. I had better go in for something else."

It was, I am very sure, a wise decision. Possibly I might have become a routine college teacher of elementary mathematics. I was assuredly not gifted enough ever to have been even respectably competent in dealing with the vast complexities of modern mathematics in what has become one of the great ages of that science. Nevertheless, I am not sorry that I learned the little I did. Now, nearly fifty years later, I might still solve a simple problem in calculus, though of differential equations I remember barely enough to recognize one when I see it, and the meaning of the formulae of the atomic scientist eludes me completely.

Fortunately I had meanwhile developed a different interest, stimulated partly by college work and partly by reading of a different sort on my own. Three of Dr. Bruce's courses—in the Romantic Poets, in Chaucer, and in Shakespeare—opened three new, rather different worlds all of which generated in me, not merely interest, but excitement. I can still repeat passages from Shelley and Keats which I then committed to memory though some at least of the magic has now departed from them. And I remember vividly my reaction to a rereading of *Hamlet.* It had been required in a sophomore course and in my obligatory notebook I had expressed the opinion (passed over in silence by Dr. Bruce) that while it was an interesting enough play it certainly did not deserve the extravagant praise which was conventionally lavished upon it. When I returned to the play, only a little more than a year later, I found it hard to believe that this was the same text I had read before.

Like so many thousands of other young readers, I fancied, I suppose, that Hamlet and I were very much alike and very different from anyone else. And though for me, something has faded from Shelley and Keats, and despite T. S. Eliot's opinion that *Hamlet* is "too interesting" to be supremely great as a work of art, I hold firmly to the conviction that it and *Don Giovanni* (which I did not meet until many years later) are incomparably the finest works for the stage ever written. And though I have since seen many performances of *Hamlet,* including some pretty bad ones, it has never failed to survive any of the mishandlings to which it was subjected. Incidentally, the very first *Hamlet* I ever saw was at about the time that I first really read the text and I was probably wrong in assuming that the actor who played the role was ideally suited to it. Nearly every reader of these lines has seen Charles Coburn as a somewhat portly character actor popular in the movies. More than forty years ago he was heading a traveling company which gave alfresco performances of several Shakespearian plays on many a college campus.

My conversion to literature was completed in that same library where I had pored over the bound volumes of the *Scientific American.* So far as I can remember Bernard Shaw had never been mentioned in any college course, but I came across some unfavorable references to his absurd impudence in the old *Literary Digest*—the same periodical which, after years of prosperity, suffered a mortal wound when it conducted a poll on the basis of which the overwhelming defeat of Franklin Roosevelt in 1932 was prophesied.

Shaw was represented as so irritatingly clever that my curiosity was provoked. I made a special visit to the library and at random pulled from a shelf a fortunate choice—the volume which contained *Man and Superman,* still perhaps the best introduction to Shaw's work. I began to read and I was soon caught up in a growing delight. When I came to the end of Act One where Violet, who has just listened with increasing indignation to John Tanner's passionate defense of her as an "unwed mother," turns upon him for daring to assume that she could possibly have been guilty of improper relations with any man, I closed the book to sit for a while reveling in the discovery of what literature could be. This was the light which broke upon me on my way to Damascus. From then on and for many years I was more a Shavian than I had ever been a Spencerian. Just as I supposed that my temperament was akin to Hamlet's, so I believed that Shaw and I thought alike!

It was not that, even then, I believed him "better than Shakespeare." It was only that he was different in a very important way. He demonstrated that literature was not, as I had previously assumed, something which only dead men had created and that it had not "Stopped short/In the cultivated court/Of the Empress Josephine." He established a connection between the past in which my imagination had been living and the actual world in which I found myself. The literary enterprise, I realized for the first time, was still a valid one and could do something analagous to what Chaucer, Shakespeare, and Shelley had done for their contemporaries.

The library where I found both the *Scientific American* and *Man and Superman* was not at all "progressive." It offered no "services," celebrated no "read-a-book week," had no "reference librarian," and, so far as I know, never made any effort to persuade people to patronize it. I don't think that, actually, very many people did. Most of its books had not been off the shelf for years, some of them, I am sure, not since they had been removed, water-soaked and charred, from their original home which had burned and never been rebuilt. Nevertheless the books were there, patiently waiting until someone either came to seek out a particular one as I had sought out Herbert Spencer's works or, perhaps, merely to stumble upon it by chance. The most important thing about any library is just the fact that a book can wait there until someone to whom it has something important, perhaps something crucial, to say pulls it down. And one of the most important characteristics of the book itself is just that, unlike a television program, moving picture, or any other "modern means of communication," it can wait for years, yet be available at any moment when it happens to be needed.

Many years after my experience with Shaw, the historian Carl Becker told me about a similar experience of his own. He had been born in a tiny Iowa community by no means highly intellectual. But it did have a small library, presided over by a stern-faced woman of more than middle age who must have been wise though probably not well trained. By chance he pulled down from the shelf a bulky novel and read the first sentence which happens to be one of the most famous of opening sentences: "All happy families are alike; every unhappy family is unhappy in its own way." Something about that statement, he did not quite know what, aroused his curiosity and he took the volume to the librarian's desk. "Is this a good book?" he asked.

In Nineteenth Century Iowa, Tolstoi was known, insofar as he was known at all, as a rather "dangerous" writer —certainly not food for babes. But the librarian did not tell him that it was "not for his age group." She gave him a good long look over the top of her spectacles, hesitated a moment, and then said, "Well—it's a very *strong* book."

He took it home and there his intellectual life began. He had taken the first step on the road which was to lead him to a professorship at Cornell University and the writing of a series of historical studies of real importance. The second most important thing about the little Iowa library was a wise librarian. But the most important thing was the fact that the book was there. That library would have been justified by its fruit even though no one else had ever read its copy of *Anna Karenina.*

If we knew the intellectual history of all the people who *have* an intellectual history, we should find, I suspect, that something like this happened to a great number of them. At least I know that after I read *Man and Superman* I was never the same as I had been before.

We hear a great deal nowadays about "the importance of communication" and about "improved methods of communication"; but though certain supplementary methods of limited usefulness have recently been invented there are no *improved* methods, because the printed page remains the best and most flexible "means of communication" ever devised.

Even some colleges have joined what seems to be a conspiracy to ignore this fact. A year or two ago I visited a campus where they no longer had an English Department because it had become a Communications Department instead. And I remember saying to one of the professors whom I met on the campus that I thought it a sad day when a professor was seen—as at the moment he was—carrying under his arm, not books, but three film cans.

Just suppose that the radio, the phonograph, the film strip, and all the rest of it had been in existence since the Fifteenth Century but that books had just been invented. What a marvelous advance in communication that would be! And how many advantages the book would be seen to have over any previously known means, including ready availability and the possibility of wide choice. What comes over the air is chosen for you by somebody else and you must receive the communication at a particular moment, or not at all. A book, on the other hand, you can choose for yourself and you can read it at your own convenience. It is always available while a broadcast is gone, usually forever. And how much more economical in time a book is! Deduct from a half-hour broadcast the musical fanfare, the station announcement, the sponsor's commercial, etc., etc., and you can learn by five minutes with a book more than you can get in a half-hour broadcast. "Why," we would say, "this marvelous new invention, the book, just about makes radio obsolete."

But perhaps the greatest of all the advantages of the book as a means of communication is simply that by reading you learn to read, become more and more capable of receiving more and more completely more subtle and complicated communications. By listening to the radio or looking at film strips you become only more and more passive, less and less capable of giving your attention.

Despite my attempts as a freshman to irritate Dr. Burke I was, in general, a docile student and one of the last from whom anyone would have expected any action likely to embarrass the University. But Shaw was heady stuff for an innocent like myself and he inspired me to the creation of a very small tempest in a very small teapot.

Somehow or other—probably because no one else wanted a job which carried very little prestige—I was appointed editor of the chronically languishing "literary magazine" which expired annually after the publication of one or two numbers. Just how much I myself wrote of the issues for which I was responsible I do not remember but I do recall two essays. The first was a glowing review in which *Androcles and the Lion* (just recently published in an American magazine) was expounded as an embodiment of true Christianity. To my great delight a refutation appeared by an equally impassioned undergraduate in a magazine emanating from a Catholic college. The second essay, an attack on that Noble Experiment which Tennessee was among the first to make, was more successful, from my standpoint at least.

In brief space I attacked Prohibition as an institution and the character, motives, and intelligence of its proponents on all fronts and from every point of view. As for the proponents, they were either hypocrites, who didn't practice what they preached, or they were blue-nosed puritans compounding for "sins they were inclined to/ By damning those they had no mind to." As for the institution, it was an outstanding example of all misguided attempts to protect people from the vices and follies which should be always available if they were to grow strong by resisting them. There were many quotations to enforce all points (drawn for the most part from Ward's *English Poets* which had been the text of a sophomore course) and I leaned heavily on Milton's low opinion of "a cloistered virtue." I have no copy of the piece, but it was quoted in a recent article which appeared in a University of Tennessee publication and I note that its title was "On Being One's Brother's Keeper" and that I went far enough afield in criticizing, not only Prohibition but all "blue laws," to declare: "There is no more reason why theaters should be closed so that people will go to church than that churches should be closed to induce people to attend the theater."

I remember that Dr. Bruce, who was certainly no prohibitionist, confined his criticism to the dry remark that the Lord's Prayer with its "lead us not into temptation" seemed to imply an anticipatory disagreement with Milton. But somehow or other the state legislature (of which the University stood in constant terror) had its attention called to my diatribe and reacted violently enough to cause real concern on the campus. Tennessee was, after all, in the Bible Belt and less than ten years later it was to make an international spectacle of itself by bringing to court a school teacher accused of teaching the Darwinian theory.

The Dean of my university summoned me to his office and solemnly warned me that, though I was only a few months away from graduation, I would be expelled if I published any more such offensive articles. Since no more issues of the magazine could appear that year, I found myself in one of the most delightful of situations. I had established myself as what my literary hero called a Devil's Disciple but was prevented by circumstance from the necessity of exposing myself to any risk.

As June approached, I and two of my friends agreed not to shave our upper lips until we had received our diplomas and, for I know not what reason, the modest mustache resulting from the agreement has remained in place ever since. Came June and I was graduated "with honors" though whether they were "Summa," "Magna," or merely plain, I no longer remember. Because there was no chapter of Phi Beta Kappa at Tennessee I had previously been elected to the lesser known honorary fraternity Phi Kappa Phi whose motto I had forgotten until I saw it a few years ago on a brass plaque in the entrance hall of the University of Arizona: "The Love of Learning Rules the World."

On this occasion it struck me that, of all the lies which have been cast in eternal bronze, this is probably the most barefaced.

3

A few months before I graduated from the University of Tennessee I told my father that I wanted to enter the Columbia Graduate School. He asked how much I thought it would cost and then said "All right." My mother, on the other hand, was mildly perturbed. "You have never been away from home for more than a week or two at a time," she said. "How will you get along without me to tell you what clothes to wear and when to change them." "Oh," I replied, "just send me a post card when you think I need a clean shirt." And without further ado it was settled.

Secretly I was far less debonair. Self-distrustful since early childhood and temperamentally inclined to fear the worst, I had a somewhat exaggerated idea of the prodigious talent and industry that would be expected of a candidate for the Doctor's degree, and I doubted that I would be equal to either. In fact, I am not sure I would have had the courage to face anticipated failure, even with the help of the desperation which had long been my defense against the dark estimates of my chances I habitually set up before undertaking anything, had it not been for a motive I have not mentioned so far. "At least," I said to myself, "you will have a chance to see something of Life as it is lived beyond the narrow confines of Knoxville." One of the attractions of Literature as opposed to Mathematics was simply that the best place to study the latter was said to be Chicago and Chicago, in the imagination of most provincials—especially Southern provincials—was not to be compared with New York as an embodiment of everything the home town was not.

Though I had, of course, some knowledge of college professors and admired two or three of them greatly, I had never met a man or a woman who had written a book addressed to other than an academic audience, and never, with the exception of one touring pianist, anyone of more than local reputation in any of the arts or sciences. Those who did write books, paint pictures, or perform in public seemed to me members of a species different from that to which I, my family, and my acquaintances belonged. The most I hoped for myself was that I too might become a minor college professor. But at least I could hope also for a closer view of what writers and artists were like.

Moreover—and like most young men and young women who persuade their parents to send them to a metropolis where they will enjoy "cultural opportunities"—I had also considerable curiosity about opportunities not ordinarily classed as cultural. In Knoxville there was no choice except between respectability and dissipation of a very unglamorous kind. "In England," said Sidney Smith, "there are only two amusements: Religion and Vice," and had I known this remark I would have thought it not inappropriate to the situation in my own home town. But in New York, so songs and musical comedies discreetly hinted, there was a Gaiety on the edge of Wickedness intoxicating to imagine.

Today, when the glamour of even Paris, Vienna, and the Riviera are rather a *vieux jeu* so far as the young are concerned, it is hard to remember how writers for the stage (led I suppose by George M. Cohan) had built up the image of New York as precisely what O. Henry called it: Bagdad on the Subway. "Give my regards to Broadway" sang one of Cohan's homesick exiles,

Remember me to Herald Square
Tell all the boys at Forty-second Street
That I will soon be there.

Was not Knoxville nearly twenty-four hours rather than "forty-five minutes" from Broadway? Was not, therefore, Cohan's scorn for New Rochelle appropriate *a fortiori?*

Oh, this place is a bird
No one ever heard
Of Delmonico's, Rector's or Brown's.
With a ten dollar bill you're a spendthrift,

If you open a bottle of beer
You're a sport, so they say,
And imagine Broadway
Only forty-five minutes from here.

Several times during my adolescence brother Charlie had taken me on one of the trips to New York which were then the Knoxville equivalent of the Grand Tour. We had seen the sights, gone to the theater, and gaped at the tall buildings as visitors were expected to do. Now that I have developed a strong distaste for all cities it is hard to remember how I stood long on a street corner fascinated by the crowds, and I suppose that had I then known Samuel Johnson I would have echoed his exclamation over "the full tide of human existence" which he thought he had seen at its flood in Charing Cross.

We made even somewhat timid visits to "Delmonico's, Rector's and Brown's." I well remember one such to a well-known "cabaret" which we choose, I presume, because it had borrowed its name from the Parisian restaurant celebrated in *The Merry Widow* which had been performed in Knoxville with the original American stars, Ethel Jackson and Donald Brian. "I go off to Maxim's/Where fun and frolic beams." Though in the New York namesake also the "Ladies smiled so sweetly" we did not, I confess, "Catch and kiss them neatly." But it was the only occasion of my life when I was intoxicated enough on the return to our hotel actually to see the pictures bouncing up and down on the walls and the keyhole rising and falling as they do in the funny papers.

If none of the lyrics I have just been quoting seem worthy of one who was soon to become a professional student of English Literature, the fact that I quote them from memory is a sufficient indication that they made at the time a deep impression. Now, it seemed, I was to be, not a mere tourist, but a real New Yorker. At the University of Tennessee I had been a good boy and almost a model student. Now I was mature enough, I hoped, to be reaching years of indiscretion.

If all this now strikes me as comic I believe, nevertheless, that it was the right attitude for me to take at the time. And I shall insert here as the best comment something I wrote nearly forty years later just at the moment when I was about to say good-by to cities—at least as places to do more than visit.

> At some time in the course of his experience every man should rub shoulders with his fellows, experience the excitement of a metropolis' nervous activity, live close to the great, the distinguished, the famous, and the merely notorious—if for no other reason than because only so can he learn properly to discount them or at least learn in what ways they are, and in what ways they are not, to be taken at their own and the world's valuation. Those who, for example, have never seen an author are likely to take books with the wrong kind of seriousness. Urbanity seems to be literally that: something impossible to acquire except in cities. But one need not, and one should not, I think, spend a lifetime in getting it, for in that respect, as in so many others, a city pays a diminishing return. The years between eighteen and thirty should be amply sufficient to polish anyone capable of being polished. If he is not urbane by then, something more drastic than mere residence in a city would seem to be called for. And if I have never felt at home with anyone who had never had any experience of cities, I can say much the same thing of those who have never had any other kind.

Before the great day of departure arrived it was decided that brother Charlie should go with me on "the Vestibule." We were together in New York for a few days until I was settled in the Furnald Hall dormitory on the corner of Broadway and 116th Street. There I soon discovered other new arrivals, some of whom were almost, though not quite, as apprehensive as I was. In those days the Graduate School of English was small enough to make it not only possible but inevitable that members of the hard core composed of those who had resolved to aim at a

Ph.D. soon knew one another. Six or eight of us quickly fell into the habit of eating most of our dinners at the same boardinghouse and all of us met regularly as members by invitation of a Graduate Club where we solemnly practiced being scholars either by reading papers to one another or by listening to some outsider who could be persuaded to perform. One businessman from downtown whose hobby was *Tom Jones* came to talk about the various ways in which he studied the masterpiece he had chosen and to exhibit the manuscript index he had compiled. Here one of us promptly discovered the following entry: "Bitch, Tom called son of a."

If I was heartened by the humility of other new students who did not seem so much brighter or more learned than I as to outclass me, I was on the other hand cast down by some of those farther along the rocky road who enhanced their own importance by vivid accounts of the nearly insuperable difficulties ahead. One such, who had just passed his orals, gave the impression that nearly everybody failed and that so far as he could judge most of us were doomed. But at least ultimate catastrophe might be a long way off. The usual procedure was to spend two years taking the required courses, an indefinite time in private preparation for the comprehensive Oral Preliminary, and several years in writing the thesis which had to be "defended" before the degree was finally granted, usually at least five or six years and often much more, after the first courses were taken. Frequently the candidate was compelled to get a job somewhere while preparing for the oral and almost always did so while working on his thesis.

Several members of the little group which soon coagulated were later to fill academic chairs in important institutions: Robert Bolwell, who retired only a few years ago from George Washington University, Walter Graham at Western Reserve, and four of us (a really astonishing number from one academic generation) at Columbia itself. The four were, besides myself: John Lyon, for many years a pillar of the Department of Extension; Emery Neff, a remarkable scholar in the field of Comparative Literature; and Mark Van Doren, equally well known as teacher, critic, and poet. Neff was, by the way, the hero of the moment because he had just returned to the University to continue work on his thesis after having been fired from a small denominational college where he was accused of corrupting the students with immoral literature: to wit, some of the plays of Bernard Shaw. By comparison with this exploit my own little undergraduate brush with college authorities was hardly worth boasting about.

At Tennessee I had had only two even moderately intimate friends and enjoyed no reputation except as a rather tiresomely assiduous student. The gayer crowd certainly regarded me, if it regarded me at all, as not even potentially a member of that group. Among my new companions at Columbia I was astonished as well as delighted to discover that I was considered "sophisticated," an amusing if somewhat reckless talker, and even a bit of a wit. I promptly adopted the new role which I found very congenial and played it in a fashion which must have been extremely callow but seemed to be effective among those who were, no doubt, almost equally so, each in his own way. Inwardly I was too self-distrustful not to work hard and seriously at my studies, but to be accepted by my fellows as something of a personality was a great and novel experience. It was also certainly one of the reasons why I recovered quickly from the first two or three weeks of desperate homesickness, recovered, in fact, so completely that when I returned home for the first Christmas holidays I already regarded Columbia and New York as my spiritual home and had no desire to stay long away from them.

So far as academic work was concerned I enjoyed two important advantages. My Knoxville teacher, Dr. Bruce, recommended me to his life-long friend and fellow Virginian, William Peterfield Trent, one of the most distinguished and influential members of the Graduate Faculty, who took me more or less under his wing and was to be in charge of the thesis I ultimately wrote. Through my soon developed friendship with Mark Van Doren I met his brother Carl, one of the most respected younger members of the Graduate English teaching staff, and I had the advantage of his intimate advice and encouragement. For this and for many other reasons Mark became so important a part of my life that I must say something, but much too little, about him.

I do not remember when we first met, but I remember very vividly when we first became aware of one another. And so, Mark has said, does he. We had arranged to go downtown together, perhaps to a matinee, and were standing on the rear platform of a subway car. That is assuredly not the ideal place for a conversation, but we began one which has been continuous ever since in the sense that it has always seemed to be resumed at the point where it was interrupted whether, as was for long the case, the interruption was only a few hours or a few days, or, as during the last decade, several years elapsed between meetings.

Mark was almost precisely my age and had arrived in New York at the same time. Academically, however, he was a year ahead of me since he had already taken his

M.A. at the University of Illinois. In other, more important respects, he was still further ahead. Because his older brother Carl had helped to guide him, and because as undergraduate teacher he had a man of the vigor and originality of Stuart Sherman, Mark had already acquired a real familiarity with literature and a maturity of judgment far beyond mine. I fancied that in certain respects I was more "sophisticated" than he, but in what really mattered he was far more sophisticated than I. His master's thesis, *Henry David Thoreau: A Critical Study,* was about to be published by Houghton Mifflin, publishers of Thoreau's own works, and only those with some experience of master's essays can realize what an astonishing achievement this represented. He was already a marked man, and I was well aware how completely incapable I was of any such accomplishment as was already his.

Years later Mark confessed to me that he, on his side, had been secretly somewhat overawed by my callow iconoclasm and my pose as an *enfant terrible.* Nevertheless we took to one another from the very beginning and shared interests, ambitions, and plans, auguries that our long friendship was to be based in part, not upon an identity of temperament or intellect, but upon our complementing one another in ways which we both understood.

To have always at hand someone from whom understanding and sympathetic attention can be taken for granted is itself a priceless boon, and it is one which friendship with Mark conferred upon me in the days when I was a callow and he a more responsible student. But to be sure that this sympathetic listener will also "come back" with something which is illuminating because it is not merely sympathetic and understanding but is also a new insight from some different point of view or perspective is to have a perfect intellectual companion. And I have no doubt that it was because his students later sensed something approaching this kind of response that they also could be so greatly helped to develop their own varied personalities and to find their ways along such divergent paths. As a teacher no less than as a companion he has exercised a mysterious gift for influencing strong minds in ways and in directions he neither intended nor was aware of. No one who was listened to with attention by men whose subsequent careers were as different as (to take two amusingly extreme examples) Thomas Merton, the Trappist monk, and Allen Ginsberg, the Beatnik poet, can be accused of merely encouraging reflections of himself.

"Discourse," "dialogue," and "dialectic" are words much favored today in intellectual discussions and they threaten to become cant. But when I think what it has meant to me intellectually to have been able to call Mark my most intimate friend for forty-three years I cannot avoid using those words for the inescapable reason that they define precisely the essential character of the relationship. People sometimes speak of the ideal friend as an *alter ego;* but talking to an *alter ego* is too much like talking to oneself—soothing, no doubt, but otherwise not very profitable. There should, of course, be some fundamental compatibility as well as the sense that one will be comprehended, and I flatter myself there is that compatibility between Mark and me. I believe, that is to say, that at bottom we believe the same things and value the same things. But we have arrived at our convictions by different routes, and he, at least, has learned things along the way I would never have known had he not led me to them.

I have often wondered just how this fundamental difference, not inconsistent with equally fundamental similarities, might be defined, but I am afraid that I will never be able to do better than to say that it has something to do with the fact that Mark is a poet through and through while I have never been able to achieve anything except prose. I hope and believe this does not mean that I am incapable of understanding poetry or, for that matter, incapable of poetic feelings on my own. But my approach, even in the case of such mildly mystical inclinations as I am proud to confess, is always the plodding approach of prose.

Mark is a poet twenty-four hours of the day as well as through and through, and to say that means much more than to say simply that the writing of poetry has been, ever since I first knew him, his greatest interest—indeed, as he would probably say in his somewhat extravagant way, his *only* real interest. It is to say also that his approach is always via the leap and flight of a poet's perception, so that in our intercourse I have often found myself compelled to follow ploddingly after him, sometimes not really understanding what he had said until days—in a few cases years—afterward.

I think it significant that when I felt impelled to write, some quarter of a century apart, two books of nontechnical philosophy in which I tried to state what I believed about man and the universe I thought the appropriate motto for each to be a few lines from two of Mark's poems, written, I believe, with about the same interval of time between them. This, I think, does not mean that I borrowed my ideas from him and I am quite sure that he did not borrow his from me. But it does illustrate how we arrived at compatible conclusions by different routes, and it makes clear why our relationship has always been, to me, so rewarding.

Because of my close friendship with Mark I soon came

to know his brother Carl more intimately than a student ordinarily knows one of his professors. I benefited enormously from his advice and encouragement, not only during these student years, but long after, when he gave me an opportunity to write for *The Nation* of which he was Literary Editor, and when he recommended the first book I wrote after my thesis to the publisher, Alfred Knopf. The vice most characteristic of the writer is envy. He is likely to feel that the literary success of anyone else detracts from his own. But I have never known another man of letters who seemed to rejoice as Carl did in the achievements of others or who was so eager to help them. I do not mean that he himself was not ambitious, or that he was not proud of his most imposing work, the biography of Benjamin Franklin. But he seemed to rejoice almost as much in the success of others as in his own.

The avowed purpose of the Graduate School of English and Comparative Literature was to train scholars more or less after the pattern introduced by the German universities, but this was somewhat more rigidly adhered to at Harvard than at Columbia. At the former institution "Modern Literature" meant primarily literature at the time of Shakespeare. At Columbia even Victorian literature was studied, but we began with Anglo-Saxon (Old Gothic was required at Harvard) and the stress was upon history and other factual knowledge. We were expected to be thorough and that meant, for instance, that we were required in the course in Elizabethan Drama to read and take notes on one play a day until we had got through the entire surviving corpus of something more than two hundred plays written in English before 1642, when the Puritans closed the theaters. But courses were not the only or the most important thing. We were constantly aware that when the day of judgment came and one of us presented himself as prepared to face the oral, he would be expected to have mastered a never clearly defined body of knowledge and to answer a majority of the questions a group of our instructors cared to ask, whether or not the candidate had ever "taken a course" which supplied the answers.

Most of us worked a hard six-day week attending lectures, reading well into the night what had been assigned, and, at the same time, trying to acquire somehow or other the requisite knowledge of books and men concerning whom we had never received any formal instruction. We knew that between the completion of the required courses and the examination we would certainly have to spend a good many months filling in the gaps; but we knew also that we had better pick up what we could as we went along.

Sooner or later before going up for the oral we would also have to pass sight-reading tests in French, German, and Latin. For the first two I was just barely prepared already but I had pretty well forgotten the little Latin I had ever known. In desperation I registered for a night Extension Course in "Latin by the Direct Method," taught by an enthusiastic spinster who believed that Latin was a language, not a cryptogram, and that it was time to get away from the usual methods of language teaching—which have been accurately described as "treating living languages as dead and dead languages as buried." After a few months in her class I was able to pass my test which consisted of sight reading a passage from Ovid's *Metamorphoses*. That is, of course, rather easy Latin, but I doubt that most students who had taken three or four years of the then conventional high school instruction would have been up to it.

Fashions change in graduate instruction as in everything

else and today many universities put less stress on history and factual knowledge, more on "criticism," especially of the "new" variety. I shall not attempt to pass judgment upon the relative value of the two approaches, but I will say that I am not sorry to have been subjected to the Columbia discipline, and that I rather doubt the advisability of putting so much stress, as is often put today, upon contemporary and nearly contemporary literature. Instruction should, in the sciences, of course, be as fully abreast of today as possible, but I have always felt that the real business of college or university courses in "the cultural subjects" should be to bring the student up to date on the best that has been said *up to his own time.* His contemporaries he will learn about for himself and in all probability he will understand them better than his instructors ever can. But he is far less likely to get around to absorbing all he should learn from the past unless he is led to it by his elders. Having long held this opinion I was interested to find recently quoted a remark by T. S. Eliot to the effect that he did not believe either his or any other modern poetry should be "taught"; and that students should be required to read the English and other classics instead. When my own time came to teach courses at Columbia I preferred to lecture on Dryden and Pope rather than on my contemporaries.

All the fellow students whom I met during that first year were earnest and hardworking, and a few of them stuck almost fanatically to their task. One (later also himself a teacher at Columbia) was invariably to be found either in a classroom or tucked away at a table between the library stacks devoted to English literature. Here he was working his way slowly from volume to volume like one of those real, not metaphorical, bookworms which exit from the back cover of one volume only to enter the front cover of its neighbor and so advance until a whole set of quartos could be suspended from a string passed through the neat holes its progress leaves behind.

Most of us, however, had at least some curiosity concerning New York City as something more than the home of Columbia University though the extent to which this curiosity extended beyond its "cultural aspects" varied considerably. Most of us visited museums, attended the theater or the opera, occasionally at least, and "saw the sights." Since I had, as a small child, visited the Statue of Liberty and ridden a swan boat on Central Park Lake I felt it unnecessary to repeat these adventures but, as I have already hinted, I had an eager interest in the less conventional aspects of metropolitan life. Bohemia as I imagined it interested me greatly and I aspired, as the young often say, TO LIVE—that being a broad phrase which may include anything from dinner in an Italian restaurant to activities necessarily involving a member of the opposite sex.

Only a few weeks after my arrival in the city I spent a Saturday evening wandering about Greenwich Village looking in vain for the Washington Square Players of whose daring experiments with "sophisticated" plays I had somehow heard. When I learned later that, despite the designation of the company, it played at the appropriately named Bandbox Theater on 59th Street near Third Avenue, I not only attended all of its performances but made my way afterwards to the neighboring restaurant where I could admire from a distance the performers themselves. Later, of course, the Washington Square Players grew up to be the Theater Guild, and after it had done so I came to know more or less intimately some of the very persons who seemed, when I first saw them, inhabitants of a world unfortunately quite discontinuous with mine. In 1915, however, even to be in the same room with them was thrilling enough since, despite my serious interest in academic learning and my almost awed respect for its most distinguished representatives, the members of artistic and literary Bohemia represented glamour of a more potent kind.

In one respect fortune favored me just as it had by arranging that I should meet Professor Trent because of his friendship with Dr. Bruce, and Carl Van Doren because of Mark. I soon acquired two less respectable friends who quickly introduced me into a world I might otherwise have been long in discovering.

The first of these was an extremely pretty girl whom I had known only slightly at the University of Tennessee from which she had disappeared a month or two before my graduation, possibly by request, though I never knew. Now she miraculously turned up in New York where she introduced me to an establishment not quite like any I have ever known before or since. It was located in midtown, west of Broadway; it was inexpensive; and though I suppose it served dinner, I never ate there. The real fun started about nine o'clock, by which time it was crowded with young people who ordered drinks from time to time, mostly, as I remember with horror, liqueurs, since most were inexperienced drinkers, and who mingled freely on the small dance floor. This was not quite, I realized, Maxim's; but fun and frolic certainly beamed there.

A month or two after I had become familiar with the customs of this utopia my sponsor turned up with a new hairdo and a complete new costume to announce that she was engaged to be married to a man from upstate whom she was joining immediately. I never saw or heard of her again. Nearly ten years later another young woman, with whom my relations were even more casual since I never "took her out" but once, performed on that occasion another function that proved to be vastly more important and of which I shall speak later. Remembering the two incidents, I have been led to wonder if Providence had not created both girls only to be useful to me. Indeed, one of my few attempts at fiction was a story based remotely on this theme; I am grateful that no editor was foolish enough to accept it.

Though my pocketbook was not sufficiently plump to stand the strain of "Delmonico's, Rector's or Brown's," there were a number of other more modest eating and drinking places which had "atmosphere." Occasionally I took Margarite Valentine, the English pianist whom I had met in Knoxville, to the Kaiserhoff on 43rd Street just west of Broadway where we ate Welsh rabbit and drank Rhine wine after the theater and where (as I remember, to illustrate the changed manners) she was asked to put aside the cigarette which, as an English woman, she took for granted.

More often I went for dinner to a similar but humbler German restaurant called Sheffel Hall, east of Union Square, and on other occasions to the then famous tourist attraction, "Little Hungary," on the lower East Side, where it seemed to a provincial like myself quite devilish to drink imitation Tokay from the long-necked decanters permanently installed upside down on the tables and dispensing the wine from a valve against which one pressed a glass. Once I persuaded the prettiest female student in the graduate English department, who had also recently arrived from the South, to accompany me there. But though my intentions were strictly honorable the dangerously "foreign" atmosphere kept her rigid with apprehension and she seemed perpetually on the point of exclaiming in the words of the popular song:

You may tempt the upper classes with your villainous demitasses
But Heaven will protect the working girl!

Although it was not until the beginning of my second year that I made the acquaintance of the other person who was to prove most useful in providing relief from academic responsibilities, this seems the place to pay him the tribute of gratitude. He was Glen Mullin, an old Illinois friend of the Van Dorens and about the same age as Carl. By first ambition a painter, he had studied at the Art Institute in Chicago and also passed through a Wanderjahr he described later in a book called *The Scholar Tramp*. Now, encouraged by the Van Dorens, he decided to come on to New York, take a Master's Degree in English, and make a livelihood as a teacher. So indeed it all turned out, for until his death a few years ago he taught writing in Columbia's Extension Department and I accounted him one of my close friends.

During his first few years in New York Glen lived in a studio and kept on with his painting in his spare time. The first of these studios was in an extraordinary rabbit warren unsuspected by the general public and given over to minimum rent studios in what was called the Lincoln Arcade just behind a moving picture theater in Lincoln Square. The second was on Fifteenth Street, just west of Union Square, where a number of lofts were provided with skylights. So far as I was concerned the important thing was that I was free of both and got an intimate glimpse of a *vie de Bohême* rather closer to the operatic than one might imagine. So far as I know, all the denizens of the Lincoln Arcade were perpetually stony broke, but on Fifteenth Street the studio next door was occupied by Glen's close friend Rolf Armstrong, then reaching the height of his commercial success as a magazine cover artist whose pretty girls appeared month after month on *Cosmopolitan Magazine* and led after that a long life on calendars and advertisements. A few years later Glen was to marry Armstrong's favorite model Jean, whose face was anonymously familiar to a vast public.

Jean, who was to be a close friend for many years, was an extraordinary woman in many respects. Girlish in face and figure for many years after middle age, she seemed also eternally youthful in spirit, simple, debonaire, seemingly flippant and unpredictable, but actually so competently responsible that she managed with tact and cheerfulness on a teacher's small salary a family which often included her husband's father and mother as well as, permanently, the little daughter of her deceased sister. Glen is now dead and I have not seen Jean since I came to live in Tucson, more than ten years ago, but I can imagine her still youthful in spirit.

> *What boots it with uncessant care*
> *To tend the homely slighted Shepherds trade*
> *And strictly meditate the thankless muse?*
> *Were it not better done as others use,*
> *To sport with Amaryllis in the shade*
> *Or with the tangles of Neaera's hair?*

To such a question I gave during my early years in New York an easy answer. It seemed quite possible to do both and not necessary to tend the shepherd's trade "uncessantly."

Was I wrong? Would I have been better at my own trade had I stuck closer to my books? Perhaps. And students such as I was are now very much out of fashion, for in these days a typical graduate student, and a not untypical undergraduate, is married, has a child if not two, by the girl with whom he has, as likely as not, been "going steady" since he was an adolescent.

"Going steady," so I am told, is explained by those who engage in this new "behavior pattern" by saying that they like to be sure of a "date." But this explanation requires an explanation. Why so much stress on "security" and so little upon adventure and experience? To me it seems that a healthier attitude was revealed by that great spokesman for unregenerate human nature, Charlie McCarthy, when he responded to the observation that it was difficult to find the one woman with whom one wanted to spend the rest of one's life by remarking, "Yes . . . but then it sure is a lot of fun looking."

Student marriage raises similar questions. Both the young men and the young women of my generation were supposed so consistently to prefer freedom to responsibility, and "sex experience" to procreation that the bugaboo called "race suicide," invented a generation earlier, was regularly paraded. Nobody has any occasion to worry about that now. Planned parenthood has turned out to mean just that and not, as the moralists once feared, planned sterility. And the plan is usually put into operation just as soon as the certificate is signed. Is this playing safe or is it being reckless?

One's first impulse is to say that it is being reckless. To marry while still in college, to set up housekeeping on the installment plan, and to beget children one is not ready to support does not look like overcaution. Yet there is another way of looking at it. When John Tanner is proving that no normal man or woman actually wants to get married even when the Life Force has him in its merciless grip, he ends his list of matrimony's penalties by adding the necessity for abandoning "the romantic possibilities of an unknown future." Has this become not a penalty but a boon to a conformist generation anxious above all else to know what is going to happen to it? Are the romantic possibilities of an unknown future the last thing it wants? Does it prefer to settle as soon as possible into a pattern of life more or less fixed once and for all? Does it want immediately the responsibilities of a family as a steadying influence? Is it afraid of that "freedom" which its elders were once accused of rating too high? Whether early marriage is or is not an important symptom of the trend to conformity, it is certainly a condition that promotes it. Hostages to fortune do not encourage the taking of chances. They increase, and they also furnish an excuse for, the desire to be secure. And that may be one of the greatest appeals which these hostages make.

Those years, when there are any, that lie between the advent of maturity and the responsibility of a family are the freest most men and women ever know—in significant as well as in trivial ways. As children they were under the control of their parents. As heads of a family they will be largely dominated by the needs of that family. No one else is so free to venture as the unmarried adult. No one else pays so light a penalty for any sort of nonconformity, or is likely to feel so free to risk a play for some big prize. He can, if necessary, "go up to the garret." There is neither anyone to forbid nor to be dragged along with him into poverty. The world is his oyster, and he can risk trying to open it. He can march to his own drum, and he is freer than he ever was before, or ever will be again, to set his own values. But there are fewer young people in that position than there were a generation ago. The epoch which used to lie between adolescence and family life has been all but abolished. Whether with deliberate intention or not, it is now the usual thing for young men and young women to deprive themselves of it. They pass almost without interval from tutelage to domesticity. Is it any wonder if they are most unusually conformist?

The term "wild oats" is commonly used with very limited implications. Even in that limited sense, the sowing of a few was widely recommended during most of the Eighteenth Century, and in the Twenties the practice was—with characteristic solemnity and a careful avoidance of the raffish term—again defended as the last prescribed course in that curriculum of "sex education" that should precede the final "adjustment to matrimony." "Wild oats" in this sense are again generally frowned upon, and we need not reopen the debate. But there are various species of wild oats other than the sexual. At least there ought to be some general term which would cover the whole exuberant process in the course of which youth questions, and criticizes, and rebels, before it "settles down"—some word to name the epoch of adventure and risk, of free experiment with attitudes and aims, with projects and standards of value. When no wild oats have been sown, no unconventional crops can be reaped. And I do not see how anything other than conformity can be expected of a generation which willingly foregoes the opportunity to sow even a few.

4

▲
▲▲▲

During the first year Carl Van Doren conducted the seminar for those who planned to take an M.A., whether or not they meant to go on from there. He suggested that I take as the subject of my Master's Essay the Nineteenth Century Philadelphia dramatist, George Henry Boker, of whom I had never heard but who was well known in his own time as the author of several poetic tragedies of which one, *Francesca da Rimini* had been acted with success by Laurence Barrett. I fear that what I turned out was routinely undistinguished. Though I managed to get a short article based on it published in *The Sewanee Review,* I was well aware how small an achievement this was by comparison with Mark's commercially published book. The latter is still cited in all bibliographies of Thoreau and was youthful in only one respect of which Mark himself was afterwards well aware. Years later when we were discussing a passage from some writer whose relevance to Thoreau was not very immediate I remarked that he had quoted it in his first book. "Oh, yes," he said, "I quoted everything I knew." And that, of course, is a habit of young writers.

Despite my failure to make much of my Master's Essay I was apparently an acceptable student. Brander Matthews gave me a "B" on the examination which I took at the conclusion of his course in Molière and which was, I believe, the only one of the examinations of the year where I was not awarded an "A." It would have comforted me greatly and no doubt disgusted Brander had we known that I was one day to climb into the Chair of Dramatic Literature which had been founded and named in his honor. At the end of the term I was awarded a modest scholarship, sufficient to pay the tuition for my second year.

The succeeding summer I spent in Knoxville, a considerable part of it passed in traditional Southern fashion on the front porch. It was there that I had in childhood read both the Alger books and Edgar Allan Poe and there that, later, I mused on Fate, Free Will, and the unfairness of God in the company of Omar Khayyam. Now, sobered by my aspirations toward learning as a graduate school defined it, I devoted myself to various "important" books which would not be discussed in any of the courses I planned to take during my second and last year of class attendance.

Somewhere or other I once read an anecdote about a child who had secretly resolved to run away from home and who, having given up the enterprise a few hours later, was amazed to discover on his return that he had not been missed. Casting about for some way of calling attention to his long absence and return he finally remarked: "Well, I see you have the same old cat."

My own situation and my reaction to it was somewhat similar. Knoxville had hardly noticed my eight months' absence. As I sat on the porch where I had passed many a previous summer and when I looked up from the pages of, for instance, Thomas Hobbes' *Leviathan* I saw the same slow-moving pageant of Main Street, still little changed from what it had always been. The same pedestrians, most of whom were familiar to me, passed by, and some of them stopped for a word or two, though not always aware that during the winter just passed I had been farther away rather than merely indoors. I, so I felt, was different, if Knoxville was not. So far as I was concerned I was already nearly a stranger. Nothing, I was sure, had happened to those who had remained there. I felt proudly, if a bit unjustifiably, that I now inhabited a different world. And despite the affection in which I held my father, my mother, and my brother Charlie I was almost, though not quite, as homesick for New York as I had been only a few months before for the members of my family if not for Knoxville itself.

After this summer spent at home I returned to Columbia in the fall of 1916, proudly past the first if minor hurdle, the Master's Degree, and now a young member of what we regarded as an aristocracy composed of those determined to face the rigors of the Ph.D. I entered the seminar conducted by Professor Trent and concerned with English literature of the late Seventeenth and the Eighteenth Centuries. There I promptly indicated that I hoped to find some thesis subject relating to the comedies of the Restoration—*i.e.,* Wycherley, Congreve, Van Brugh, Farquhar, and their lesser contemporaries.

Why did I make this choice? Partly no doubt because I had a stronger interest in plays and the theater than I quite realized. Partly also because I had liked jokes and wit for so long that, so I have been told, I began to tell anecdotes of one sort or another almost as soon as I could talk. I still do, and I like to rationalize my fondness for this sort of thing by believing that I am fundamentally a tough-minded idealist who insists upon subjecting my own as well as others' idealism to the test of corrosive common sense and even the cynicism toward which wit so commonly tends. Just as a religious faith which is terrified by blasphemy is often rather insecure, so, I like to think, is any idealism which shrinks from the criticism of wit.

There was also, I am afraid, a less worthy reason. I was still under the influence of my adolescent desire to shock and the consequent tendency to pretend to like even more than I actually did both the raffish and also the "decadent," as that term was understood during the Eighteen-nineties. The comic drama of the Restoration was notoriously the naughtiest section of English literature. Who could treat it with a profounder understanding than I?

Reading the dialogue I found it hard to believe that conversation so completely cynical and so overloaded with double meanings often not always very double, could have been tolerated in a mixed company. And it is another commentary on changed manners that there are few interchanges in Restoration comedy which would raise eyebrows at a present-day cocktail party. Four-fifths of the corpus I had undertaken to study is actually pretty sorry stuff. The simplified Hobbism which furnished what passed for the underlying philosophical and psychological assumptions was extremely shallow as well as false. Nevertheless a few of the writers did sometimes achieve moments of high if limited expressiveness, and I have always remembered one short passage in Congreve which aroused what was to me a fascinating speculation.

What was then called admiringly "a woman of pleasure" (an upper-class female libertine) at one moment exclaims:

> But say what you will, 'tis better to be left than never to have been loved . . . For my part, my youth may wear and waste, but it shall never rust in my possession.

The contrast between "wear and waste" on the one hand and "rust" on the other is a finely comic bit of discrimination; but that is not what struck me. "Better to be loved and left" is identical except for one word with " 'Tis better to have loved and lost/Than never to have loved at all." Were Tennyson's lines entirely original or were they an echo, conscious or unconscious, of Congreve? If they were either of the two last, then what went on in his mind when he substituted "lost" for "left"? The change of the one word changes the whole sentence from comic realism to romantic melancholy. It also illustrates one of the important differences between the modes. "Left" is crystally unambiguous. "Lost" covers too vaguely defined an area to be other than fuzzy. You know precisely what Congreve's character meant. Tennyson's might have meant quite a number of different things.

Professor Trent accepted my proposed field of study and later in the year I read to the seminar a general report on Restoration Comedy and my attitude toward it. He then suggested that as my special subject I should choose what is referred to in literary history as "The Collier Controversy" which, so he said, had never been closely studied.

Jeremy Collier was a stiff-necked clergyman and, technically, what was called a Non-Juror; *i.e.,* one who had been willing to pay the considerable penalties involved in refusing to renounce his allegiance to the exiled Stuart kings and to accept the new dynasty of William and Mary. He was a man of considerable antiquarian learning, also of the most narrow-minded opinions of the sort commonly described as "puritanical." In 1698 he startled the intellectual world of England by publishing a book called *A Short View of the Immorality and Profaneness of the English Stage* in which, with considerable rough eloquence, he denounced as an abomination the whole tradition of the English theater with especial emphasis on the ribaldry and cynicism of recent comedy. It was a fanatical as well as an able book, but Collier risked ruining his case by making little distinction between obvious obscenities and explicit ridicule of religion or morality on the one hand, and the most farfetched interpretations of mild and innocent remarks on the other.

Collier's world was so remote from that of the fashionable writers and their audience that one would have expected him to be either ignored or ridiculed. Contrary to what may well have been his own anticipations, the book created a sensation in both worlds. Other clergymen, literary commentators, and several of the dramatists themselves entered the fray. Within a few years thirty or forty books and pamphlets directly provoked by Collier were published and it was soon obvious that the defenders of the theater were feeble, the attackers strong. Plainly, England was ready for what Macaulay was later to call "one of its recurrent fits of morality," and whether or not Collier was as much a symptom as an effective cause, the fact remains that within a comparatively few years the whole Restoration comic tradition died and English comedy turned so strongly towards sentimental moralizing and so squeamish a regard for the proprieties that it all but ceased to be comic at all.

Professor Trent's suggestion was that I should first study the whole literature of the controversy—much of which had probably never been read for a century and a half—then consider all the other influences, sociological as well as literary, which resulted in what is traditionally called Sentimental Comedy. Some of my research could be done at Columbia but ultimately I would have to go to England to find documentary material as well as many of the rarer printed items of the Collier controversy. How I was to manage this I did not know, but after all I still had my orals to prepare for and a completed thesis would be some years away.

Having finished the required courses in the usual two years, I learned, before I returned for another summer in Knoxville, that I had been given what was much sought after—namely an appointment as instructor in the undergraduate Columbia College. Concurrently it was expected that I would go on with my own work.

I was neither very successful nor very happy as a beginning teacher. From the first few months I spent trying to find my way in a classroom I remember only two things with pleasure, of which the first is the beautiful incomprehension of a sophomore. We were discussing Christopher Marlowe's *Dr. Faustus* and in all innocence he asked me why Faustus had been so disappointed when he saw Helen of Troy. Since the exclamation she provokes is one of the most purple of purple passages, I inquired what caused him to suppose that Faustus had been disappointed. "Well, all he said was 'is *that* the face that launched a thousand ships?' "

The other thing I remember with pleasure from this dismal period was watching from the sidelines the battle for the minds and souls of the coming generation, which was already being waged between Teachers' College and the Graduate School of English. I was especially delighted by some sniping behind the lines undertaken by the shy, seemingly inoffensive Professor Allan Abbott, himself a member of the English faculty at Teachers' College. One of his exploits was to publish in a technical journal devoted to Education a burlesque essay proposing an "integrated" English course. The essay was called "A Fish-Centered School" and the "project" was a course to be built around Henry Van Dyke's essay on fishing. Students were to investigate fish from every standpoint: literary, scientific, recreational, aesthetic, etc., and it was suggested that, among other things, they be required to compile a notebook illustrated with pictures cut from the encyclopedias in the school library. The cream of the jest was that many readers took the proposal seriously, though at least one raised apologetically the question whether or not mutilation of the encyclopedias should be encouraged.

Another of Professor Abbott's enterprises, semiserious in intention but productive of an hilarious result, was inspired by the growing mania for psychological testing. It consisted of a device for measuring Poetic Appreciation. A considerable number of short passages commonly recognized as of high literary merit were each rewritten in several ways intended to vulgarize them—by making the rhythm too insistent, by obtruding a farfetched moral, by inserting lines of outrageous sentimentality, obvious clichés, etc. The victims of the test were asked in each case to select the version they thought best. Most of them preferred one or another of the debased versions but that was not all. After a year's course in Poetic Appreciation they were then given a similar test. Most of them did even worse than before.

By now the First World War was raging towards its climax, and like many, I suppose, I was more than half-relieved to see a way out of suffering present evils by flying to others I knew not of. During my second term as instructor, I volunteered into the Army ahead of the draft.

I shall pass rapidly over my "army career" since it was as uneventful and inglorious as possible. I was promptly assigned to the new Psychological Branch of the Medical Corps and sent to Fort Greenleaf, Tennessee, where we were given a very sketchy basic training along with instructions in the method of giving the newly devised Army Intelligence Tests, Alpha and Beta. During one of my first tours of duty as sentry, solemnly carrying a gun to defend Fort Greenleaf, I faced, at the limit of my post, another Columbia graduate student, he from the department of Philosophy, whom I had never met before. Thomas Munro was from then on and for many years one of my friends. He became for a time an instructor at Columbia, then was attached for several years to the Barnes Foundation in Philadelphia, and is now, as he has been for many years, one of the curators of the Cleveland Museum of Art.

Because some congressmen thought psychological testing a ridiculous frill the commissions we were supposed to receive at the end of our training period were held up (in fact they never came through) so that Munro and I were shipped to Fort Travis, Texas, as corporals.

San Antonio where the camp was located turned out to be a sleepy old-fashioned town, and life in the barracks was not unpleasant or, except during occasional rush periods, too demanding. From time to time a contingent of five hundred or more newly inducted men would arrive and as a part of their "processing" they were given in groups either the Alpha test for those who could read and write, or the Beta for illiterates. It was my first real experience with intelligence tests and, though I soon came to the conclusion that one should be careful not to expect too much, they nevertheless served very effectively to make rough distinctions that were very useful indeed in this special situation.

Primarily the object was to divide the recruits into three classes: those who might be sent to an officers' training camp with a high degree of probability that they would not be flunked out; those who could be trained promptly into acceptable soldiers; and, finally, those who were so dull that, at best, they would seriously slow the progress of the other common soldiers in any large group.

Experience soon proved, by the way, that a score of "B" indicated nearly the same probability of success in officers' training camp as did an "A" but that only about fifty per cent of the "C" men sent as an experiment finally won their commissions. Under the circumstances the sensible thing to do was to take a chance on the "A's" and "B's" only; but I could not help wondering even then if there were not potential General Grants among the "C's" who would never get a chance. And I have often wondered since whether the increasing tendency to make irrevocable decisions on the basis of tests of one kind or another doesn't mean that safe mediocrity is given an increasingly sure place in the world while offbeat genius is relegated to the labor battalions.

Those who failed either of the group tests were usually given individual interviews or tests to check the results and to eliminate psychopaths. This was more interesting work and we soon discovered that one question would place the subject in the appropriate large category almost as reliably as a whole series of tests. "What is a spoon?" we would ask. If the answer was a true definition—something like "It's an implement" (or even just "a thing") "used in eating"—that meant either "A" or "B." If the response was a "definition by use"—"A spoon is what you eat with"—the subject was a "C." And if he gave a "pseudo-definition by iteration"—"A spoon is a . . . . well it's a spoon ain't it"—he was "D" and likely to be a nuisance in anything but a labor battalion. We got not only quite a few of such but, since draft boards were fanatically determined not to miss anyone, we got also several low-grade idiots and a few obvious psychopaths.

The problem of avoiding confusion between low intelligence and lack of education or any other kind of experience was not in most cases as difficult as might be expected so long as no fine discrimination was attempted, but a contingent of several hundred Negroes from the Louisiana rice fields, some of whom spoke no English, was a real problem. Not only were some of these men completely illiterate but many had never seen anything except the fields within a radius of a few miles from where they lived. I remember two amusing incidents. Asked if he thought he could walk to the battlefields if given enough time, one hesitated a long time before he said "No." "Why not?" "Well I think there is some water somewhere." Obviously not a moron. A not-infrequent answer to the question "Who is the president of the United States?" was "Uncle Sam," but another Louisiana Negro looked up with an ingratiating smile and answered with another question, "It ain't you is it boss?" Obviously, like the boy who had shined my shoes in Knoxville, a diplomat.

We scored as well as administered the test and compiled statistics, the latter sometimes involving Karl Pearson's "Coefficient of Correlation" which we had learned to compute in the course of our training but of which I am not sure I ever really understood the mathematical basis. Between rush periods we had a reasonable amount of leisure, a good deal of which Munro and I spent in extending our reading by drawing books from a rather large if naturally miscellaneous camp library. The captain in charge of our company grunted once when he found me in my bunk deep in Taylor's *The Medieval Mind* which he evidently thought unnecessarily remote from the effort to win the war, but I devoted most of my time to catching up with the most esteemed recent fiction. This meant so many shelves full of Wells, Bennett, Galsworthy and George Moore that I have never had much inclination to read them since.

The thing I remember best from my stay at Fort Travis was a moment of embarrassment among the most acute I have ever suffered. The commissions we thought we had earned were still blocked in Washington but I did get elevated to the rank of Sergeant. We were not a company very much concerned with military punctilios but, still, the army was the army and shortly after achieving my new rank I was approached by one of the privates assigned to our barracks to perform some of the humbler duties. He began a question with "Corporal, do you want . . ." At that moment my left arm itched and I raised my other hand to scratch it—just where the new chevrons had been sewn on my sleeve. "Oh, excuse me," he said, "Sergeant, I mean." I tried to explain; but I don't think he believed me. And to this day I vehemently repudiate amateur psychologists who insist that whatever I may have thought in my conscious mind the itch was an unconscious awareness of my new rank. This always reminds me of one of my father's favorite jokes, brought I imagine by Grossmother across the Atlantic.

It concerns a German soldier who had reached middle age before he finally rose from private to corporal. The great event was the only subject of conversation in his family for months before and for months after the new dignity was achieved. "Mother," asked one of the children, "are we *all* corporals?" "Certainly not. Only your father and I are corporals."

The great lesson I learned in the army was that fearing the improbable worst (which I have always been inclined to do) sometimes can serve a useful purpose. Within a day or two of the armistice an order came through that all members of the Psychological Corps should be given their discharges. It was a Saturday afternoon and I went immediately to our captain and asked for mine. "Well," he said, "it's Saturday. You can wait until Monday can't you?" "No," I replied, "the order says 'immediately' and to me that means right now." He laughed scornfully but said, "O.K." My fellow psychologists laughed also, but I stood firm. On Monday the order was rescinded and I soon departed gaily while the others remained behind. It was months before some of them got their release because they were presently, as officially members of the Medical Corps, shifted to hospitals where, so one of them told me later, there was nothing to do in the nearly empty wards which were maintained as nominally in operation by young members of the medical staff not anxious to return too soon to the uncertainties of civilian life.

Naturally, I congratulated myself on my prudence, but there was another moment at which I was astonishingly imprudent. In the course of the pre-discharge medical examination I passed under the hands of a young doctor who, seated at a table, was making certain routine tests. He reached over his head, turned on an electric light, and peered into my eyes. Three times he repeated the maneuver and then exclaimed in dismay, "You don't have any pupillary reflex!" "Well," I replied, "I might have one if you didn't put your head between me and the light every time you turn it on." Even now I tremble to think that he might very well have sent me back for a few months "to learn military courtesy," but he must have been a decent fellow. He merely laughed with some good-natured embarrassment.

Thanks to him I was soon on my way back to Knoxville where, after a few weeks, I departed again for Columbia to pass my days and some of my nights in the library until such time as I felt myself learned enough to ask for an oral examination.

The end of the First World War brought no such flood of students to the colleges and graduate schools as was to overwhelm them after 1945. Columbia was much the same as I had left it, and Prohibition rather than war was responsible for the most obvious change in New York City. The cafés and restaurants which had seemed to me so large a part of its glamour were either dead or dying and the era of the speakeasy was about to begin. But since I had come prepared to work harder than ever, I accepted the change with a shrug.

Far more important to me was the fact that I now fell "seriously in love" for the first time. This, I know, is a vague phrase, but one of the comedies I had chosen to study supplied me with a precise criterion. The hero, in a very ecstasy of reckless passion, permitted himself to exclaim, "I love you to the point of matrimony itself—

almost, egad"; and my own state was ultimately so much worse that I was presently prepared to abandon the "almost." Since mine was not an unrequitted passion, circumstance rather than mutual intention frustrated one of those early marriages of which I have already expressed disapproval.

The young lady in question, a contralto preparing for a career by studying Italian at Columbia, will appear briefly again in this account; but at the moment the important thing is that she aided rather than interfered with my preparation for the ominous day when I must appear for question before a solemn committee of the faculty. Full of gloomy prognostications, I might well have worried myself into a decline had I not been able to console myself with the day, or rather the evening, ahead.

Since World War II Doctors of Philosophy have become "plentiful as tabby cats." Forty years ago they were by no means so numerous, but even then the general public was not, I fear, very heavily impressed by their right to put Ph.D. after their names. On the other hand, this highest of academic degrees meant a great deal, both practically and in prestige, to those who hoped to win it, especially if they intended, as most of them did, to become teachers in some college. Moreover, one had to go through a good deal to get it.

Over most of us there hung like a threatening shadow the prospect of the two-hour Oral which would determine whether or not three or four years of work had been wasted and for such as were, like me, temperamentally disposed to fear the worst, the date fixed long in advance looked like approaching doomsday. We spent most of our nights as well as our days anxiously considering which known gaps in our knowledge it was most important to fill and, worse yet, what areas of ignorance lay unsuspected on this side or that. Since in those days not more than five or six candidates per year were likely to present themselves to the Graduate School of English and Comparative Literature, our spirits rose or fell as each of our predecessors succeeded or failed, and we anxiously compared our estimate of them with our estimate of ourselves.

The successful not only gave counsel but staged mock examinations in which they were the questioners and we the candidates. J. H. H. Lyon and Donald Clark, both of whom later taught for many years at Columbia and were in my time already two or three years past the Oral, acted as unpaid tutors and Lyon, especially, as a guide, counselor, and friend who generally took each candidate for a calming walk in the hour preceding the great event.

Nearly every successful candidate had some story to tell and John Lyon's story was especially well known. At the end of his examination he had been asked, according to custom, to withdraw for a few minutes while his fate was discussed. A short time later Professor Ashley Thorndike, head of the department, appeared and said, "A very good examination, Mr. Lyon." Naturally, Lyon left the building on clouds and lay down that night for what he thought would be the first good sleep of the week. Sometime after midnight he awoke in terrible doubt. Had Professor Thorndike said, "A very good examination," or "Not a very good examination"? All possibility of sleep was gone. At daybreak he dressed and sat on the steps of Philosophy Hall until Professor Thorndike appeared, many hours later. Until then he had not been able to be sure that the damning "not" hadn't preceded what he had at first taken for a gratifying phrase.

When, in the late spring, my own day of doom arrived I went for the ritual walk with Lyon and entered trembling into the awful chamber. As I quitted it two hours later I noticed that the chair upon which I had sat was surrounded by so copious a semicircle of fragments plucked from its cane bottom that it is a wonder the seat had continued to support me to the end. As I waited in the outer office for the verdict Miss Wallace, the aging and kindly secretary who knew everybody's business, offered her congratulations. "Rather premature," I said. "Oh, I know it will be all right," she replied. "Well, it is taking them long enough to decide." Miss Wallace looked at her watch. "You have been here exactly twenty seconds." A little later I sent a telegram to my parents in Knoxville and went out to dinner with the young lady whom I loved "to the point of matrimony itself."

Twenty-five years later when I was one of the group assembled in the chamber where I had passed my ordeal, but this time to question rather than to be questioned, the Chairman of the department, successor to Professor Thorndike who had died some years before, turned back a hundred pages in a record book still being used to the corresponding date in 1919 and read aloud the notes on my own examination. They concluded "A very good examination." At least *I think* there was no "not" before "a very good." In any case I intend to lose no sleep in worrying.

5

▲
▲▲▲

Mark Van Doren has told in his own recent autobiography how it happened that a few months later we sailed together for our first stay in Europe, but I must repeat, briefly at least, the happy little history. Nowadays there are so many agencies and foundations dispensing grants of one sort or another that one is reminded of Mark Twain's description of the membership conferred upon him in the Legion of Honor, "a distinction which few manage to escape." In 1919, on the other hand, Columbia's Graduate English Department had only the one annual Cutting Traveling Fellowship (1200 dollars) to bestow and naturally enough both Mark and I wanted it. Nevertheless, we were so close that only after discussing the matter together could we bring ourselves to make competing applications.

Having done so we both departed, he for his home in Urbana, Illinois, I for Knoxville. Pessimistic as usual, I dismissed the matter from my mind and when a telegram arrived announcing that I had been given the fellowship my surprised exaltation was tempered by embarrassment. How could I tell Mark that I had won and he lost? Meanwhile, in Urbana, Mark was the unhappy victim of similarly mixed feelings. Because the war had made European travel impossible during 1918, two grants could be made for 1919 and we each had one.

As soon as this fact was known there was no question but that we would enjoy the boon in company. We booked passages on a boat sailing from New York, had them canceled by a strike, and finally departed from Philadelphia on the *S.S. Haverford* which took two weeks to Liverpool. Two weeks was not, however, too long a voyage for two young men who had never crossed the ocean before, especially not when there happened to be aboard a very pretty young English girl for whose favorable attention we immediately became entirely amiable rivals. Mark had, I remember, an edge on me. Come to think of it, he always did have the edge on me when members of the opposite sex were around. Unlike me he had no great desire to be regarded as a devil among the ladies, but the ladies always wanted him to be a devil among them, and that gets you farther, quicker. But what woman, young or old, would completely discourage either of two young men when she could have them competing for her time and attention? Very little time she certainly had to herself but I don't think she suffered much from this fact. After the boat docked neither Mark nor I ever saw or heard of her again, but neither of us, I think, have ever had days and nights at sea pass more entertainingly.

All Columbia English students fortunate enough to get to England headed toward the great library of the British Museum, but we allowed ourselves first a short walking tour in the Lake Country where we read Wordsworth's "Michael" on the very scene of that sad pastoral tale. In London ten days later we followed the classical pattern by engaging "bed and breakfast" in a rather dismal lodginghouse in Guilford Street just around the corner from the Museum and were plunged at once into the atmosphere of innumerable realistic novels: Kippers or finnan haddie at a breakfast table presided over by a landlady whose husband spent all his time reading the racing sheets; beds in a cold room heated only by a fireplace for which nearly incombustible coal could be had at the rate of one shilling per bucket.

For months thereafter neither Mark nor I very often skipped a day in the great reading room to which our Columbia credentials gave us admission. I was soon deep in the books and pamphlets of the Collier controversy while Mark, whose subject was John Dryden, checked or added esoteric bits to a thesis farther advanced than mine. For all I know some work as world-shaking as that which Karl Marx had prepared in that same room may have been taking shape around us, but our nearest neighbor was a turbaned and rather smelly Oriental who sat all day nearly hidden by the pile of astrological works with which he had surrounded himself.

So old-fashioned were the museum's atmosphere and facilities that they had changed little since the Nineteenth Century and it was easy to imagine the penniless George Gissing doing his laundry in one of the wash basins until the day when he found himself faced with a new sign: "For casual ablutions only." Going to or from the reading room we often turned aside for a few minutes into one or the other of the great exhibition rooms, and my old mentor William P. Trent (who was so bitterly anti-English as to have become pro-German) would have been pleased that I noted certain striking variations in the vocabulary used to give the history of this object or that. Replicas were likely to be labeled with strong words like "destroyed by the Germans" while a certain famous original from Egypt confessed only that it had been "acquired at the capitulation of Alexandria." From time to time Mark and I also followed a tradition long established by Columbia Traveling Fellows which was to pay a visit of respect to the glass case containing the most famous of all manuscripts pertaining to English literature—namely Cotton Vitellus A 15, the sole surviving manuscript of the Anglo-Saxon epic *Beowulf*. Incidentally, the second most famous English manuscript, the fine copy of *The Canterbury Pilgrims,* beautifully illuminated about the year 1400 is similarly exhibited at the Huntington Library in California. "Westward the course of Empire"—and sweeps along with it various waifs and strays.

Week ends we usually spent (dutifully but also with excitement) visiting the places and the objects whose associations with English literature we were proud to know: the tomb of Nell Gwyn, somewhat inappropriately located in the fine church of St.-Martin's-in-the-Fields; the tall column erected in 1666 to commemorate the Great Fire and still bearing on its base that mendacious inscription charging the Catholics with having deliberately set the fire, and responsible, therefore, for the Catholic Alexander Pope's fine line about the district where this monument "like a proud bully lifts its head and lies." Also, of course, Hampton Court, famous for its gallery of

Restoration beauties painted from life by Sir Peter Lyly, but each head provided with "the sleepy eye which tells the melting soul" and then set above a standard body equipped with the inevitable swelling, well-exposed breasts. Proud that we knew how street and place names like Theobald's Road and Cavendish Square should be pronounced, we were saddened to discover that the man on the street usually did not.

During that preliminary tour of the lake country we had met Mr. Langton Cole, an architect then responsible for the maintenance of St. Paul's Cathedral. With him and his family we were to spend many pleasant and instructive week ends—instructive because they made us familiar with one segment of English life; pleasant because, like most of the foreigners I have met, he was cordial to Americans even when (as was not here the case) they disapproved of us as a people and sometimes paid that most insulting of compliments: "But you are not a bit like an American."

The Coles lived in Sutton within commuting distance of London and seemed to me so typical that they might have come out of a novel, so perfectly did their manners, attitudes, and habits correspond with the class to which they belonged. Mr. Cole was exactly what a professional man charged with a public responsibility should be; his wife, a large, no-nonsense woman who was somewhat lame charged about the village in a tricycle without regard to dignity for the simple reason that she knew and expected everyone else to know just precisely what her somewhat better than mere middle-class dignity was. There were five unmarried daughters, one of whom was preparing herself to become a mistress in a girls' school. A somewhat younger sister lived chiefly for the sake of cultivating a common obsession with the virtues and sorrows of the sainted martyr Charles I and was appropriately shocked when I declared my preference for Charles II. The house, comfortable and uncomfortable in the typical British fashion, was so cold that I was only moderately successful in concealing the fact that my trembling hand had difficulty in conveying the breakfast egg to my mouth without spilling, and I once unjustly suspected irony when one of the daughters, looking out the window at a cold drizzle, exclaimed: "What a fine day for a walk."

Commenting on his daughters' rather dim matrimonial prospects, Mr. Cole explained that there was really no one in the village with whom they could associate. There were some members of the minor nobility who were above them, and of course the sons of tradesmen far, far below. But there were no other families of professional men such as would have been their equals. I was bold enough to ask, "Well, what about me; for all you know my father might be a greengrocer"—knowing as I did from novels that, for some reason or other, a retail seller of vegetables ranks as perhaps the humblest of tradesmen. In obvious surprise at my incomprehension he replied: "That wouldn't make the slightest difference; you are an American." Whether this meant that since no American is a gentleman there is no use making distinctions among them or, possibly, something less insulting, I have never been able to decide.

Since Mark and I felt that we should investigate also some other segments of London society we adopted what seemed at the time a rather daring, even slightly rakish, device. We had inserted for one time only the following in *The Times* famous "agony column": "Two young Americans, literary but interested in everything, desire London friends."

The result was astonishing. In due time the newspaper forwarded to us some thirty or forty letters whose signers ranged all the way from a professional dance-hall "hostess" and a teenager from Wimbledon (eager to escape from that notoriously restrictive environment) to a Baroness who, as it turned out, was a passionate Americanophile with a son at Harvard. Accepting an invitation from the latter, we felt that we were entering a rather dizzily exalted circle and the tea was so agreeable that we were only slightly disappointed to learn that the Baron was a banker so recently elevated to the peerage that, in W. S. Gilbert's phrase, "the paint was hardly dry on his ancestral portraits." From the other letters we selected those which seemed most promising and some meetings thus arranged were quite rewarding. A few took place in an atmosphere more or less faintly illegitimate but others, including several with entirely normal males, were simply with gentlemen who had a curiosity about Americans analagous to ours about Englishmen.

One other incident I feel impelled to mention. Reading in the *Athenaeum* an article in praise of port wine we were delighted to discover that it was signed by George Saintsbury, the famous retired Professor of Literature from Edinburgh University whose books were obligatory for graduate students. In his honor we went out to the nearest pub, drank a glass or two of what purported to be the beverage he had celebrated, and then wrote him a letter describing how we had been inspired to do so. Back came a reply from the Royal Crescent, Bath, in which Saintsbury expressed pleasure that he had been able to corrupt two refugees from the land of prohibition, hoped that the port had not been too awful, and added that were his own cellar not now only a memory he would invite us to a glass of port as it should be. When his little volume

Notes on a Cellar Book appeared shortly thereafter we received a copy signed and inscribed, "Authenticated, especially note to p 40," which note reads:

> "One of the most agreeable incidents of my life in connection with port is quite recent. Soon after I had published something about wine in the *Athenaeum* and since America 'went dry' two students of that misguided country wrote to me saying that they had found it impossible to refrain, after reading the article, from sallying forth, purchasing some so-called Port Wine (I hope it was not very bad), and drinking my health in it. It would be difficult for a teacher to have a more gratifying testimonial to the efficacy of his teaching; especially when he remembers the boasts of prohibitionists as to bringing on prohibition by sowing pseudo-scientific tarradiddles in U. S. school-books."

Very little of my working life has been devoted to the primary historical research for which the Columbia Ph.D. was intended to train us. Temperament and circumstances turned me in a different direction. Nevertheless, I have never regretted that I learned the little I did and during the years when I was preparing my thesis I tasted to some slight degree the pleasure which can be felt in pursuing forgotten documents and discovering historical facts until then unknown. In the library of the Archbishop of Canterbury at Lambeth Palace I turned up documents indicating that the antitheater party in London had attempted to draw the Church authorities into their campaign, and among the vast collections in the Public Records offices a petition in the names of the three famous actors, Thomas Betterton, Elizabeth Barry, and Ann Bracegirdle, which was unknown to historians of the stage and had remained, for I know not how long, tied into a bundle with other documents thrust into a canvas sack. For me such minor discoveries were a glimpse down "the road not taken" and at least they make me feel that I understand better than I would have otherwise how and why the historical scholar operates.

When spring came Mark and I both concluded (perhaps the season had some influence) that we had done what we came to London to do and that we might cross the channel to Paris, there to remain until our money ran out.

It is strange how intermittent is the record which memory preserves for us, how complete blanks often alternate with images and recalled emotions forty years old still more vivid than some scarcely more distant than yesterday. I remember that Mark had decided to make a side trip to the Netherlands whence his ancestors had come, and that he joined me in Paris a week or ten days after my arrival there. But I have no memory whatever of leaving the Guilford Street lodgings, of whether I proceeded to Portsmouth or Dover, or even of the channel crossing. Of the journey by train from a French port to the metropolis I recall (but here very vividly) only two incidents: my pleased surprise at the Normandy country with its queer red houses strangely high and narrow, and the fact that I broke the journey at Rouen to visit the cathedral where, exhausted by walking the town, I fell asleep in a pew until I was awakened by a costumed beadle carrying a staff who indicated somewhat indignantly that a cathedral was not a dormitory.

Then the fog descends again not to lift until Mark and I are established in the ancient Hotel Corneille on the street of the same name, close by the Odeon. It was only a few steps to the colonnade surrounding the theater where a leading bookseller displayed a huge collection of books which were, at the prevailing rate of exchange, almost incredibly cheap. It was also only a short walk to the quais of the left bank and the so-often painted, etched, and photographed *bouquinistes* who displayed in boxes their collections of mostly worthless second-hand books and magazines some of which nevertheless found purchasers ranging from collectors, always hopeful of finding some unrecognized treasures, to urchins who paid a penny for a catalogue or an outdated almanac which, as the *bouquiniste* would point out, was worth acquiring because it did after all boast "des images."

For such as we in search of the exotic and, especially, of the past, Paris was, if anything, more exciting than London. It was more completely foreign, and its antiquities, if not more numerous, were more graceful and seemed also somehow more assured—less like preserved relics than a still integral part of the city. All that we saw had been seen by many generations of the students who had preceded us and was to be seen by at least one or two succeeding generations. That was part of the charm. Returning to Paris repeatedly until the outbreak of World War II, I was always amazed to discover not, of course, that Notre Dame and the Louvre were still there but that one might be reasonably sure that nearly every little shop, café, or even newsstand would be precisely where and what it had been before, even though the proprietor might have died and his widow or his son-in-law taken over. The sense of stability which this gave is something no one brought up in an American community can have experienced at home. It is the antithesis of Progress but, when met for the first time, it may strike those of a certain temperament as something reassuringly better.

What Mark and I saw, felt, and thought about the revelation which is Paris was too little different from what countless others have seen, thought, felt, and described to need recording once more. But I was then, and have continued to be, so aware of the curiously ambiguous attitude of the Parisian to the outlanders who incessantly come to camp on his doorstep that I must, in a moment, quote what seems to me the best description I have ever met of that attitude.

On the one hand, no nation was ever more chauvinistic than the French. It believes that its intellect and its culture are not only the best in the world but also so nearly the *only* intellect and culture that all men but Frenchmen are barbarians. A reply made to me a few years later by a young man connected with the theater with whom I happened to be crossing the ocean is not untypical of this attitude. When I happened to remark that the Odeon was preparing to present a translation of a play by Eugene O'Neill he said positively: "You are mistaken. No American could possibly write a play which the Odéon would be willing to perform." Once I also remember asking a Parisian who was discoursing upon what he regarded as an undisputed fact if he thought it part of politeness to insist so strongly that you are politer than anyone else. But the point of my question was not understood.

On the other hand, Paris' tolerance of the barbarian seems often to go beyond tolerance to become cordiality, and it is certainly true that I, as an individual, have seldom met anything else. Perhaps the explanation is that complete assurance of superiority renders unnecessary the defensive rudeness of those less sure that they are better than the intruder. Here, in any event, is the analysis and description referred to above. It occurs in Logan Pearsall Smith's *Unforgotten Years* and though it refers especially to art students the extension to all is easy.

> Paris welcomes would-be artists with its urbane, heartless grace; it provides them with every facility for learning the art they will never learn to practice; it appropriates with a charming smile the savings they have brought with them, and with the same smile it watches them fade away or perish, knowing that new generations will soon appear to occupy their little hotels and lodgings.

When, not long ago, I wrote a review of Mark's autobiography I twitted him with having failed to mention what I did not believe he could have forgotten, namely, the only quarrel we ever had in the course of more than forty-five years of association and friendship. I shall put some account of it here because it illustrates an aspect of Mark's character which sometimes comes as a surprise to those who have not known him long.

John Dryden, one of his first great enthusiasms and the subject of the thesis on which he was working while we were together in Europe, might have had him in mind when he wrote, "Beware the fury of a patient man." Mark is patient, so patient, for instance, that though he certainly does not tolerate bores and fools *gladly* he tolerates them (up to a point) so patiently that they often think they are pleasing him. But when the storm breaks it breaks astonishingly out of a clear sky. As an illustration, I remember that years later, when we were both teachers at Columbia, I heard a roar which shook my adjoining office when the lightning finally struck a crank who had paid repeated visits, sure that Mark was listening sympathetically to his plan for an Owls Club—to be composed of Mark himself, along with the eleven other wisest men in the world, who would decide all policies for the universe and would have them accepted just because those who made them were so obviously the wisest men. "Damn it I don't *want* to be an Owl and I *won't* be an Owl. Get out of here!" Nor is it likely that even some of his favorite pupils will forget the times when, having listened with what seemed sympathy to some excuse, or evasion, or folly, he reached the end of his patience and the storm broke without so much as a single premonitory rumble.

The only time I was so unfortunate as to be on the receiving end of his wrath was when we were returning late at night on foot to our Left Bank hotel from some foray into Montmartre, not strictly part of our academic work. For some time we had been walking in silence, I—and this was the occasion of the outburst—a foot or two ahead. Suddenly, in the same voice later to be used in declining the invitation to be an Owl, I was informed vehemently and profanely that he would not be bullied into walking faster than he wanted to walk. Though guilty, I was so unaware of my crime and so astonished at what came out of the darkness behind me that I made no reply whatever. We reached the hotel in silence. We parted for the night without a word. Next morning all was serene again and neither of us ever mentioned the incident to the other until I wrote my review of his autobiography. Mark's anger is as short-lived as it is seemingly sudden, and I say "seemingly" because I have no doubt that it has usually been building up like the electrical charge in a cloud.

During 1918-19 twelve or fourteen hundred dollars (for some mysterious reason my grant was of the latter sum) went amazingly far in England and even further in France. Mark and I put aside barely enough to pay our passage home and resolved to stay in France until the last franc left over had been spent. Dramatically the end came when I discovered an imminent hole in the seat of my only wearable pair of trousers. The pilgrims would be compelled to return.

Seldom if ever have I departed more reluctantly from any city or country. What had happened to me was merely what has happened to so many Americans that there is no point in attempting to describe it again. We all flatter ourselves that Paris is not so much our second as our true home, and for a time I suffered from the absurd delusion that just as I belonged in New York more than in Knoxville, so I belonged more in Paris than in New York. It is not that Parisians "make us feel at home" but rather that, with their great and indifferent tolerance, they permit us to make ourselves at home there.

Before the beginning of the Second World War I returned a number of times to France, once for a stay of more than a year, and I returned always with delight. That I have no strong urge to do so again is due partly to the fact that I have lost most of my interest in cities, partly that, from the reports I get, Paris seems to have changed as much as I.

For one thing, though tourists and temporary residents were already numerous in 1920, they still did not dominate the scene as it is said they now do. For another thing, the city itself is changing. "Modern" buildings are transforming the appearance of the ancient city and whatever may be said in favor of modern buildings they are almost precisely alike no matter where they are constructed. It is hardly worth while to cross the ocean to contemplate another huge structure of steel and glass. Oh yes, of course the museums are still there. But the charm of the past as one used to experience it was the charm of something still alive. As for museums we have them too. Cities, like individuals, are growing more and more conformist, and I am told that a modern hotel now occupies the site where the dear old Corneille had stood for so many years.

Departing, Mark and I had at least the great satisfaction of feeling that our mission had been accomplished. His thesis was finished, I had written a good part of mine, and collected the material for all the rest. With the terrible Orals behind us we felt that our Ph.D.'s were almost assured.

Perhaps this is the best time to say that Mark's *John Dryden,* like his Master's Essay on Thoreau, quickly found a commercial publisher and was immediately recognized as the best critical study of a great but at that time unappreciated poet. Reviewing it in England, T. S. Eliot wrote the essay later reprinted in one of his most influential volumes and thus shares the credit for having brought Dryden back as one of the comparatively few writers with whom intellectuals and "new critics" invariably speak with respect and enthusiasm.

My own *Comedy and Conscience After the Restoration,* which I completed in Knoxville within a few months of my return, remained unpublished until 1924, partly because a University press dallied with it long before deciding to risk a certain grant at its disposal upon another book.

When it was finally printed at my expense (and at a cost to me of approximately half what I had spent on the European expedition) it received, as is usual in the case of theses which appear frankly as just that, comparatively few reviews. But two that it did get served to teach me that reviews should not always be taken with the seriousness it is hard for an author not to accord them. One said that though the book was an admirably thorough and scholarly presentation of its subject it was not very interestingly written; the other that though it was very interestingly written it was not, unfortunately, as thorough as it ought to be. It would have been a great satisfaction then, though it is only a mild one now, to know that it was to be reprinted three times and has recently become available in paperback.

During my stay in England and France I had kept up the more or less agitated correspondence which can be easily imagined with Stella Bonnard, the singer with whom I found myself in love "to the point of matrimony itself." Meeting her on my return to New York I saw her for a week or two but learned the stunning news: she was soon to depart in order to continue for an indefinite time preparations in Germany for an operatic career. Since I myself had been absent for almost a year in the furtherance of my own career, there was not too much logic in my ineffective protest that hers should not come first. In any event she thought it did and, when I left her for Knoxville, she was on the point of departure.

I never saw her again and she died a few years ago. In Germany she first studied, then for a time she sang in one of the more important provincial operas; and when it became evident that her stay in Europe was indeed indefinite we broke off our correspondence. This much of her subsequent career I do, however, know. She married a German who died not long thereafter, then returned to Superior, Wisconsin, whence she had come, married again, and taught vocal music for many years.

After we had said our last good-by in New York I departed, feeling much bereft, for Knoxville where I assumed that I would stay until fall when I would take up the job which had been promised me at the Brooklyn Polytechnic Institute. The head of the small department there was Professor S. Marion Tucker, an ex-student of Professor Trent who had recommended me to him. But in Knoxville I was restless. After finishing the writing of my thesis, that restlessness became so evident that my father, indulgent as always, offered to give me whatever money I needed to tide me over in New York until my salary at the Polytechnic should begin. I accepted eagerly and with less embarrassment than I ought to have felt at wanting to get away from parents and a brother to whom I was nevertheless deeply attached.

An additional reason for my restlessness was an incident which seemed at the moment—perhaps actually was—of enormous importance to me.

Shortly after my return from France, and while I was still pausing in New York, I had written an essay which I sent to the Messrs. Mencken and Nathan who had been for the past six years editing an ancient pulp magazine called *The Smart Set.* This monthly had already had a long but ambiguous history. It was founded originally by the notorious William D'Alton Mann, editor of the disreputable *Town Topics,* who is said to have planned *The Smart Set* as an outlet for the literary efforts of the high social group whose doings he chronicled and whom he sometimes, it was said, blackmailed.

When this group proved less fertile in literary production than he had anticipated, he sold the magazine to one John Adams Thayer, proprietor of the very successful *Everybody's* and Thayer later made Willard Huntington Wright editor. Wright promptly turned it into a now almost forgotten pioneer in the just beginning revolt against the genteel tradition. He paid very little for contributions, but he accepted those which the more respectable publications would not touch and under his editorship, as well as that of his erstwhile contributors Mencken and Nathan, it published an astonishing number of firsts as well as the less salable work of established writers. O. Henry was paid seventeen dollars for one of his first stories, and Somerset

Maugham got a very small check for the short story "Miss Thompson," later made into the sensationally successful play *Rain.* In its pages appeared also very early work by Theodore Dreiser, Ezra Pound, F. Scott Fitzgerald, Waldo Frank, Dashiell Hammett, Aldous Huxley, D. H. Lawrence, Sinclair Lewis, Edgar Lee Masters, Eugene O'Neill, and many others.

How much I knew about it or just why I thought it a suitable place for my own somewhat naughty essay I do not know. But send it in I did. Then, while I was busy with my thesis in Knoxville, the unexpected answer arrived, a check for twenty dollars and a note which read, "Your essay amuses us. Mencken and Nathan."

Previously, I had, to be sure, seen in all the improbability of print my Knoxville reports to *The Footlight* and, eight or ten years later, the article based on my Master's Essay. But no one had ever *paid* me anything for words set down on paper. At that very moment, so I felt, I had become "a writer." What a dizzying prospect seemed to open! I don't mean that I even dreamed I might make a living that way. But at least one thing I had composed had a tangible market value.

I kept for years, but long ago lost, the tattered pulp magazine, the issue of January, 1921, in which my essay finally appeared but it is permanently preserved in a *Smart Set Anthology* edited by Burton Rascoe where it was reprinted along with very early work of my betters.

A few of its phrases as well as its general tenor have remained always in my memory, but to read it now is to be amazed again at how callow I still was. After all, I had previously written a doctoral thesis still considered solid enough to be kept in print more than forty years after it was written. Yet for what I hoped was a literary debut I chose to imitate the precious "decadence" of the Eighteen-nineties even though, as it comforts me to realize, it was the spoofing, Beerbohmish tone rather than the solemn Oscar Wildish, that I chose to imitate.

The theme was suicide aesthetically considered, and the thesis that in this, as in everything else, we were indifferent to drama and beauty. The ancient suicides—Petronius and Empedocles given as notable examples—considered aesthetic effect; moderns cared for nothing except "getting themselves dead." I don't remember what my own title had been but the editors called the piece "Threnody on a Decadent Art" and I well remember without consulting a text the opening sentence: "In no department of human activity is our decline from the grace of the ancients more evident than in that of suicide."

One reason that this has stuck in my mind is that it has seemed to me to demonstrate that every man has a natural rhythm which tends to persist through all changes of opinion, taste, and subject matter. Perhaps it is only fancy, but it seems to me that the first sentence of a very serious, not to say gloomy, book which I wrote eight years later is cast in almost the same mold: "It is one of Freud's quaint conceits that the child in his mother's womb is the happiest of living creature." Incidentally, there is also a difference of only two in the number of words in the sentence.

Here, copied out from the anthology, are a few of the passages which I regarded at the time as especially choice.

> In no department of human activity is our decline from the grace of the ancients more evident than in that of suicide . . . We achieve our ends with devastating thoroughness, but with all our effectiveness we are crude . . .
>
> Even had illuminating gas been known in the days of the Ptolemies, it is inconceivable that Cleopatra should have used it. Death by such a means suggests stuffy hall bedrooms

and unfortunate shopgirls, and is incompatible with "immortal longings" . . .

Anyone with the authentic taste in suicide will feel at once the exquisite fitness of her final choice—the asp, for such means smacks neither of the lamp nor of the laboratory, but brings one in touch at once with Nature—the source of all genuine beauty. Cunningly compounded poisons would have suggested the ignoble labor of vulgar apothecaries, puttering in dirty shops, but the venom of the asp was quietly distilled in Nature's alembic . . .

The austerity of Tacitus prevents him from fully appreciating the genius of Petronius, but a sympathetic imagination can easily reconstruct the picture from the bare skeleton given in the *Annals*. Gathering a few friends about him at the bath, he descended leisurely into the tepid water, and, reclining negligently, he began to discourse with his companions. Casually, he drew the curved bronze razor over his wrists and lowered his arms into the water. A slender stream like crimson smoke curled upward and dispersed itself through the crystal water, which, after a time, began to blush faintly and then to grow more deeply incarnadine. Being a man of pleasure, he avoided the usual deathbed topics and indulged in convivial songs and stories. From time to time he arrested the course of his too rapid dissolution by stopping the flow of blood, but, intermittent though the loss was, he gradually grew weaker and weaker, until with the breaking of the last jest and the emptying of the last bottle he was no more. Petronius Arbiter was dead, but he left a name that is to endure as long as the art is revered . . .

Socrates, involuntary though his suicide was, showed what could be done in this branch of the art. Surrounded by an audience capable of appreciating the best he could give them he tossed off the lethal bumper, not only like a man, but like an artist. Your modern, on the other hand, buys his vial of laudanum and, sneaking off to a corner, dies like a dog.

Indeed I am not aware that hemlock, with all its noble associations, can even be bought. No single fact could show more clearly how blind to their opportunities suicides have become. Etc., etc.

When my new Columbia friend Raymond Weaver—of whom more later—read the piece, he made a remark which sank deep and I think did me a great good. "The trouble with you, Joseph," he said in his somewhat lofty manner, "is that you try 'to get something off' in every sentence. That is not the way decent prose is written."

Hugging the memory of the letter and check from Mencken and Nathan I returned to New York where I found that Glen Mullin, the painter, had gone to Connecticut for the summer, accompanied by Jean to whom he had just been married. I could await the opening of the Brooklyn Polytechnic Institute in his Fifteenth Street studio under the roof of an ancient commercial building. Rolf Armstrong's studio was next door, all sorts of queer characters drifted in and out, and during the night stray cats wandered in through the open skylight in search of food. I felt a gratifying assurance that one couldn't be much more Bohemian than that, and I suppose I was right.

Soon I sent another essay, this one called "A Defense of Book Reviewers" to the *Yale Review.* It came back promptly with the suggestion that it might be just what Henry Seidel Canby would like for the new Saturday Literary Supplement which he had undertaken to edit for the *New York Evening Post.* A few weeks later my essay occupied the first page of one of the earliest issues of what was later to detach itself from the *Post* in order to become *The Saturday Review of Literature,* to which I have contributed from time to time ever since.

I fear that this essay (of which I no longer have a copy) was also a bit old-fashioned. "Serious criticism," as sponsored by Pound and Eliot, was about to become the mode among intellectuals. My Defense, I seem to remember, was nothing of the sort. It maintained, I believe, that just as the artist arranged Life into a pattern interesting to him, so the reviewer (and critic) arranged these various "interpretations" into some pattern interesting to him. This is, I suppose, pretty much what Eliot had in mind when he dismissed impressionistic criticism as the result of merely "a weak creative impulse" rather than a genuinely critical one. The great difference was, however, that I took a tolerant, even an admiring, view of what Eliot despised.

Though up to that time I had never written a book review, Canby immediately decided to try me out. By the time the term opened at the Polytechnic I had turned in several short notices of unimportant books and was beginning to think of myself as one who might continue to practice this humble occupation while earning my living as the teacher I had long assumed I would be.

6

▲
▲▲▲

The Polytechnic Institute of Brooklyn is now, like the University of Tennessee, a greatly expanded, flourishing, and highly respected Institution. When I joined it in 1921 it occupied only one old-fashioned building on Livingston Street, and I was the only member of Professor Tucker's English Department staff. Our function was chiefly trying to teach the would-be engineers, many of them very ill prepared, to write with a barely acceptable minimum of decency. Since many saw not the slightest reason why they should be required to do so, the job might have been dismal had it not been that Professor Tucker, with the support of Dr. Fred W. Atkinson, the president, organized voluntary activities and elective courses for those who had any aspirations toward "culture."

Enthusiastic about the theater—he was at one time

President of the New York Drama League and the author of several books and anthologies concerned with the modern drama—Professor Tucker sponsored amateur dramatics while I led a reading and discussion group in the contemporary novel. I taught sixteen classes a week, mostly freshman composition, and that included evening classes on Tuesday and Thursday, when I was in the office or a classroom from nine A.M. until nine in the evening.

Professor Tucker was exceedingly kind to me, so kind indeed that though I lost track of him for many years I was delighted to meet him again only a few weeks ago when he came in his hale eighties to spend the winter in Tucson. Though from time to time my path crosses that of a former student of the Polytechnic there are two whose careers interest me particularly because they illustrate a favorite thesis which is that how the twig is bent may be less important than the way it bends itself—even when it may seem otherwise.

One of these cases is that of Theodore Fuchs whom I have never seen since he was Professor Tucker's eager assistant in arranging the lights for theatrical performances and said then (rather improbably it seemed to me) that he would make theatrical lighting his life work. In actual fact he is the author of a standard textbook on the subject, has had wide experience, especially in connection with ceremonies, pageants, etc., and is now in charge of all illumination for plays, ceremonies, etc., at Northwestern University.

The other case is that of Professor Eleseo Vivas, a member of my very first class at the Polytechnic. I soon learned that he was the son of a South American political refugee, but he first attracted my attention by some intelligent remark during the course of a group discussion. I stopped him as he was leaving and politely asked where he came from, and then about the intellectual life in his native land. "Well," he replied, "in Venezuela any man who himself owns two pornographic French novels ranks as an intellectual."

Presently it developed that he was at the Polytechnic because his father refused support for any education other than that of an engineer; later Eleseo was indeed cast off when he decided, a year or two after our meeting, to study philosophy at New York University. He all but starved in the process but was unshaken in his determination, finally got his doctors degree, taught at the Universities of Wisconsin and Chicago, then passed to his present position of Professor of Philosophy at, oddly enough, the same Northwestern where Theodore Fuchs is occupied in spreading a different kind of illumination. Eleseo is the author of several books, especially in the field of aesthetics, and is a frequent contributor to technical publications.

Now I am willing to grant (though I have my doubts) that Professor Tucker and chance were responsible for the direction which Theodore Fuchs has taken. But though Eleseo in the course of a recent biographical note has given me credit for his discovery that he had a mind, this is of course nonsense. No one who has a mind can be long prevented from discovering the fact. My inexperienced teaching was certainly not skillful, and I doubt that any teaching could have been bad enough to delay for more than a few months his finding of himself. I know that students often give large credit to some teacher or other and also that the teacher often takes it complacently. But it is to me a sobering fact—and I state it without any pose of modesty but simply as what I believe to be true—that, though I was for many years a teacher and saw pass through my classrooms a considerable number of young men who have distinguished themselves in various very different ways, I do not believe that I ever contributed anything of crucial importance to the education of any of them.

While on this subject I would like also to anticipate a little and give another example of the twig which bends itself. Not many years after Eleseo defined a Venezuelan intellectual for me I met the son of Oswald Garrison Villard (then my boss) at his father's country place near Watertown, New York. Oswald junior was perhaps twelve or thirteen years old and one of the first of the radio hams. Though his father had no interest in technology or science and ardently hoped that his namesake would carry on the family tradition of liberal political activity, the boy had passed the required tests and was the licensed operator of a rather elaborate transmitting and receiving station. Of his subsequent career I knew nothing until I went to Stanford University a few years ago to deliver some lectures and was startled as well as pleased to receive a note from the Professor of Electrical Engineering—who was, of course, Oswald Garrison Villard Junior and distinguished especially in the field of electronics. To clinch the point I must be indiscreet enough to say that when I asked one of his colleagues about him I got as a reply high praise plus a rather regretful remark that he was extremely conservative in his political attitudes.

So much for the twig-bending efficiency of family tradition and fatherly guidance, as well as for that of the teacher. Of course it will be said of Professor Villard's alleged political conservatism that it is a *reaction* against the family tradition. *De post facto* explanations are always possible, and if the son had become a radical political scientist it would have been said that he was, of course, following in his father's footsteps. But I have little faith in the soundness of a psychological science which cannot predict whether a given individual will be conditioned by, or will react against, the influences supposed to have been responsible for his development.

Any student of the social sciences will of course point out that all this is mere "impression," if not prejudice, and ask scornfully for statistical support. I have none of my own to offer but it happens that within a few days of writing the preceding paragraphs I came across something which may not be entirely irrelevant. In the spring 1961 issue of *Daedalus,* the official quarterly of the American Academy of Arts and Sciences, Joshua A. Fishman presents a study called "Childhood Indoctrination" in the course of which he cities "a large scale, thorough study of nearly two thousand boys attending Catholic high schools" which revealed that the athlete ranked first as their ideal, with Jesus taking third place. As for aspirations, money came first, material possessions second, eternal happiness and salvation third.

Sixteen class hours a week, plus theme reading and conferences with the writers and the various other chores in a small college, did not dampen my modest literary ambitions. I continued to write an occasional review for Canby at the *Post* and was delighted when Carl Van Doren, helpful as always, suggested that I do a few short notes for *The Nation* of which he was then literary editor though still teaching at Columbia. Not long after that he gave me a series of short books which included Nietzsche's *The Anti-Christ* and four other brief works by authors all at least vaguely influenced by the former. I had fifteen hundred words, I headed the essay-review "Anti-Christ and the Four Disciples," and it brought me my first letter of approval from a famous man. Carl showed me a characteristic note to him from H. L. Mencken to which was added on the back a postscript. "By the way who is this man Krutch? That was the best short piece on Nietzsche ever written. Some damned hun I suppose." I was, naturally, so exalted that I forgave the writer for his astonishing failure to remember me as the contributor only a year or two before of that brilliant essay on suicide in his own magazine.

Perhaps I should have mentioned earlier that when I surrendered to Glen Mullin his studio in which I had spent the summer Mark Van Doren, who was returning to an instructorship at Columbia, joined with me to rent the top floor of an old brick house in Greenwich Village where we shared a kitchen and bath while each had his privacy in a large bed-sitting-room-and-study combined. So far as I know, the building, which dated from the period when houses not very different from Seventeenth Century London town houses were a metropolitan style, still stands on Barrow Street. Moreover, our landlord and lady might have come from a novel not very different from the one from which our London hosts seemed to have emerged. The real head of the house was a buxom, good-humored Irish Catholic whose frequent malapropisms nearly always had an ecclesiastical or theological flavor. She told us on the day we moved in, first, that we would no doubt be glad to have a home of our own where all our belongings could be "consecrated" and, second, that the "consummation" of gas in the heater which warmed my room would not be great. Anxious also to assure us that she was no spy she remarked that since this was not a rooming house we were free to receive visitors of either sex, provided it was all "above board"—whatever that might mean.

Her husband was a heavy drinker of the saturnine type

whom I remember chiefly because he supplied me with a remark of deep psychological significance which illuminates the workings of that "inferiority complex" of which one was just beginning to hear much. One day when Mark and I were climbing the third floor steps together we glimpsed him lying on the floor with blood streaming from his forehead. It was nothing serious for he had simply rolled off the bed, but when we roused him he looked at us with obvious resentment and muttered: "You think you are very smart. You teach at Columbia and you write for *The Nation*. But as for me I"—long pause during which he searched for a superiority—"as for me, I wear my B.V.D.'s all the year 'round." This was, reduced to its simplest form, the eternal defense of the he-man against the intellectual.

For me, however, the most fateful member of the household was the landlady's daughter—though for a reason very different from what such a statement might suggest. She was a rather tough-minded young woman with an eye on the main chance and not in the least interesting to me even as the most casual of acquaintances. Nevertheless, she played in one instance a crucial role in my life for which I am still grateful.

This is how it happened. My brother Charlie had come from Knoxville to visit me just before Christmas, 1920, and when we prepared to sally forth one evening we found that, due to the season no doubt, no girls seemed to be available. In desperation we invited the landlady's daughter, who was agreeable, and then proceeded to dinner at a Village restaurant with a dance floor and a blind pianist who doled out fox trots or *The Blue Danube* as impulse dictated. Shortly after we had finished dinner, three young ladies entered alone. One was quite commonplace, the two others very pretty, obviously sisters, and somehow or other just faintly exotic. Before they had advanced more than a few steps into the room I said with a sincerity at which I myself was astonished, "That's the girl for me." "Which one?" asked the landlady's daughter, and when I pointed to the slightly older of the two sisters she went on: "I don't know her but (indicating the uninteresting member of the trio) I do know that one." "Call them all over," I said.

Now I had never before "taken out" the landlady's daughter and I never "took her out" again. By an odd coincidence this was also both the first and the last time that the two sisters had ever spent an evening with the young woman whom the landlady's daughter knew. The two of them were links in a necessary chain of communication which had no further function once the communication was established. In fact, when the landlady's daughter died of a mysterious disease not so very long after, it seemed to me additional evidence that she had been put on earth merely to bring Marcelle and me together.

Marcelle and her sister Celestine were, as I was presently to learn, slightly exotic in appearance because they were French Basques from the little village of Hendaye on the Franco-Spanish border. They had come to Boston shortly before the outbreak of the First World War to visit a third sister who had married an American. When war came they remained, and Marcelle patriotically trained as a nurse at the Massachusetts General with the intention of serving in a military hospital. Now, since the war was over, the next most useful thing seemed to be social service and she had recently joined the workers at the famous Henry Street Settlement on New York's East Side.

Introductions over, I immediately asked for a dance and the pianist went into *The Blue Danube* which is certainly more appropriate to True Love than a fox trot. As the evening wore on, I became more and more sure that my exclamation when Marcelle had entered was not recklessness but inspiration. Before we parted I got (after what seemed to me rather ungracious hesitation) an address and a telephone number.

Next day and for several days thereafter I asked for "a date," only to be always refused. As I afterwards learned, Marcelle and her sister, after discussing the matter, had agreed that I had not struck either of them as very attractive, that I had seemed, as a matter of fact, rather "fresh," and that they wanted nothing more to do with me. Finally I wrote a note in which I told them the anecdote about the Swede who had been three times thrown out of a saloon and who at last shouted back at the bouncer: "You can't fool me. I know what it is. You don't want me in there." Improbable as it may seem, this did the trick. If I cared to enlist a male friend, the two sisters would accept a joint invitation. Thomas Munro, whom I have mentioned before, and who was to become one of the curators at the Cleveland Museum of Art, was agreeable, and we went, I forget where, for dinner. Soon we were a regular foursome and then separate twosomes, though Tommy ultimately married someone else.

Late that winter Celestine returned to France; Marcelle stayed in New York. By summer she and I were spending nearly every evening together, and the evenings were so long that, as she has since complained, she got little sleep because she was due early at Henry Street while I, enjoying that greatest of academic privileges, the summer vacation, could lie abed as late as I liked. All this was very satisfactory indeed. But there was also a very dark and threatening shadow.

Why should girls have careers and why should these careers always (as it seemed to me) take them somewhere else? Stella had gone to Germany to study music and had not come back. Marcelle was committed to going to France in the fall, there to enter upon her duties with the Rockefeller Foundation. And she, like Stella, thought that duty came first. Despite all my pleas she sailed away before the end of summer. But my letters must have been persuasive for less than six months later she was back in New York. A little more than a year later we were married and we have remained very happily so ever since.

Some little time before the marriage actually took place but when it was already obviously inevitable, I began to be a little concerned about having to tell Mark that our highly satisfactory living arrangements would have to be broken up. The difficulty was solved as happily as that in connection with the traveling fellowships had been. In short, he, with some embarrassment, told me first. He had decided to give up bachelorhood in favor of Dorothy Graffe whom he had met not long before in the office of *The Nation* where she was one of the editors. They too are still very happily together.

I think it bad taste for a man to talk too much about the charms of his wife. It is only what Oscar Wilde called "washing one's clean linen in public." But perhaps I can permit myself to touch upon the subject indirectly by saying that to this day new acquaintances who become friends invariably get around to asking me confidentially if I realize not only how attractive but also what a perfect wife in every other respect she is. Once a physician who had attended us both put the question in a different way. "I am interested," he said, "for scientific reasons, to know whether you picked her out because you realized how perfectly you complemented one another or whether it was instinct, or, possibly, merely a happy accident."

My own opinion is that "instinct" would be the truest

answer, with reasoned judgment and good luck making minor contributions. In most respects we are opposite but compatible and complementary—physically, temperamentally and intellectually. I am tall, thin, and pale blond. She is black-haired, dark-rosy of complexion, and inclined to the rounded rather than the angular. I lapse easily into melancholy; she is merry. I tend to withdraw into solitude; she likes people, and must know anyone very well before she dislikes even the unlikable. At every proposal for society, travel, or anything else, my first impulse is to say "no," hers to say "yes." Yet, fortunately, we nearly always agree on mature consideration.

I usually anticipate the worst; she usually the best. I am a worrier; she is not, and almost the only thing she has ever blamed me for is that I have taught her a little of that unfortunate art. That opposites attract is true but relatively unimportant. The question is, does the attraction last? And in my case the answer is "yes." If I have any complaint it is that of the speaker in Browning's "My Last Duchess," namely that she so readily likes people that I can take less credit than I might otherwise award myself because of the fact that, apparently, she likes me. At any rate, I can say what it seems comparatively few married couples can: I do not think either of us has ever considered the possibility of parting.

This, it must be remembered, was at the beginning of the now so-famous Twenties, the great age of "parties" many of which were proudly described as "wild" whether they were private or open to all, like the once so well-known all-night dances at the very public and very Bohemian "Webster Hall." Our social life was active, but at our age one could work and play both, and I had never worked so hard before and never have since.

This is how it came about. Ludwig Lewisohn, the drama critic of *The Nation,* contributed every other week a review of whatever novel seemed to him worth discussing. Carl Van Doren asked me if I would take a look at all the rest, pick out two, three, or four which seemed at least passably interesting, and write a group review for the alternate weeks. The task was formidable and my heavy teaching schedule left me only Saturdays and Sundays on which to tackle it. On my doorstep the postman deposited great bundles of books, mostly by writers unknown and destined to remain so. It was up to me to discover which could be made to seem worth talking about and to say, if possible, something at least mildly interesting about them.

I adopted a routine which I would not today dare to face. One week I would devote the whole of Saturday and Sunday to sampling ten or a dozen books, deciding which seemed most promising and reading carefully as far as I could through the chosen ones. Next week end I finished the reading and then (usually on Sunday) devoted the whole day to writing a thousand words.

Like most young reviewers I was as eager to attract attention to myself as I was to damn or praise a book and I had a low opinion of most group reviews which tend to fall into a pattern something like this: "If Mr. Smith and Mr. Jones are serious but somewhat dull Miss Williams is sprightly if trivial, while of the four it is Mrs. Wilkinson who has the truest novelistic gift." I hit upon the scheme (partly I suppose because it tended to put me into the foreground) of finding two or more novels which could be made to support a generalization I hoped would not be too farfetched. One result was that a reader presently paid me the dubious compliment of telling the editor that though my pieces were usually interesting they did not always seem to have much to do with the books under discussion.

I no longer have copies of any of these efforts but only yesterday I consulted the bound volumes of *The Nation* in the library of the University of Arizona and find that the very first of my group reviews (March 8, 1922) was devoted to four lady novelists of whom only Sheila Kaye-Smith is still remembered. Though I have completely forgotten all four, it seems that they all dealt in some fashion with heroines roughly classifiable as "new women." The first two sentences of my review are: "Ever since it became generally acknowledged that the cosmic oyster was not for man alone, the female Hotspurs, Quixotes, and Sanchos have sallied forth in incredible numbers each resolved to open it according to her chosen technique. Four women have here told the story of such an expedition and all have described, for the most part unconsciously, a phase of the illusion that a mere change of manners can make women free." Obviously I had not entirely recovered from the tendency for which Raymond Weaver had rebuked me—to try to "get off something" in every sentence.

Having immodestly quoted both the dubious compliment of one reader of the novel reviews and Mencken's sweeping approval of the essay on Nietzsche, I should correct any impression which the present reader may have that I am trying to suggest a universally cordial acceptance of my early efforts. Actually, it was a cause of almost complete despair to me that I was taken to task rather more frequently than I was lauded. Two instances stick in my mind. Ernest Boyd, the red-bearded critic who assumed personal responsibility for French literature in the United

States, ridiculed me for using an impossible French pseudo-word and implied that no one so ignorant should be trusted to review a novel by André Gide. Worse yet, when I gave what I thought a favorable notice to a work by one of the older but still well-known American "realists" who happened to be also a friend of editor Villard, the novelist wrote the latter a letter which began something like this: "I know that it is impossible to persuade any but inferior minds to write book reviews but that of my recent book was so far below even the usual level that I feel compelled to cancel my subscription."

Despite such blows, I replaced Ludwig Lewisohn as drama critic in the fall of 1924. In anticipation, I had left the Polytechnic Institute at the end of the preceding spring term and I did not return to the academic world (except for a few part-time appearances) until I became a Professor in the English Department of Columbia University in 1937. Few people envy book reviewers and no one ever asked me how he might fulfill a life ambition by becoming one. But the country is full of would-be drama critics and a good many of them have begged me to tell them how they might become one. The answer is that there isn't any way, because in nearly every case known to me it has just happened. John Mason Brown was, so far as I know, the only one of my colleagues who determined early that reviewing plays was what he most wanted to do and who found that, in Thoreau's words, "If one advances confidently in the direction of his dreams . . . he will meet with a success unexpected in common hours." Like most of the others I simply fell into a vacuum, this one created when certain domestic difficulties made it advisable for Mr. Lewisohn to reside abroad for a time.

I hope it is safe now to make this last statement. When,

shortly after the event, I was called upon to reply impromptu over a radio network to a denunciation of drama critics by the obstreperous producer, William A. Brady, I remarked that these creatures were not, as he seemed to assume, a special breed, not men of unusual ignorance, malice, and perversity, but merely ordinary people who found themselves performing a strange function. "Take me," I added, "the real reason I am a drama critic is simply that Ludwig Lewisohn couldn't get along with his wife." I had barely reached home when the phone rang and the former Mrs. Lewisohn exclaimed angrily that I had libeled her and that I would hear from a lawyer. Incidentally, the only other occasion when I was threatened with a libel suit was about the same time and arose out of a review I had written for the *Evening Post* of a novel by a young man who had achieved considerable fame by a first book now pretty well forgotten. His new opus told the story of a writer, suspiciously like himself, who had fled Puritanism into Greenwich Village where he had achieved Freedom. Since I was already beginning to be a bit suspicious of Freedom as a pure abstraction I asked: "Freedom for what? Apparently freedom to write this novel." Again it was the wife who was enraged, though this time I got a letter rather than a telephone call. I had implied, she said, that the novel was autobiographical and in it the wife had had an abortion. Since this implied that she had had an abortion it was clearly libelous. Fortunately I never heard any more of either of these threats.

It was lucky for me that I began to review plays at the very moment when it was commonly assumed that the American Drama was about to enter a period of mature glory. The dawn—whether a true one or a false—had begun nine years earlier when the amateur group calling itself "The Washington Square Players" waved a manifesto in the face of the New York Drama Critics and opened with a bill of one-act plays at the Bandbox Theater at 57th Street and Third Avenue. This first of what are now called Off-Broadway playhouses developed later into the Theater Guild under the management of much the same group which had founded the original company. It was joined the next year by "The Provincetown Players" who opened their reconstructed carriage house just off Washington Square with another program of one-acters which included *Bound East for Cardiff,* the first play by Eugene O'Neill to be performed in New York.

Elsewhere (in *The American Drama since 1918* and in the introduction to Alice Lewisohn Crowley's *The Neighbourhood Playhouse*) I have tried to describe the effect of these two "little theaters" upon the whole Broadway scene. Here I must say only that though World War I slowed down their activities, they picked up energy again as soon as it was over and that by 1924, when I entered the scene professionally, they had attracted attention, and audiences, sufficient to convince even some of the commercial managers that playwriting was not merely "a trade" (as one critic had said without regret that it was) but an art in the practice of which a writer might be as serious, as unconventional, and as excellent as he found it within his ability to be. Also that the public which read "serious literature" in other forms was quite willing to accept plays written at the same level of ambition.

The very first play I reviewed happened to be *What Price Glory?* by Maxwell Anderson and Lawrence Stallings. It was followed a few weeks later by Sidney Howard's *They Knew What They Wanted* and a little later by O'Neill's *Desire under the Elms.* Finally, during the same season came *The Little Clay Cart,* this last staged at the Neighborhood Playhouse operated on Grand Street by the Lewisohn sisters as an activity connected with the Henry Street Settlement House.

How good were any of these plays? Of the three new ones only *Desire under the Elms* is vividly alive today though *They Knew What They Wanted* has been once revived (not too successfully) and was more recently made into the popular quasi-operetta, *Most Happy Fella.* On the other hand it could, I think, be said that no other American play had, like each of the three, so successfully broken the grip of that deadly convention which had made the theater a mere cultural backwater. All three were "contemporary," not Victorian, and whatever their defects or limitations they were those of the authors, not something forced upon them by the tradition that plays had to be a generation behind the times. The playwright had "won his freedom" and he had now only to use it—if he could.

At bottom *What Price Glory?* was perhaps essentially a robustious melodrama and its pioneer introduction of profanity and ribald humor was not quite so important a cultural advance as was then often assumed. But at least it was original to the extent that it invented a method of presenting on the stage the modern soldier in a light very different from that of either the romantic hero or the nobly pathetic victim. Moreover, its method and tone were theatrically so effective that the most successful of even remotely similar plays about the Second World War imitates them without significant change. *Mister Roberts* is merely a seagoing *What Price Glory?* and the debt of the book of *South Pacific* is hardly less.

Since I was incapable of competing with the man-about-town knowingness of my colleagues of the daily papers among whom, about this time, were Alexander Woollcott, Heywood Broun, and the now almost forgotten but then very well-known Percy Hammond, I attempted an "intellectual" approach and my review of *They Knew What They Wanted* furnishes an amusing example of the difference between what an "intellectual" critic can make of such a play and what the author thought he had in mind —especially if the author happens to think of himself as first of all a practical man of the theater. To me *They Knew What They Wanted* had a thesis suggested by the title which was, I still think, illustrated by the plot. This thesis was that when, as so often happens, you can't get precisely what you most want it is wiser to choose a second best that may turn out to be quite tolerable after all, rather than to plunge yourself into the tragedy to which "all or nothing" is likely to lead. If I had known then Samuel Johnson's statement I would surely have quoted it: "The remedy of the ills of life is palliative rather than radical."

A few years later I found myself returning from Italy on the same boat with the author and we spent a week almost constantly together. Inevitably his plays were discussed. He told me that he had had no thesis at all in mind, that he was interested only in telling a story, and that the story was obviously that of *Tristram and Isolde* —the story, that is to say, of a man who sends an emissary to fetch a bride, only to discover that she has given herself to the emissary. He was right of course—on one level at least—and had the tendency to interpret new literary works in terms of "myth" been as popular then as it is now I should probably have noticed the fact, perhaps even added the now equally obvious remark that *The Courtship of Miles Standish* is a genteel version of the same story. Nevertheless, there is often more than one interpretation of any work of fiction and I still maintain that *They Knew What They Wanted* does have a thesis and that this thesis is quite simply: "Better half a loaf than no bread."

Before I took up my new duties Mr. Villard gave his opinion that no drama critic was any good for more than a few years and that all should be hanged at the end of five. I remained at my post from 1924 to 1952 (except for three seasons when I was in Europe or elsewhere away from New York) and I finally escaped without a rope around my neck.

When the time comes I shall have something to say about the situation in the theater when I turned my back upon both it and all metropolitan life. But this is the place to add that, though the promise of the Twenties was never quite fulfilled, it still seems to me that I was lucky to have been a spectator then, because this was an era of novelty and adventure when it was possible to hope that next week might reveal something nearer true greatness than anything that had yet appeared. American plays were undoubtedly better than they had ever been before. O'Neill was our first playwright to deserve and ultimately win world-wide acclaim and equals might, we hoped and believed, be about to make their appearance. This we kept on believing until the great depression put an end to the age of confidence and even the critics of the conservative press began to assume that Art is a Weapon.

Though I admired and praised several of the new playwrights (Behrman, Rice, Anderson, and Howard especially) I had no doubt then, as I have none now, that the most impressive, both as writer and man, was Eugene O'Neill. I had seen all of his earliest plays but I did not meet him until 1926 when I was immediately struck by the passionate sincerity which shone through his great shyness, and I am proud of the fact that he seemed to take immediately to me as I did to him. After 1926 he was so seldom in New York that the time we actually spent together was not great. Nevertheless, he talked freely when we did meet and we sometimes exchanged letters. I feel that I know him better than many with whom I have spent many more hours.

Soon after our first meting he was off to Bermuda and he paid me the compliment of sending me the first draft of *Strange Interlude.* In a letter from Hamilton, Bermuda, dated June 10, 1927, he wrote: "I hope I made it clear that this is a first draft which will have to be cut a great deal before it is a finished product . . . I am particularly keen about this play and 'Lazarus Laughed' because by using one or the other or both of the techniques employed in these two I feel that one can do anything one is big enough for in the drama, that there is no theme, no comprehension difficult to handle in the theater. But 'technique' is a word worn groggy and it only blurs what I am trying to say. What I mean is freedom from all modern formulas that restrict the scope of the theater to the unreal real and the even more boring unreal unreal. Which sounds a bit scrambled! I'm a bum explainer—and 'Strange Interlude' is clearer about it than I am."

To my letter written after reading the manuscript he replied with another of nearly a thousand words, some of which I think worth quoting inasmuch as the letter has never before been published and throws light on O'Neill's own conception of the play and its meaning.

> Your appreciative criticism of "Strange Interlude" was deeply gratifying—especially that you found that there was something of a novel's comprehensiveness in it. What you say about the slightness of even the best modern plays is exactly what I feel . . . but on the other hand, even the best of modern novels strike me as dire failures in another direction. They are all so wordy, so padded with the un-

important and the insignificant, so obsessed with the trivial meaning of trivialities that the authors appear to me as mere timid recorders of life . . . No. I think the novelists worse than the playwrights—they waste more of one's time!

As for the "complexes" of the characters in "Strange Interlude," I must confess that before or in the writing I never thought of them in any Freudian sense and that's probably why no exposition of the theme obtruded. I'm no great student of psychoanalysis although, of course, I do know quite a bit about it, without having gone in for a complete analysis myself, and I am enormously interested to see what will eventually emerge as a science out of all these theories and the behavioristic ones. My position is sort of half way in one camp and half in the other. But to get back to "S I," I feel that, although it is undoubtedly full of psychoanalytical ideas, still those ideas are age-old to the artist and that any artist who was a good psychologist and had a varied and sensitive experience with life and all sorts of people could have written "S I" without ever having ever heard of Freud, Jung, Adler, and company. This doesn't apply in my case, of course. I'm simply making the statement because it seems to me that there is a tendency now to read psychoanalysis into an author's work where ordinary psychology offers a sufficient exclamation—let alone imagination and intuition. All of the author's peals of thunder will be stolen now if this keeps up! . . .

I've almost finished with the cutting and minor revisions of the play. Your scheme is about the one I had been following in making the cuts. My fear in writing a first draft is always of omitting something, so there are bound to be many repetitions. I usually have a first draft at least one-fourth too long—almost intentionally, for I've gotten so cutting is a labor of love with me and I get a keen satisfaction out of it second only to the actual writing.

The Guild are going to do "Strange Interlude" next season, or I will have to get it done elsewhere. Their option, on my insistence, is only for next season's production. I can't afford to wait. Waiting years for production while your mind passes on to other things is the most trying experience—financially trying too, let me add!

During the Twenties and early Thirties my high opinion of O'Neill was, of course, shared by most of those who had a special interest in the theater, though certain critics of general literature sometimes dissented. His European reputation grew rapidly and he was to be the first American playwright ever to receive the Nobel prize for literature. But no new play of his appeared on Broadway between the unsuccessful *Days without End* (1934) and *The Iceman Cometh* (1956). In the meantime a reaction had set in. Several of the critics who considered themselves the most serious and the most responsible attacked his reputation, sometimes with great vehemence, and continued to do so for seven or eight years. No successful revivals were staged and it began to look as though O'Neill might be forgotten both in the theater and out of it.

I continued to write about him defensively from time to time and presently (I don't mean to imply any connection between the two facts) the tide turned again. Various of his plays were successfully revived in the newly important Off-Broadway playhouses and the posthumous *Long Day's Journey into Night* achieved a great international success. This resurgence of his fame he did not live to enjoy, and the last time I saw him (sometime in the late Forties) was in a hotel in New York. Though still strangely handsome and still capable of his shy flashes of enthusiasm or humor, his palsy was so far advanced that he could not lift a coffee cup to his lips unaided. Carlotta Monterey, who had played the elegant passenger in *The Hairy Ape* back in 1922 and whom he had married shortly after he wrote me the long letter about *Strange Interlude,* hovered over him to give the assistance he must have. She is now his literary executor and the guardian of his fame.

Without pretending to assess O'Neill definitely, I would like to state my own opinion, which is still what it was, namely, that of all those who have written plays in the United States either before or since his time, he is the most likely to endure. Half a dozen other dramatic writers may seem at the moment to be "important." Several of them may seem to some "better." But O'Neill is the inevitable writer with whom the others must be compared.

You may cite him to prove how good or how bad his own work is, or how bad American playwriting has always been. But you cannot leave him out, and there is no one of his contemporaries of which the same can be said for long. He imposes himself upon even the most unwilling. Eric Bentley, for example, does not admire him and, to mention another who has expressed herself freely, neither does Mary McCarthy. But in recent books both find it necessary to devote a number of pages to explaining why they do not. And there is no other American playwright who imposes that obligation. Old-fashioned dramatists used to talk about "the obligatory scene." For critics of the theater, O'Neill is the obligatory subject. Bernard Shaw called him "a banshee Shakespeare"; but this also is in its way a compliment.

That his many plays vary enormously in merit is obvious. So too is the fact that he is often clumsy. Half a dozen contemporaries and successors write smoother dialogue and technically smoother plays. But the passion and sincerity with which he expresses a tragic sense of the human dilemma is unrivaled.

All this has carried me somewhat ahead of the story. I

must return now to my first years on *The Nation* and to some matters unconnected with the theater.

Any writer anxious to avoid the suspicion that he is tainted by even a trace of the mere journalist will like to believe that he never wrote anything—even an article, much less a book—for any reason other than inner necessity. Some of my own writing has been, I hope, of that sort, but though my first book (assuming that a doctoral dissertation doesn't count) was one which I undertook with enthusiasm the prompting came from the outside. Alfred Knopf wanted a biographical critical study of Edgar Allan Poe, asked Carl Van Doren to suggest an author, and Carl suggested me. Knopf agreed to give me a try under the rather unusual condition that the decision whether what I produced was or was not worthy of publication should be made, not by the publisher, but by Carl.

It seemed to me then (as it still does) that if the psychoanalytical approach to literature, just then beginning to be made here and there, would work anywhere it should work on so obviously abnormal a writer as Poe. During my first winter as Drama Critic I used such time as I could find in rereading his work and much of what has been written about him with this in mind; and at the beginning of the following summer we retired to a rented cottage in Cornwall, Connecticut, where I hoped to get ahead with the project.

Cornwall was chosen because Carl and Mark Van Doren had both bought farmhouses there, as had also Lewis Gannett, an old friend from *The Nation,* and various other acquaintances connected in one way or another with the literary, journalistic, or theatrical worlds. The next year Marcelle and I also bought a house in the township and that was, I suppose, the first step in that alienation from city life which was ultimately to make me turn my back on it permanently. But I confess that at the time I considered myself so completely urbanized that I was reluctant to leave New York for even a few months. The next year I bought the house for the same reason that, I imagine, most houses in the country are bought—my wife wanted it. And I have no reply to her occasional reminder that this was one of occasions—we differ as to how frequent they have been—that she knew better than I what I really wanted.

But the first summer in Cornwall was not to be uninterrupted work on Poe. The famous "monkey trial" at Dayton, Tennessee was imminent and beginning to assume the proportions of a grotesque *cause célèbre* involving all the elements most likely to interest the mid-twenties when "censorship," "Bible Belt," "liberalism," etc., suggested the most lively issues of a happy decade during which war seemed to have been disposed of, prosperity seemed permanent, and world revolution so remote that Communism was merely "an interesting experiment," Fascism an aberration not to be taken too seriously. Since I had been born and had grown up only about fifty miles from Dayton where the trial was to take place it seemed reasonable that I should join the many reporters being sent to cover it.

7

▲
▲▲▲

The Monkey Trial at Dayton was a teapot tempest which attracted international attention and is now enshrined in the intellectual history of Twentieth Century America. More than thirty years after it took place it was almost simultaneously the subject of a successful play and of a widely read, completely documented study. References to it still turn up not infrequently in the conversation of intellectuals, and I can still become the center of attention if I announce portentously, "All of it I saw and part of it I was."

Nevertheless, it is difficult to see the whole affair in any true perspective and it has almost always been oversimplified by those who have attempted to describe or to assess. If it was partly a witch hunt, it was also a jape elaborately staged for their own amusement by typical intellectual playboys of the exuberant Twenties, and the real villains were not either the benighted rustics nor the playboys but the responsible citizens and officials of Tennessee who should never have allowed it to happen.

When Marcelle and I arrived at Dayton the little town was already in a state of excited bewilderment and almost of shock at the discovery that it had been selected as the site of an Armageddon. The great world had never noticed it before. Now it was swarming with reporters, a whole galaxy of famous warriors had descended upon it, all because astonishing attention had been called to a local political farce of a familiar sort and one which would probably have been soon forgotten had not several unexpected things happened.

It all started unsensationally enough. A backcountry member of the Tennessee legislature had been distressed to hear that the daughter of one of his constituents had lost her Fundamentalist faith when she heard at school something of the Darwinian heresy. Inspired by the same naïve trust in the efficacy of moral legislation which had saddled prohibition on even the most sophisticated parts of the United States, the legislator introduced into the lower chamber a bill forbidding the teaching of the theory of evolution in any part of the state's educational system. No politician wanted to go on record as opposing God or religion, and the bill was passed in the lower house by legislators, some of whom later stated that they had confidently assumed it would be killed in the Senate. The Senate thereupon passed the buck to the Governor, certain, so they said, that he would veto it. But the Governor was not disposed to center all the ire of the Fundamentalists on himself alone. Accordingly he signed the bill with the remark that he did not expect it to become an operative law.

Probably it would have been soon forgotten if John Scopes, athletic coach and professor of biology at the Dayton High School, had not called the attention of his principal to the fact that the textbook he was using seemed to violate the law. He was told to ignore the fact and would no doubt have done so had it not been for a local citizen (an outlander by the way) named George Rappelyea who was manager of a local coal mine. He had been increasingly irritated by the antics of the Fundamentalists and he asked Scopes if he would be willing to co-operate in a test case by submitting to an indictment brought against him. Scopes consented, and the Civil Liberties Union in New York agreed to subsidize the defense.

Originally the Civil Liberties Union had intended to employ only local counsel, but when William Jennings Bryan, whose star had been waning fast, announced that he would come to Dayton as the champion of Christianity against Atheism, the Union revised its plan and enlisted the services of three oddly assorted national figures shrewdly selected for their diverse talents: Clarence Darrow, coat-sleeved wizard with all juries including those of such "plain men" as he himself pretended to be; Arthur Garfield Hayes, veteran of many civil liberties suits who knew the ins and outs of the law as Darrow did not; and Dudley Field Malone, a silver-tongued orator whose talents had been most often employed in divorce cases but whose ornate rhetoric might be expected to fall persuasively on the ears of the simple. John R. Neal, an eccentric teacher of law in his own private school at Knoxville, tagged along.

Probably Dayton had been slow to believe that all America and much of Europe would take seriously what was happening there, but by the time we arrived excitement was running high and the little town was doing its best to acquit itself well in the role of host to guests of a very unfamiliar kind. The circus and the religious revival were the only festive occasions with which it was familiar and the atmosphere was strongly suggestive of both. Signs and banners—some welcoming the strangers, many of the where-will-you-spend-eternity? kind—adorned the principal street. Preachers, official and self-appointed, had come into the town to harangue from soapboxes whomever they could persuade to listen. Private citizens offered bed and board to the many who could not find accommodation in the one hotel and the overcrowded boardinghouses. The Chamber of Commerce, which saw the whole thing as a chance to put Dayton on the map, gave separate dinners in honor of the two champions, Bryan and Darrow, while the more intellectual citizens, though firmly asserting their loyalty to Bible and Church, expressed frank satisfaction in the anticipated opportunity to hear the great questions debated by the most famous defenders of religion and atheism.

As for the hangers-on like myself, we quickly converted the soda fountain in the drugstore into a café where not only we but most of the leaders and many of the interested citizens discussed everything which was happening in full amiability, though one paradox was soon noted. Only the Great Commoner held himself aloof. Guest of a leading citizen he fraternized with no one—not with his opponents, nor with the reporters, nor with the ordinary citizens. He was glimpsed only occasionally in a large black limousine, and on the one occasion when he entered the drugstore he let it be known that he was not amused by the soda clerk who asked if he would have grape juice, of which he was a famous advocate.

Here, there, and everywhere was the broad beaming face of H. L. Mencken. A few days later he enjoyed in the courtroom what were perhaps the happiest moments of his life contemplating, and in a sense presiding over, a spectacle which semed arranged for his delight. He was in the middle of that Bible Belt he had done so much to make famous and its inhabitants were behaving precisely as he had always described them. Had he invented the Monkey Trial no one would have believed in it, but he had been spared the necessity of invention. He fraternized exuberantly with everyone; and everyone, including even the street-corner preachers, were delighted with him—until the first of his dispatches got back to Dayton and many of those with whom he had genially conversed could hardly believe that he could be the author of the brutally contemptuous account he gave of them. One preacher, I remember, protested more in sorrow than in anger, that Mencken had seemed to listen with sympathy to his arguments; then had flung into his face the reply: "Oh well, I have always said I would be converted to any religion for a cigar and baptized in it for a box of them."

Much as I admired Mencken, this was one of several occasions when I found in him a brutal rudeness too strong for my taste and at the time I could not help contrasting it with the courtesy of the Fundamentalist proprietor of a little boarding house at one of the "Springs" which served Dayton as summer resorts. I had driven out for dinner with Darrow and several others, each of whom introduced himself and was cordially greeted. Darrow came last and when he murmured his name the host recoiled for a moment as though the gates of hell had just opened in his face. Then he remembered his manners, swallowed twice, and extending his hand he said: "I am glad to meet you, Mr. Darrow." A prince, even a Prince of Darkness, obviously deserved no less.

▲

Though I am no lawyer and hence subject to correction, I assume that, from a strict legal standpoint, the defense did not have a leg to stand on. John Scopes had obviously violated a duly enacted statute and "guilty as charged" was the only possible verdict. Most of the strangely mixed crowd which moved from the drugstore and the streets into a courtroom crowded to the doors and windows must have been aware of this fact and it must have been in part responsible for both the calm confidence of the inevitably prejudiced judge and that section of the audience which genuinely believed in its own essential rightness. The Lord had delivered the enemy into their hands—and on home ground too.

But the defense had, of course, no interest in the inevitable verdict or even in the question of the constitutionality of the law which, if raised, could only have been settled at some distant day in some other court. Since it was interested in propaganda rather than in a verdict, the defense's strategy was to turn nominally legal proceedings into the meeting of a debating society, and the question to be discussed was not the legal guilt or innocence of John Scopes but Fundamentalism versus modern thought as typified by the theory of evolution. Its thesis—and a very strange one to be defended by the Ingersolian atheist Clarence Darrow—was simply that the theory of evolution was in no way incompatible with either Christianity or the essential truth of the Book of Genesis.

Since this was not, after all, the question which the jury would be called upon to decide, the locally elected Judge Rawlston, who presided, might, I presume, have ruled out as irrelevant almost everything which was said in the course of the trial. Probably he was not shrewd enough to do so, and it is even less likely that he wanted to do anything of the sort. He was known to all as a staunch supporter of those to whom the fantastic statute seemed sound common sense. He had probably never in his life heard anyone question in other than timidly apologetic terms the combination of ignorance, superstition, and (sometimes) hypocrisy for which he stood; and he was confident that, so far at least as *his* world was concerned, the debate as well as the legal verdict would be in his and his community's favor.

After perhaps fifteen minutes during which shutters clicked and flashbulbs flashed while the judge basked in this recognition of his importance while protesting feebly against it, he gravely welcomed the visiting counsel. "Rest assured," he seemed to be saying, "we shall annihilate you as gently as possible." The first hint that the defense did not intend to be polite had come when Darrow astonished the court by objecting to an opening prayer on the ground that it was prejudicial. But after the objection had been overruled, the atmosphere was again relatively calm until the fourth day of the trial. Then Darrow, coatless and conspicuously suspendered as though to assure Dayton that he was as plain a man as any of its own citizens, rose to launch his impassioned if legally irrelevant attack.

He began, as all before him had begun, with trivial courtesies. He ironically thanked the judge for having bestowed upon him the title "Colonel" and the judge, with a twinkle of good fellowship in his eye, bade him "take it back to Chicago." The vicious circle of empty courtesies seemed to have been re-established when Darrow, after a transition too quick to be noticed, was suddenly in the midst of an impassioned oration, shaking his finger in the face of the astonished judge and denouncing in angry, insulting words what he called the ignorance, intolerance, arrogance, and bigotry of that community of which the judge was known to be a typical member. Upon the face of the latter was written shocked amazement, and the correspondents rubbed their ears to be sure they heard aright. "With flying banners and beating drums we are marching backward to the glorious age of the Sixteenth Century when bigots lighted fagots to burn the men who dared to bring any intelligence and enlightenment and culture to the human mind."

Much that followed was farce, though not without sinister overtones. When the prosecuting attorney made his principal harangue he accepted the assumption that Darwinism rather than John Scopes was on trial and he translated the question into East Tennessee terms. Long, drawling, lanky, and with an air of rustic simplicity which was, like Darrow's, partly synthetic, he reached the climax of his performance when, taking the jury into his confidence, he asked them to contrast Genesis with Darwinism. "The defense has told you that they mean the same thing. Let's look at the record. The Bible says that God made man" (here he stooped to the floor and then flung his hand into the air) "out of the dust of the earth. What does this theory of evolution say? It says that God set some sort of a scum floating on the water and then said 'Give me a few million years and I'll *try* to make something out of you.' "

Darrow's reply was in the form of a brief cross-questioning of the obviously not very bright adolescent whom the prosecution had summoned to establish technically the fact that Scopes had indeed taught the forbidden doctrine. The cross-examination went something like this: "Now, son, I understand that you were taught the theory of evolution. Tell me exactly what you were taught." (Long pause and with hesitant embarrassment) "That all life comes from an egg." "Was that all you were taught?" "Yes, sir." "Well, son, I suppose that when you heard that all life comes from an egg you stopped going to church, didn't you?" "No sir." "Witness dismissed."

As tension mounted it was obvious that even many of the Dayton citizens who had come to see the infidel discomfited and then destroyed had begun to take a genuine interest in the drama. Plainly impressed by the vigor, the confidence, and the competence of the enemy they tended to forget which side they were on and to take delight in the contest for its own sake; sometimes even bursting into applause which the judge not too sternly repressed when a good hit had been made or some rhetorical flight was executed by Darrow in a style not too different from that they had learned to appreciate at a Fundamentalist camp meeting. But they were also reassuringly aware that their own champion was merely holding himself in reserve and that when the time came he would know how to deal with those who now threatened to mislead them.

Many a time during the days when the heathen raged or when Darrow, Hays, or Malone rose for a few seconds to voice some legal objection in terms which unmistakably implied their contempt for a court from which they expected no fair play, the eyes of the spectators turned toward the Peerless Leader from whom they awaited vindication and triumph. Though for several days Bryan continued unbroken the silence he had been maintaining, the reddening of his neck, the tightening of the lines about his mouth, and the increasing speed with which he waved his palm-leaf fan showed that some of the arrows were reaching home and that his heart was stung by the realization that here were men of undoubted if undeserved eminence who scornfully refused him the respect he had once been accustomed to enjoy. Finally he could stand it no longer. He rose to say merely that in due time he would answer. And the applause which greeted this statement showed clearly how satisfactorily his audience expected him to fulfill his promise.

At last his moment came and he began with a plea for the exclusion of all testimony from either scientists or theologians. Though he himself, he boasted, had been certified as learned by the many colleges which had bestowed honorary degrees upon him there is no such thing as a Bible expert. Learning is useless. The opinion of a bushman just converted is as good as that of a scholar who has devoted a lifetime to the study of the text. Faith alone counts.

His case could hardly have been stated more ineffectually and the audience which had long awaited some convincing retort to the heresies it had been hearing, was aware of the fact. He used the word Faith but it was no glowing or even positive thing. It was not something which triumphed over difficulty and doubts but which fled from them. Almost as in a parody, he equated it with ignorance and reduced it to something of which no one could be proud. Any passionate revivalist from the hills could have been ten times more effective. He would have believed. Bryan merely refused to doubt. The Champion upon whom Dayton depended had let it down and Dayton knew that he had. At that moment not only confidence but hope went out of its heart and it was prepared to applaud, as presently it did, the flamboyant oratory of Dudley Field Malone—not primarily, perhaps, because it believed or even understood what he was saying but because he at least had in his liberal platitudes the Faith which Bryan seemed to lack.

Malone was a spellbinder of much the same variety that Bryan had once been, and his audience responded as similar audiences had once responded to Bryan's spell. He pleaded for fair play, stated the simple case for light against darkness, then taunted Bryan as a coward who had first declared before the world that the trial at Dayton was a duel to the death between religion and science and then refused to fight the battle he himself had so loudly called for. When Malone, swelling with pride over his triumph, stalked over to Mencken to receive the praise he obviously expected, what he got was: "Dudley, that was absolutely and without any possible exception the *loudest* speech I ever heard." Coldly considered this was perhaps a just assessment, but the most effective debater is not necessarily the one who stands best the test of cold consideration, and Malone was precisely right for the occasion. The applause which broke out from a predominantly hostile audience was twice as great and twice as long as that which had greeted Bryan.

Under cross-examination the defeated champion provided an even sorrier spectacle as he retreated further and further into boastful ignorance. Asked if he did not know that there were records of civilization far older than Biblical chronology could include, he replied that he was not accustomed to seek evidence which might damage his faith. Asked finally if he denied "that man was a mammal," he replied, "I do," probably because he had only a very vague idea what the word meant. And it was at this point that Mencken fell with a loud crash from the table upon which he had climbed to get a good view of the show. Perhaps it was the accident he pretended it to be, but I have always suspected that it was to mark with an exclamation point an interchange which he wanted no one to forget.

One was almost sorry for the great leader who had fallen so low. Driven from politics and journalism because of obvious intellectual incompetence, become ballyhoo for boom-town real estate in his search for lucrative employment, and forced into religion as the only quasi-intellectual field in which mental backwardness and complete insensibility to ideas could be used as an advantage, he already knew that he was compelled to seek in the most remote rural regions for the applause so necessary to his contentment. Yet even in Dayton, as choice a stronghold of ignorance and bigotry as one could hope to find, he went down in defeat in the only contest where he had met his antagonists face to face. Dayton itself was ashamed for him.

It knew very well who had won the debate, though many may have still believed that it was Truth which had been defeated in what was, after all, no more than a debate. So far as the legal verdict was concerned it was no more in doubt than it had been before the trial opened. From a legal standpoint the judge was, I suppose, quite right to have kept the jury out of the courtroom during most of the technically irrelevant proceedings. It had, as a matter of fact, been present for not more than fifteen minutes during the entire trial. And it did not, of course, take long to agree that John Scopes was indeed guilty of having taught the theory of evolution in defiance of a law passed by both houses of the legislature and signed by the Governor.

A few days later William Jennings Bryan died suddenly while still in Dayton. It was commonly (and probably truly) said that gluttony had prepared the way for his death; but I suspect that a broken heart was the immediate cause. Mencken staged a grotesque dance over his grave in one of the best and most characteristic of his essays, "In Memoriam: W.J.B." A few days after we had left Dayton he wrote me a note: "God aimed at Darrow, missed him, and hit Bryan. But our loss is Heaven's gain."

And it is interesting to imagine what Bryan himself would have said had it actually been Darrow rather than he who was struck down at the end of the debate.

Meanwhile I had been fulfilling my own duties by sending to *The Nation* three articles. The first—to which Lewis Gannett in New York supplied the inflammatory but not inappropriate head, "Tennessee: Where Cowards Rule" —states so clearly what is still in my opinion the most significant aspect of the whole affair that I shall reprint a few paragraphs from it:

Dayton, Tennessee, July 5

> Even those who do not happen, like the present writer, to have been born and bred in Tennessee should not find it difficult to forgive Dayton. A tiny town set in the midst of fruitful strawberry fields, it had never heard of any Darwin except the one who keeps the local dry-goods store until Mr. Bryan enlightened it, and to this day it is ignorant of that famous meeting of the British Association when Huxley and Wilberforce threshed out the question which has now arisen, some sixty years later, to puzzle it. Its faith is no narrower than that of every other community equally remote; its temper is better than was the temper of Oxford half a century ago; and if some of its inhabitants turn to the law to protect their children against the teaching of a dangerous theory, it is with a simplicity of mind which has no conception of the questions of academic freedom involved.
>
> Dayton, moreover, once the law was passed, was ready and anxious to deal as best it could with all the questions, legal and scientific, involved. While the president of the State University sat in his office praying that he might be allowed to violate the law in peace; while he was quietly issuing (as several members of his faculty have assured me

he was) unofficial instructions to his teaching staff that they should make no changes in their instruction; and while he was, at the same time, seeking to retain the friendship of both sides and accepting the congratulations of various fundamentalist bodies for his stand against evolution, Dayton was arranging to settle in simple honesty what the representatives of science, education, and enlightenment were anxious only to dodge.

And so when I sit at the little table in Robinson's drugstore where the argument began and discuss with the county superintendent of schools his attitude as one of the prosecution, I feel that the shame of Tennessee is not in Dayton. There is no State of the Union, no country of the world, which does not have communities as simple-minded as this one, and if Tennessee has become the laughing-stock of the world it is not because she has her villages which are intellectually a half-century behind the centers of world thought but rather because among her sons who know better there is scarcely one who has the courage to stand up for what he thinks and knows instead of flying quickly to cover lest he might have to sacrifice to his convictions some political advantage or some material gain.

At Dayton no one is afraid to tell me what he thinks. But when I go to Knoxville, seat of the State University and one of the three largest cities in Tennessee, I enter a different world. One of the most important members of the university board of trustees takes me aside to whisper in my ear; the president of that institution, telling me I am a good fellow, takes me confidentially by the arm; the editor of one of the leading newspapers, distinguished by the safe piety of its editorials upon the subject, closes the door of his office; and the remarks of all might be summarized in what were the actual words of one: "Of course it's a damn-fool law—but I won't be quoted." These and other Knoxvillians are defensive and indignant; they resent in various terms the publicity they have attracted and they protest against being judged by the laws their legislature passes; but these Knoxvillians will not admit that, fundamentally, they are to blame. In Tennessee bigotry is militant and sincere; intelligence is timid and hypocritical, and in that fact lies the explanation of the sorry role which she is playing in contemporary history. Dayton's only crime is the naïve belief that a law may be intended to be enforced.

Not even those who voted for the bill wanted it to pass. As a member of the legislature told me, he thought he might as well win the favor of a few fundamentalist constituents by saying "aye" because he felt sure the Senate would reject so preposterous a measure; the Senate, following the same admirable political logic, decided to put the burden upon the Governor, who, as the last responsible party, would hardly dare write himself down an ass; but the Governor, so it is said, remarked only: "They've got their nerve to pass the buck to me when they know I want to be United States Senator" before he signed the bill. And strangest of all, even the politicians make no particular effort to conceal their dishonesty because they feel that while the fundamentalist will be satisfied with any obedience however venal, the rest of the population will acquiesce in any amount of political corruption and cowardice. Thus the Governor, who had accompanied his signature with a letter stating, in effect, that no one expected that the law would be enforced, became an earnest supporter of the bill when the letters from the Epworth League and the Baptist Young People's Association began to arrive; and Senator Graves, who has distinguished himself by the firmness of his utterances in favor of the same bill, amazed me by giving me permission to quote him as saying that though he very much regretted that the bill had been passed I would have understood why he voted for it had I been in the Chamber to hear the cheers and jeers of the fanatics who had caused it to be introduced. "I am no politician," he added cryptically, "but if I were one I should have had to vote for that bill whether I wanted to or not."

Meanwhile the law is accepted by the people of the State in a manner worthy of the legislators whom it elected to represent it. The average businessman is puzzled by the furor created in the outside world; he cannot understand why anyone should care whether evolution is taught in the schools or not when obviously neither business nor industry is affected by questions so highly abstract. The president of the university, who ought to know better, can think of no plan more courageous than weakly to disobey the law when necessary, while pretending to the legislature that he approves of its acts or, more accurately, gives it to understand that he will not embarrass it by publicly stating his opinion of the law which both he and it know to be asinine. Concerned above all else with his precious appropriations, it never occurs to him to ask whether his chief duty might not possibly be something other than wangling money from a cowardly legislature.

If these paragraphs, written thirty-six years ago, still seem to me true and just, I cannot say quite so much for some of my other pronouncements which now seem naïve in their oversimple liberalism and inclined to see the threat of rural fundamentalism as more serious than it actually was. Thus, for instance, I added, rather in the tone, I fear, of Dudley Field Malone, this peroration to my second article:

The affair at Dayton has taught several valuable lessons. It has shown conclusively that the danger, often referred to by liberals, of laws that will reduce the United States to a bondage more complete than that of the darkest puritan village of colonial New England is no fantastic danger but one real and present; and it has shown also that the only possible way in which that danger can be fought is with a bitterness and vigor equal to that of those who provoke it. The mob is up; it has tasted blood and smelled smoke. Fair words are useless, for with every concession it grows in strength and determination; and it will not do to rest quietly behind the Constitution, for the Constitution is not an impregnable wall. It is subject to change and, as Mr. Darrow said in a quotation from Bancroft which we may have occasion to find all too true, "it is right to preserve freedom in constitutions, but when the spirit of freedom has fled from the hearts of the people, then its matter is easily sacrificed under the law." So far as Tennessee is concerned the only question worth asking is "How many are her Neals?" And so far as the country at large is concerned, "How many are her Hayses, her Darrows, and her Malones?"

Some of "the bigots" were, to be sure, bitter enough. The cowards were more bitter still against those who insisted upon speaking out instead of running for cover. But vigor was exactly what was lacking. Bryan's sorry performance disheartened even his admirers. It is impossible to imagine him leading a successful crusade. And when a superior court declared a mistrial on the technical ground that the judge had fixed the penalty which should have been left to the jury it added a recommendation that Scopes should not be retried. So far as I know there was no protest against this inconclusive conclusion. The law is, I believe, still on the books. But it had become what the Governor had hoped it would be: "not an operable statute."

Those who wrote the recent book and recent play are too young to have known at first hand the atmosphere of the Twenties and their interpretations seem to me for that reason to miss the tone of the proceedings as well as what time has made the most significant aspect of the whole affair. Almost inevitably they see it in terms of the grim ideological conflicts of our own day rather than as, in part at least, a typical jape to be gleefully reported in *The American Mercury*. They see a witch trial and miss the fact that it was also a circus; that the defense had deliberately baited their victims; that they had nothing to fear for themselves at least; and that they were enjoying themselves thoroughly.

What took place was more farcical than ominous for the simple reason that Bryanism was not, as it has been made to seem, roughly equivalent to McCarthyism but was, instead, as typical of its decade as McCarthyism was of the Fifties. Bryanism could not possibly have become that Wave of the Future which communism or fascism may be because it was only a backwashing ripple from the past. No one (except Bryan) got hurt and no one on the side which was unpopular only in Dayton and other Fundamentalist communities could conceivably have been hurt very much. The wooden swords with which the antagonists fought provided a fine theatrical spectacle but it was a sham battle—not because Bryan was not in earnest but because he had nothing to fight with. Neither the principals, nor such camp followers as I, were Freedom Riders who would be beaten and jailed. Is it any wonder that those who were young then look upon the much maligned Twenties as in some respects a golden age?

The attitudes of Knoxvillians toward a native son who had first deserted his community and then returned ten years later to call "coward" both the legislators and the educational leaders of his native state are revealing. When I went to the University to ask why no protest had emanated from it, the pompous dean hedged and gravely refused to comment when I asked if he would be content to have his curriculum established by the legislature. But when I put to the president the same question he rose from his chair, put his arm over my shoulder, and exclaimed reproachfully: "Now, Joe, you *know* there is no sense in asking me such a question."

One newspaper (Scripps Howard) reprinted a large portion of my first article without editorial comment other than the remark that *The Nation* was generally considered "one of the most important journals of opinion." On the other hand, the locally controlled evening *Sentinel* let itself go with the following editorial (July 10, 1925) which I was, of course, delighted to be able to take back to New York.

WE ARE NOT PROUD OF HIM

There has come to our desk an "advance copy" of *The Nation* for July 15 which contains an article, marked for our benefit, entitled "Tennessee: Where Cowards Rule." The article purports to have been written by one who is not ashamed to record therein that he was "born and bred" in the state he so maligns. We had become resigned to the inevitable when we were told when the Dayton test case first befell of the hosts of characters and human oddities, the cranks and fanatics, religious and irreligious, the journalistic muck-rakers, the literary high brows and know-it-alls, the agnostics, atheists, free-thinkers, free lovers, socialists, communists, syndicalists, psychoanalysts and what not that were preparing to descend upon us. But we confess we were not prepared for the native son character whose "heart within him burned" as homeward he turned his wandering footsteps with the ambition to shine and stink in the public prints by muck-raking his native land and retailing all of the idle gossip, the whispered scandals and exaggerated stories current among the people from whom he sprang as characteristic of them and deserving the gibbet of publicity in which it appealed to his peculiar pride and taste to place and damn them as a whole.

Our Tennessee people and Knoxville folks are as God made them and they have no cause to complain of His Handiwork in their case when compared with others. They are of all sorts and conditions, and have their mixtures of good, bad and indifferent, as other peoples and communities. It is not our purpose to defend them from the dirt-dubbing to which they have been subjected by this native son after the delectable methods developed and acquired in the putrescent atmosphere and reeking environs of Manhattan's moral and physical slums. We would not so insult them. But we wish this native son to know that we are not proud of him, in view of his odorous exploit. Knoxville and Tennessee will not reserve for him any niche in the future halls of fame and enroll his name among the sons to whom they will point with pride. We presume he was born for some good purpose. There is nothing in nature or creation that is without design. The humble tumble-bug serves a purpose in the wondrous plan. But we do not envy him his job or covet his company.

That was bitter enough to be sure. But though sticks and stones might break my bones hard words are honey to such a young rebel as I fancied myself. Members of militant minorities do not always get off so easily today.

Marcelle and I returned happily to the rented cottage in Cornwall and before the new theatrical season began I had finished *Edgar Allan Poe: A Study in Genius*. It was published the following spring and, though its sales were no more than modestly good, it had an excellent press including full-page feature articles in both *The New York Times* and *The Herald Tribune*.

On the other hand, many members of the Poe cult—a

notoriously sensitive and sentimental group—were highly offended. Despite the obvious fact that their hero was one of the "sickest" of writers ever called great and that his true distinction is the fact that he was the first to exploit fully what Baudelaire was to call the neurotic *frisson nouveau,* they have usually preferred to regard as most typical of his genius the feeblest of his lyrics in the manner of Mrs. Hemans and Letitia Landon. Naturally they were highly offended by a biographical-critical essay which undertook to explain him (almost to explain him away) in more or less Freudian terms and as an example of the essentially neurotic origin of genius.

Looking back upon the book I still think (as at least a few commentators apparently still do) that my hypothetical reconstruction of the origin and character of Poe's obsessions does at least fit more aspects of his life and work into a coherent pattern than any other theory with which I am familiar. I will go even so far as to say that there may be something in some of even my more exuberant flights, like that in which I attempted to resolve one of the oddest of paradoxes: the division of Poe's work into contradictory parts. On the one hand, there are the poems and stories which are dominated by horrors; on the other hand, there are both the essays which insist that all art is created by a coolly rational process and the detective stories in which Poe invents the "thinking machine" detective who has since appeared in stories by many writers of detective fiction from Conan Doyle to the present day. Poe, I declared, was obviously trying to protect himself from the knowledge that he was a victim of irrationality. Or, as I put it in a phrase of which I was very proud, "He invented the detective story in order that he might not go mad."

What does surprise and now somewhat embarrasses me

is that I seem to have been so taken by popular Freudianism as to all but equate neurosis and genius. I know that only a few years later I was myself protesting that though psychology, normal and abnormal, might often to some extent account for certain of the characteristics of a great writer's work, the very fact that neuroses are common while genius is rare is sufficient to suggest that the two are not identical. I was also to use a similar argument against the more respectable methods of historical criticism and the attempt to describe literature as the product of social forces. It is easy enough to show that Shakespeare was an Elizabethan, but such interpretative explanation leaves unanswered the question why all Elizabethans were not Shakespeares. In the case of Poe I seemed to be suggesting that his neurosis *was* his genius and even, I am afraid, to imply that such is always, even though not always obviously, the case.

Dr. Beatrice Hinkle, early translator of Jung, and at the time the best known practicing psychoanalyst except, perhaps, for the Freudian A. A. Brill, wrote me a letter of criticism relevant to what I have just said but going so far in an opposite direction as to require comment.

Dr. Hinkle began and ended with high compliments. "I wanted to read it through first and had so much on my desk I could not get to it. But since taking it up I have not been able to get away from it. You have done a most excellent piece of work in analytic psychology and it made a fascinating and at the same time real biography. It marks the advent of an entirely new approach to the understanding of historical characters as well as contemporary ones . . . If you ever had read Spitteler's *Imago* you will recognize there the complete picture of the psychic mechanisms in which the image or symbol is utilized instead of the object. Excuse this long letter but your masterly handling of this most complex material has not only given poor Poe life again but it has gratified me greatly that understanding is being brought to the study of these persons."

Between the first and the last of these compliments came the criticism: "However, I cannot accept, as I gather you do, that Poe's personality difficulties account for his genius. The analysis of his character is so characteristic of a whole group of individuals who differ among themselves in emphasis or degree only, that they constitute a special psychological type. Among them are normal (although deviating markedly from another type) and abnormal members. I would say that Poe as well as some of his French brothers was a genius in spite of these disturbances, not because of them. I am too familiar with these individuals not to recognize and appreciate their problems, but there are few geniuses among them although practically all have artistic leanings and capacities in some degree. The sexual inhibitions and variations are also a general problem from which I have never seen one of this type free."

Dr. Hinkle's objections were certainly sound, as I was soon myself to admit; but she goes so far in an opposite direction as to raise another problem. Surely Poe (like many other more or less neurotic artists) did not write as he did merely "in spite of" his obsessions. If they do not constitute his genius (as I am afraid I had implied) they certainly influenced enormously the character and tone of his creations. He might have been a writer without them. But he would not have been the same kind of writer. He would not have been Edgar Allan Poe.

Have any of those who have since dealt with the problems of the neurotic genius ever given a satisfactory account of the extent or manner in which his abnormalities are more than the mere impediments which Dr. Hinkle seems to call them?

It was the nature of these mysterious relationships between certain great artists and their neurotic quirks which I had in mind when, not very long after, I happened to meet at a cocktail party the famous Dr. Alfred Adler, inventor of "the inferiority complex," and, incidentally, a ridiculously pompous little man. Having been, I suppose, rendered by the cocktails more impudent than I ordinarily am in the presence of the famous, the following dialogue took place:

Myself: I have read a number of your books and they all seem to me to rest upon a non sequitur.

Adler: What do you mean?

Myself: Well, the first seven chapters describe how very abnormal all the great men have been. Then the last chapter says "Therefore let us be as normal as possible."

Adler: I still do not understand the point of your remarks.

Myself: Suppose a writer, or for that matter any man, finds himself psychologically troubled but functioning very successfully. Wouldn't it be dangerous for him to have himself psychoanalyzed?

Adler: I would not like to answer that question directly. But I will say this: the only two leading psychoanalysts who have never themselves been analyzed are Dr. Freud and myself . . . and I think we have made the greatest contributions to the science.

At the moment however I was troubled by no such doubts about myself and on the very day of publication I was granted a sight which is not granted to most beginning authors. Passing down lower Fifth Avenue I saw a man with a book in his hand and facing away from the street into a corner of The Macmillan Company building. I peeped over his shoulder and discovered that, oblivious to everything else, he was devouring *Edgar Allan Poe: A Study in Genius.*

"Something like this," I said to myself, "is doubtless what I shall see frequently from now on. Whenever I have doubts concerning my importance or my fame I shall simply go to some frequented place and there I will find someone eagerly devouring my words."

Fortunately I did not know that thirty-six years later I would be able to say truthfully that never since that day of publication have I ever seen any stranger reading anything—book, review, or magazine essay—that I had written. Subway riders used to be great readers of *The Nation.* But not, it appeared, of the drama column.

8

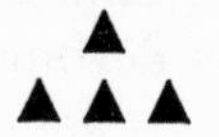

The affair at Dayton was precisely what *The Nation*'s editor, Oswald Garrison Villard, liked to call "right down our street." This meant that it involved a liberal "cause" unpopular in certain quarters yet thoroughly respectable, as the choice of the word "street" rather than the more usual "alley" may suggest, and as many of the various causes of the Twenties were not.

From his father, the railroad builder Henry Villard, Oswald had inherited a considerable fortune, much of which he spent in good works. From his maternal grandfather, the abolitionist William Lloyd Garrison, he inherited both a reforming zeal and, by a circuitous route, a journal of opinion which had had a continuous history since it was founded in 1865, with E. L. Godkin and Wendell Phillips Garrison (brother-in-law of Henry Villard) as editors. When Oswald Villard took over in 1918, *The Nation* was already much the oldest journal of opinion in the United States and it had always been "liberal" according to the changing meanings of that slippery word.

Once this had meant Herbert Spencer's *laissez-faire* capitalism with great stress upon what "liberals" of the Twenties were contemptuously calling "good government." It definitely did not mean the economic radicalism already growing at the time when I joined the staff.

The Nation had always devoted—as it has always continued to devote—a good deal of space to literary articles and book reviews, a surprising number of which were written by young beginners who would become much more widely known—as, for instance, Henry James and the Adams brothers who contributed to very early issues; Mark Van Doren, Clifton Fadiman, and James Agee (to mention only a few) who came along much later. But here even more perhaps than on the political side the tone was, in the early days, what we should now call conservative, with Paul Elmer More in charge during the early years of our century and writing the Shelbourne Essays which remain, perhaps, the most substantial body of conservative literary criticism written in the United States.

By 1921, when I contributed my first reviews, the effect of postwar changes in interests and attitudes was already beginning to be felt. Ludwig Lewisohn, a romantic "modern" whose idol was Gerhart Hauptmann, was book reviewer as well as drama critic. Later, after he had left *The Nation,* he became an ardent Zionist, but in his widely read autobiography, *Up Stream* (1922), he had described himself as "more an American than a German and more a German than a Jew." His various and well-publicized marital misadventures were to cause Villard a good deal of pain, but under his influence as well as under that of

Carl Van Doren as literary editor (1919-22) *The Nation* had turned away from Paul Elmer More conservatism to become a defender of all the "new writers"—Theodore Dreiser, H. L. Mencken, Sherwood Anderson, Sinclair Lewis, Edgar Lee Masters, and many others, some of them now pretty well forgotten.

Villard heartily concurred with some of the political re-orientations. Though still ardently championing the rights of Negroes (in a somewhat too Booker T. Washingtonish way, the staff thought) he was also an ardent champion of Peace, if not perhaps entirely a pacifist. *The Nation* was so prominent among the leaders of the attack upon the Treaty of Versailles that Villard was sometimes accused (as he had been even during the war) of being pro-German. On the other hand the economic radicalism into which *The Nation* was drifting alarmed him considerably and I remember, but can't quite date, his distress when, during his temporary absence staff member William MacDonald wrote an inflammatory editorial about New York's homeless which he headed "Take Every Empty House!"

What troubled Villard even more was the way not only the new literature, which he never took very seriously, but also liberalism in general was forming an alliance with those who advocated what he could only regard as "a relaxation of moral standards." His was the attitude of most Nineteenth Century rebels (including even the atheists) who felt it their duty to be more respectable than anyone else in order, if for no other reason, to avoid the charge that moral lapses were just what could be expected to follow from unconventional opinions on political, religious, or social questions. Still terrified of his mother, who had carried into the Twentieth Century the stern puritanism of the abolitionists, he actually trembled when a chance remark by one of the guests at a luncheon party hinted that he occasionally smoked a cigarette. And of all the new freedoms the one which distressed him most was what he was old-fashioned enough to think of as "free love."

Despite all this he surrounded himself with a staff of young men and women who almost without exception represented the very tendencies which made him uneasy and to whom he permitted a quite astonishing freedom of expression in both conversation and print. We all referred to him, sometimes affectionately and sometimes condescendingly, as "the boss," and we often thought of him as ridiculously stuffy. But I now find myself aware that we failed to appreciate sufficiently how "liberal" he was in just that respect where the liberalism of the present day is most likely to fail—I mean in his genuine tolerance of opinions different from his own. He permitted us to write things and to accept the writing of others of which he did not approve. He also allowed us to treat his opinions with sometimes ribald disrespect. On one occasion, I remember, when some scion of a prominent family had been accused of gross financial peculation he had exclaimed in editorial conference with genuine distress: "I can't believe it. Why, he is an old Harvard oarsman." Though he was momentarily disconcerted by the howl of derision which went up, he soon became used to hearing, for years thereafter, the office comment upon any prominent man who fell into disgrace: "an old Harvard oarsman, I suppose."

Irregularly, but sometimes as often as once a week, the editors invited to lunch some distinguished visitor or visitors—usually foreign, and usually political, though men of letters were occasionally included if Mr. Villard could be persuaded that they were really important. At one such luncheon the principal guests were two members of the British Labor Party and, no doubt at the insistence of one of us younger staff members, D. H. Lawrence. What happened will illustrate how benevolently naïve Mr. Villard could be in certain respects.

Lawrence had sat in complete silence while the Labor Party people expatiated on "conditions" and on how they expected to ameliorate them. Suddenly realizing that his other guest had been completely left out of all this, Villard turned to him with, "And now, Mr. Lawrence, won't you tell us what you think we should do to save the world?" Those of us who had read some of Lawrence held our breaths and he rose to the occasion. White beneath his scraggly beard, Lawrence replied with measured ferocity: "I thought, Mr. Villard, you understood that I hoped it would go to pieces as rapidly and as completely as possible."

During this period the most important members of the political staff were Lewis Gannett, who had joined it in 1919 and remained until he moved to the *New York Herald Tribune* in 1928, and Freda Kirchwey, not long out of Barnard College when she came to the office in 1918 though she remained to become, after Villard's retirement, editor and publisher. On the whole we were a happy family—much happier than we were to be when a new tension and bitterness developed here as everywhere during the Thirties. Our happiness was due in part to Villard's tolerance, but in part also to the same atmosphere which made the Dayton trial so different from what anything involving an ideological conflict is likely to be today. We were at bottom fundamentally optimistic, and we were gay crusaders. We thought we knew what Liberalism was and we were confident both that it would triumph and that, by triumphing, it would create a better world. If we had examined one another's creeds carefully we might have discovered that we were often strange bedfellows, but we were too united against the Philistines to be aware of all the things which were presently to divide us.

The war to end war was over even though *The Nation* was not sure that resurgent nationalism was not threatening its accomplishments. The minor depression of the early Twenties was passing and we were already on the threshold of that New Era which was supposed to have established a prosperity both automatic and permanent. Most conspicuously in protestant and satiric literature, but to a considerable extent in social and political criticism also, the most threatening enemies were then not Capitalism, Race Prejudice, or the neglect of the Undeveloped Countries, but Puritanism, Provincialism, and the Genteel Tradition.

Significantly *The Nation*'s most publicized series of articles during the Twenties, and one soon to be printed in book form, was devoted, not to any economic or political question, but to "Our Changing Morals." I contributed a section called "Modern Love and Modern Morals" in which—adopting the attitude which dominated the book—I implied that the only trouble with "our changing morals" was that they were not changing fast enough. Though this may seem to the young generation of today unrealistic and even frivolous it may be looked at in a different way. Just because our world seemed prosperous and safe we could try to imagine what the Good Life would be instead of not daring to look beyond the elementary concern for a minimum of security.

We were all Liberals but even more conspicuously Libertarians or Libertines—in the Eighteenth Century sense of the term, as well as, frequently at least, in the modern sense also. "Brave New World" was not yet an ironical phrase and we tended to feel that nothing stood between us and it except traditions, prohibitions, and inhibitions of a happily moribund past. Since we were in fundamental agreement insofar as this most general of general attitudes was concerned, we were all in it together and it made comparatively little difference whether we called ourselves Anarchists, Communists, Aesthetes, Social Critics, Nietzscheians, or Quakers. Anyone who has known only the situation during the last thirty years, when the dissenter has been hating no one so much as the proponent of some other variety of Liberalism, must be astonished to learn that men and women as fundamentally incompatible as many of them turned out to be could once have seemed so united.

Consider, for example, the group which was centered around the Provincetown Playhouse where the plays of Eugene O'Neill were first introduced to New York. It was presided over by George Cram Cook who was to die while trying to lead the life of a shepherd in Greece. It included John Reed, now buried beside Lenin's tomb in Moscow, Mike Gold, for many years the editor of the Communist *Daily Worker,* the aesthete Edna St. Vincent Millay, and the now all but forgotten poet Maxwell Bodenheim, who would have been called a Beatnik if the word had been invented sooner. It was true there, as it was true at *The Nation* and nearly everywhere else, that you were welcome if you were at outs with respectability and things-as-they-are. What shape the Brave New World might be taking in your imagination was not important.

I was twenty-seven years old when the Twenties began, thirty-seven when they ended. This means that they corresponded pretty closely with the epoch of my own life when I would naturally be most ready to participate in the social life of the writer, the journalist, and the actor. Perhaps I have changed more than that life has changed and possibly, therefore, I am mistaken in believing that it was not only more active but more miscellaneous than it is now, partly for the reason just given—that to be either a writer or a rebel put you into some more or less amicable relation with other writers or rebels, whatever their complexion. At least this is true: though I was never especially gregarious and made little effort to cultivate wide acquaintance in literary or theatrical circles, there was so much social activity going on that it amazes me to remember with how many writers, publishers, actors, producers, etc., Marcelle and I did at least have a nodding acquaintance.

It seemed that everyone gave parties and to many of these parties it seemed that everyone was invited. Even Theodore Dreiser—socially one of the most awkward and tongue-tied of men—felt it his duty during a year or two to preside over a weekly salon where almost anyone who had written a book might be found. But publishers were, of course, the most inveterate hosts and every new book or every visiting author had to have at least a cocktail party in honor of him, her, or it. The head of one of the new firms which published several of the most esteemed of the new writers became so much more interested in parties than in books and gave so many of what came to be known as "B Parties" (those at which literary discussion was not the chief object, and the pretty ladies present were not chosen for their interest in books) that he drank himself into a premature death. Invited guests often brought along whomever they happened to be with at the time, and I remember the host of one prodigious party (it was on New Year's to be sure) who confided to me, half ruefully and half proudly, that he had sent invitations to fifty and found himself host to two hundred and fifty. And this was in the days when bootleg liquor was not cheap.

Despite all this, serious work was done by serious men, and it is unfair that in the popular mind the "image" of the Twenties should consist almost entirely of this carnival aspect. On the other hand, I do not regret that I took some restrained part in the carnival and, especially, that I learned something about what I have referred to previously as the ways in which writers are, and the ways in which they are not, more to be admired than ordinary men.

Let me be indiscreet enough to recount one anecdote about Sinclair Lewis at a literary party. Whatever may be the permanent value of his work, he was, at the minimum, a vastly talented journalist, and there are not many such of whom it can be said that they defined and labeled with a now accepted name two social phenomena and thereby contributed to the dictionary common names as universally understood as Main Street and Babbitt. But because he was unsure of himself and astonished at being a celebrity, Lewis needed desperately to be the center of all attention. He would go to any length to be sure that he was and become almost frantic when he did not succeed.

On this particular evening the party was in honor of the late Frances Newman, a librarian from Atlanta, Georgia, who had come on to New York to enjoy the sudden celebrity which was hers just after she published a novel, more or less naughty in the accepted manner of the Twenties, called *The Hard Boiled Virgin.* Naturally she was the center of attention and Lewis, unable to endure the fact, soon disappeared. When I happened a little later to go out into a hallway, I found him there pacing back and forth in an agony. "That woman! That woman!" he was muttering to himself. Then, when he saw me: "Joe, if I was on a desert island with that woman for a year, she would be a whole lot less hard boiled at the end of it. But, by God, she would still be a virgin." Yet *Main Street* and *Babbitt* were, in their way, very remarkable books.

Once when Heywood Broun was at the height of his popularity I had occasion to go see him at his home on some business in connection with his weekly page in *The Nation*. I found him in bed, and on the wall close beside him was a huge poster with a portrait and the legend: "Read Broun every day in the World-Telegram." When he saw me glance at it he said apologetically: "My analyst told me to put it there where I would see it the first thing in the morning."

The moral is, of course: never forget that a good writer writes with the best part of himself and that the rest of him may be quite ordinary; or, as Dr. Johnson put it, authors are usually disappointing when you meet them because "unusual talents require unusual occasions for their exercise." Why should a good writer be any different at a party from anyone else?

Another moral I learned—and it is a useful one to a young writer—is that those of his calling seem even more prone than others to assume that they will never be less successful than at the moment they happen to be; that as soon as they have published even one book which brought fame and a good deal of money, they take it for granted that the success will be repeated year after year. This is certainly one of the reasons why it is so often true that "We poets in our youth begin in gladness/But thereof comes in the end despondency and madness."

Lewis, to be sure, never suffered poverty; but his last years were a frenzy of anxiety lest he should be forgotten even while he still lived; and there were a number of his contemporaries whose whole lives were embittered by one success never repeated. A certain novelist, still living I believe, whose first book was hailed as a masterpiece, found himself a decade later on the WPA relief rolls. Edgar Lee Masters, whose *Spoon River Anthology* gave him what he no doubt regarded as a secure position in American literature, never wrote another successful book. I occasionally saw him as much as twenty-five years later dragging out a dismal, embittered life in the dismal old Chelsea Hotel on Twenty-third Street. Perhaps James Branch Cabell's *Jurgen* deserves to be still read, but who does read it? How many remember that Joseph Hergesheimer's novels earned him fame as well as fortune?

1929 put an end to an epoch and a new generation was soon to dismiss the Twenties as a disgraceful decade during which those who were not hopelessly drunk on bathtub gin were criminally unaware of the various Waves of the Future (good and bad) which were soon to overwhelm them. It is true that to many of us our Bohemianism was a part of what we considered our Liberalism. We attended our own "wild parties" and we were inclined to consider sex freedom as by no means the least important of the various freedoms we believed in. Yet in all of these things we did, nevertheless, genuinely believe, and we believed in them with hope. We were not—to use the term now most often applied to the mood of a large segment of present-day intellectuals—"alienated," at least not from man and the universe, though we thought ourselves thoroughly alienated from the United States of Coolidge and Hoover.

We were not Existentialists. Our scorn was directed toward what man and society were, not against all that they might ever be. The future was bright and the present was good fun at least. We were certainly not yet troubled by the now typical conviction so well expressed by one of Arthur Koestler's revolutionaries who is made to say that "in an age of transition no one has a right to be happy." If what Wordsworth said of the early days of the French Revolution could be toned down a bit, one might be tempted to apply it to the Twenties: "Bliss was it in that dawn to be alive,/ But to be young was very heaven." So at least one is inclined to think when looking back from the seeming twilight of today when all our troubles are so much darker.

This I can still say while remembering what was said a few pages back about the disreputable aspects of the decade.

During the years when I had first begun to contribute to *The Nation* and during those when I was a staff member, both my conduct and my convictions must have fitted fairly well into the pattern. I had seen eye to eye with it in describing the Dayton trial, and as a contributor to *Our Changing Morals.* It must have seemed to me that I had made some very loose synthesis of what I had picked up from such diverse sources as the Omar Khayyam, Oscar Wilde, Whitman, and Shaw I had brought with me from Knoxville plus the Freud, Nietzsche, and other assorted writers I had read since. Never very politically minded, I also accepted almost without even superficial examination the political opinions I was presumed to have, though I think I always tended to resist even the first beginnings of that sympathy with the Communist philosophy which was already tinging many Liberals.

Despite this conforming nonconformity there were very fundamental elements in my temperament which made it inevitable that I should ultimately rebel against some of the rebel orthodoxies. Since childhood there had been a strain of melancholy and pessimism in my thoughts and an anti-utopianism which tended to make me protest against almost every proposal for the radical solution of any problem—"that won't work either." I soon began to criticize, mildly at least, the critics of our society and the premises of what was then Liberalism.

Since I have earlier confessed that in college and the graduate school I fancied myself as a naughty rather than a holier-than-thou rebel, it is not surprising that one of the first of my disagreements had to do with sex freedom, and that I took a position rather more cynical than that of the apostles of this freedom. Some of them went so far as to deny that they advocated it at all and, like Ludwig Lewisohn, celebrated the beauty of monogamy through a series of marriages each of which was defended as the only *true* marriage it had been his good fortune to achieve. Others surrounded every casual affair with all the glamour of romance and even mysticism; and I remember that I once profoundly shocked Max Eastman by responding to his statement that it was very important but very difficult to distinguish between Love and Lust with the declaration that it was, on the contrary, very easy: "If it doesn't cause you any trouble it is Lust."

All agreed, whatever else they might disagree about, that "honesty" and "frankness" were essential. Husbands and wives had the right, almost the duty, to seek "experience" where they could find it, provided only their partner was kept informed—preferably in detail. Nothing could have worked worse. "Frankness" and "honesty" seldom generated the "understanding" which was supposed to be the "reasonable" response, and marriages, instead of being stabilized, commonly collapsed.

For the failure of this aspect of the Liberal creed I had several rational explanations. One of them I had found well stated in a comment by Edwin Muir on the role played by "love experiences" in enriching the personality. The catch is, so Muir protested, that you cannot "experience love" by seeking to do so for the simple reason that the "experience of experiencing love" is all you can deliberately acquire and that is something very different from the experience of love—which can only be involuntary.

My other rational explanations were less idealistic and were founded upon the belief that human nature was (as I still believe) either something truly permanent or at least impossible to change in any radical fashion in less than many millennia. On the one hand, so I thought, the almost universal desire of the lover to monopolize the beloved is part of this human nature. On the other hand, unfortunately perhaps, the desire to be monopolized is by no means so usual. One's own polygamous or polyandrous impulses seem reasonable enough and often unimportant to oneself. But there is no use trying to explain them to wife or husband, even though the latter may understand his own similar impulses well enough. That what is sauce for the goose should be sauce for the gander is something which has been always said but never accepted.

Perhaps one should sternly repress his vagrant impulses—but repression, we had come to believe, was likely to have dire consequences. Hence the only solution of the dilemma seems to be a very old-fashioned one—which is not frankness and honesty but deceit, as kindly as one can make it. "'I believe," so I remember once announcing, "in old-fashioned marriage—by which I mean one in which both parties keep their adulteries (if any) secret." The institution of matrimony has survived the two thousand years of western civilization which have passed since faithfulness on the part of the husband became ostensibly obligatory, and survived despite the fact that an astonishing proportion of the men and women who have been distinguished enough to have left a record of their lives have been what the present-day "counselors" call "immature," *i.e.*, something less than strictly monogamous. Sexual enterprise very often, though of course not always, accompanies enterprise of other kinds. That the institution of marriage could survive more than one generation of frankness and honesty I gravely doubt. When Freda Kirchwey once interrupted some such opinions as these to ask with exasperation how I had formed so low an opinion of human nature I was proud to reply promptly: "By introspection."

Gradually I found myself privately, and sometimes publicly, dissenting from perhaps the more important of the principles and practices of what was then the Liberal creed. To me it seemed too much concerned with what it was determined to get rid of, too little with forming any clear idea of what positive things it wanted. I heartily agreed that Puritanism, Provinciality, Intolerance, etc., had blighted our civilization. But what, I asked, were we going to do when we had got rid of them? Freedom was a necessary condition of the Good Life but, as I had protested in an early review already once referred to, "Freedom for what?" A difficult question. We were getting rid of a great many things which ought to be got rid of —including the Fundamentalism over which we had won so easy a victory at Dayton—but the result was threatening to be merely the creation of a vacuum.

This conviction served to reanimate my originally pessimistic opinions which had been half forgotten in the excitements of the early Twenties and I began to feel the need to state them explicitly in the context of contemporary intellectual tendencies.

▲

During the early summer of 1926 while Marcelle and I were living in the old house at Cornwall, Connecticut, which we had bought at the conclusion of our summer in the rented cottage where I had finished the book on Poe, I sat down to write what I first thought would be simply a single essay. After it was finished I saw my way to a second which seemed to follow logically; after that to a third of what were beginning to seem chapters of a book. I continued during the autumn to write them rather slowly and I sent several successive chapters to the *Atlantic Monthly* which quite surprised me by printing them all.

That they were accepted by so conservative an editor as Ellery Sedgwick was explained to me by Irita Van Doren, Carl's wife and successor to Stewart Sherman as editor of the *Herald Tribune*'s Sunday literary section. I had continued to write many essays and reviews for this paper. Irita and I saw one another frequently at "parties" or elsewhere, and she was accustomed to have lunch with Sedgwick on his many visits to New York. He had been, he told her, bewildered and appalled by the first of the essays but had sent it to Alfred North Whitehead who advised publication. When this and several of the succeeding essays attracted a good deal of attention, both favorable and unfavorable, he continued to lay a flattering unction to his soul despite Irita's repeated correction of the error he had confidently assumed. "Of course," he would say, "the attitude is typical of the Jewish intellectual." "But," Irita would reply, "Joe is a pure blond Nordic." "Dear, dear, you don't say so," he would exclaim. At the next meeting the same dialogue was repeated. Apparently the expected opinions of a Jewish intellectual could be shrugged off. But if blond Nordics (even though not Bostonian) were entertaining any such thoughts as mine there could be no telling what the world would come to.

By early spring of 1928 about half of what was to be called *The Modern Temper* had been written, and it was to be perhaps the most widely read—certainly the most vigorously discussed—of my books. But completion was delayed for a somewhat longer time than that of the book on Poe and by a similar interruption—namely, an assignment by *The Nation,* this time involving a European trip of some months' duration. What I observed during that trip had, I think, only slight influence upon the half of the book still to be written but it was important to me in other ways and should come in here.

Shortly after our marriage Marcelle and I had spent the summer of 1923 in Europe, partly in Paris where we were introduced by Marcelle's sister Jeanne to the mixed company of painters and their hangers-on which gathered at the Dome on the Boulevard Montparnasse and which included the then famous (still somewhat legendary) model Ki-Ki. She must have sensed my underlying pessimism because she remarked one evening to Marcelle, "If I didn't know you I'd wonder what woman was making him unhappy."

We also flew to Brussels (my first experience with an airplane since 1911), visited Chartres, and went to Italy for our most strenuous session of church and museum-hopping. I was deeply enough impressed by Chartres to buy the set of Viollet-le-Duc's many encyclopedic volumes on medieval architecture and it is still on my shelves. Chartres and, in Italy, the frescos of Giotto impressed me so much that though they never quite converted me they did make me feel that the Ages of Faith had somehow blessed their artists with a serenity the world has since lost—perhaps forever. Outwardly, however, I had been more influenced by the Left Bank from which I returned with a large and, so I thought, handsome red beard which Marcelle found herself at the end of the year unable to endure any longer.

We had not been in Europe again until now when Mr. Villard decided that the time had come for me to benefit from his generous policy of sending, one by one, the principal members of his staff on a tour of inspection somewhere outside the United States. Lewis Gannett had made an adventurous trip from China across Turkistan to Russia and western Europe. I, it was decided, should depart in the late winter of 1928 and tour the theater in the chief European capitals—especially in Moscow where the actors, plays, and stage techniques were being much discussed as an important part of the new Soviet culture. I was expected to send back a few articles; but general education was the chief purpose of these *Nation* expeditions.

My two previous ocean voyages had been made in unpretentious boats so that Marcelle and I felt unusually opulent crossing this time first class on the Hamburg American line. From the dock we went directly to Berlin for a week or two where we saw, without being much impressed, some productions in the new "expressionistic" style put on by the German director who had changed his name from Fischer to Piscator and later came to America to teach at the New School for Social Research the methods he had to a large extent borrowed from the Russians—who had, in turn, found their inspiration in the Italian postwar Futurists. We saw also some fine Shaw directed by Reinhardt but soon discovered that here, as in the other capitals of western Europe, the most popular plays were, for the first time in history, translations from the American—which meant most often contemporary New York hits like the backstage melodrama *Broadway,* then a big success in Berlin.

The big adventure was, we were sure, to be Moscow which comparatively few Americans, almost no mere tourists, had visited since the Revolution. The fact that the United States had no diplomatic representation in Russia made the enterprise seem rather daring to two travelers who had never before done anything daring in the least. When we went to the American consulate to get a visa we were told sternly that we were positively forbidden to go into Russia at all; and when we said we were going anyway we were warned that our government renounced all responsibility for our safety. Then, as we left, the consul relented: "If you get into any trouble," he said, "let us know." We didn't get into any trouble at all and in Moscow I was amused to discover that if our government had no relations with the Soviets, our banks did. Our letter of credit from the National City Bank was honored there as readily as anywhere else.

As a matter of fact, our most surprising incident was comic rather than sinister. Settled in a compartment in an international Wagon Lit for the long journey across Germany and Poland to the Russian border, we were somewhat taken aback to discover that a man and a woman who shared the compartment were unimpressed by the length of our journey since they would be a week or ten days on their trip to Vladivostock; and I remember little of Poland except the sight of a group of peasants marching across the mud to Sunday services while carrying their precious shoes in their hands.

Crossing the border loomed as something more formidable. It would be necessary, of course, to leave the international train for one on the broad-gauge Russian railway. Poland and Russia were on very bad terms; the border was closed by a barbed-wire entanglement; and on either side was a line of soldiers. To make matters worse we had arrived during the night and it was necessary to stumble through the darkness from the Polish soldier who looked sourly at our passports to the waiting Russian who loomed huge in his long overcoat and peaked cap with the sinister Red Star. He had a rifle with fixed bayonet in his hand; he examined our papers in silence and, without a word, motioned us forward into Darkest Russia. Then, when we had taken half a dozen steps, he turned his head and called out in a perfect New York East Side accent: "Don't take any wooden nickels while you are here."

Had I been a better reporter than I am I should certainly have gone back to get his story. Since I didn't, the mystery of his presence is unexplained. I have known one American woman who renounced her citizenship in a moment of enthusiasm and lived to regret it when she discovered that she was regarded and treated as a foreigner whatever her technical nationality. Was my East Sider content or regretful? I shall never know.

Louis Fischer, then decidedly pro-Russian though he was later, like many others, to experience a revulsion which carried him far to the right, was *The Nation*'s correspondent in Moscow and promptly introduced us to the other members of the small group of American newspaper men including Walter Duranty, of *The New York Times,* William Chamberlain, and Eugene Lyons all of whom were then also more or less pro-Russian though the two last were presently to swing at least as far to the right as Fischer.

Other members of the little group of Americans (too small to be called a colony) were Clarina Hanks Michaelson, a proper Bostonian who had become and was to remain longer than most, a very improper Communist; and Henry Wadsworth Longfellow Dana, grandson of both *the* Longfellow and *the* Dana. He had lost his job as instructor in Columbia College for "disloyal" activities during the war, and though he was now semipermanently established in Moscow he was mildly snubbed by Clarina Hanks because she had shed every trace of her Boston upbringing and spoke only in a tough slang while Dana could not help bringing Beacon Street right into the Red Square.

He was frantically engaged upon a fanatically complete account of the contemporary Soviet theater. His hotel room was piled almost ceiling high with books and pamphlets while one wall was occupied by the poster which listed (Paris fashion) the repertory of all the theaters for the week. He hated to miss either an afternoon or an evening performance and I can still see him fidgeting in front of the poster in characteristic indecision. "I really don't know what I ought to do. Now this play here is very poor and that one is very good. On the other hand I have seen the good one seven times and the poor one only three. It is really *quite* a problem."

Soon we were established in the ancient Hotel Savoy where we ate off the former Czar's linen and wiped our mouths with napkins into which had been woven the imperial double eagle. Dinner the first night was excellent, but the quality of the food dropped off disastrously immediately thereafter, the explanation of its first excellence being, as we were presently informed, that we had been eating up the leftovers from a banquet given the night before in honor of the King of Afghanistan. Bad as the routine lunches and dinners continued to be they were not, like the food in the restaurants we tried, nearly inedible and there was always a breakfast of caviar and crisp Russian rolls to look forward to.

We "did," of course, the usual tourist sights which meant, among other things, standing in a long queue for the privilege of gazing upon Lenin in his glass case (where he looked, I must say, precisely like a wax image though allegedly embalmed by a new process which involved one of the first of the new Russia's new advances in technology), and crowding into the Red Square on May Day to see the military demonstration.

Despite its gloomy magnificence, Moscow struck me as the most dismal city I had ever seen. It was then in the grip of desperate scarcity. To find some trivial necessity like a pair of shoe strings might involve hours of shopping. On street corners, pariah members of the former middle class stood forlornly beside little collections of clothing or household goods which might include, for instance, only the left shoe of a pair which they hoped to sell for enough to keep alive a little longer. Now and then a handsome black limousine carrying some official would scatter pedestrians in all directions, but the usual form of city transportation was by horse-drawn droshkies driven by istvostchiks bundled in what appeared to be endless layers of quilted but ragged garments. The droshkies, like nearly everything else, obviously dated from the same ancient days, and one had the feeling that they were one-horse shays all of which would at some not distant day simultaneously disintegrate.

The most distressing thing of all was the helplessness of those who had the misfortune to belong to that most hated of classes, the former bourgeoisie. Louis Fischer happened to mention to me that he had recently bought a woman's hat from an ex-bourgeoise who made them secretly though, of course, she was forbidden to engage in any trade and would be imprisoned if discovered. "How," I asked, "is she supposed to make a living?" And he replied with the calmness characteristic of those who were sure that the slow extermination of a large class was necessary to the building of a new world: "She isn't supposed to." After my return I was often asked, "How does the average Russian dress?" The answer was, "In anything he can find."

On the other hand, the amiability of the ordinary man in the street was just as it has been so often described since and probably more unambiguous then than it is now. The Communist doctrine had not yet hardened into a rigid dogma from which no variation was permitted, and even the official attitude toward citizens of a country that had broken off diplomatic relations was less icily unfriendly than now when ambassadors are exchanged and summit conferences are news.

Fischer soon taught me that though it was almost impossible to buy theater tickets at the box office since all the seats had usually been sold in a block to some trade union or other, I need only make my way backstage to the manager's office and say "Correspondent—American" to get two passes without further ado. This was one of the many indications that at this time Russians were very anxious to show everything they were proud of to Western visitors—so anxious indeed that they were hurt if you were not eager to visit some primitive factory. After I expressed a desire to see some of the then famous movies, I could not manage to get away from the special showing arranged for me until I said positively that I had no time for more than the four- or five-hour program which promised to continue indefinitely. "But we thought," I was told, "you wanted to see films."

Marcelle, always interested in people and quick to respond to friendliness, was particularly impressed by all sorts of trivial courtesies. If we stood in any one of the omnipresent queues we were usually invited to take a place at the head of the line. On May Day a young girl climbed down from her choice perch to say in French, "It's your turn now." At breakfast in the hotel the waiter (also French speaking) who came to clear away pushed toward us the three sugar cubes left on a saucer with the remark: "For you. After all, you have paid for them." Yet we were sure he himself would have been very glad indeed to take them home.

As for the stage I had come to see, it was obviously the one not strictly utilitarian institution upon which money was being spent lavishly and which was obviously a vigorously going concern involving a number of different theaters, and a large repertory of classic as well as modern plays. Except for these theaters, Moscow seemed to shut down at night like a provincial village, making a drive home through the dark streets in a dilapidated droshky an uncanny experience. But the theaters were still shabbily magnificent even though the Imperial Box at the Bolshoi itself was now occupied by proletarians casually dressed and perhaps with their feet on the rail. One got the impression that Russians never tired and that no play, no speech, and no spectacle was ever too long for them. This enormous energy was probably in part responsible for the always excellent acting, no matter what the play—not only when the company was composed of surviving members of the pre-revolutionary stage but also in a trade-union theater where, so I was told, all the performers had been amateurs a few years before.

This was the time when "interesting experiment" was beginning to be a magic phrase in the whole theatrical world. Some of the Moscow theaters, notably the Vakhtangov, were wildly eccentric employing, for instance, slogans or short strips of film to provide a comment over the heads of the actors; bringing characters on or off stage on moving belts; and using all the other devices presently to become familiar to New York audiences at the New Playwright's left-wing theater in the Village and also, to a somewhat lesser extent, in the productions sponsored by the WPA. Other theaters were devoted to emerging "Soviet Realism" with what looked like a real locomotive occupying a large part of the stage in a very popular play set in a railroad repair shop and called *The Humming of the Rails.* On the other hand, various items from the pre-revolutionary repertory were magnificently performed by surviving members of the old Moscow Art Theater in what appeared to be the unchanged tradition of their generation. The new ballet, *The Red Poppy,* was essentially conventional in everything except its "message."

Since I understood no Russian we always took with us an interpreter who proved quite skillful in translating just enough here and there to make the action intelligible—though that, as I later discovered, could convey a very false impression of the literary quality of the play. No doubt because it was so beautifully staged and so powerfully acted, I assumed that *The Armored Train,* a great success at the Moscow Art Theater, must be an impressive play as well as an impressive production. It dealt with an episode of the Revolution in the course of which a band of Partisans captures an armored train sent out by the White forces and brings it triumphantly over to the revolutionary cause. The big scene in which a "hero of the Revolution" halts the train by lying across the rails at the top of a high embankment and a real train rushes towards him from the wings, ought to have aroused memories of the old melodramas I used to see in Knoxville or, for that matter, of the once famous movie serial, *The Perils of Pauline.* At the time it did not, and only some years later when a translation of *The Armored Train* became available did I realize how little it differed in either the obviousness of its heroics or the banality of its dialogue from the thrillers which Owen Davis once turned out by the dozen for touring stock companies.

(One of these last, by the way, I heard described by its original producer, William A. Brady, at a dinner in honor of Davis who had by then become respectable as the author of *Icebound,* one of the first specimens of "The New American Drama": "In Act I the villain tried to throw the heroine off the Brooklyn Bridge; in Act II he attacked her with an ax; in Act III he roped her to a railroad track; in Act IV he tied her onto the moving platform of a buzz saw. Then when, in Act V, he attempted to make love to her and she shrank away from him, he exclaimed: 'Why do you fear me?' ")

What interested me most was the evolving communist "ideology," especially as it concerned artistic and intellectual affairs. The general atmosphere was one of uncertainty and there was a good deal more freedom of opinion and expression than was permissible only a few years later. The post-revolutionary play which had enjoyed the longest run was *The Days of the Turbins,* dealing very sympathetically with the decline of an aristocratic family under Soviet rule, and Dana rather apologetically recommended that I see it though he could not bring himself to approve.

The most popular comic writers were the collaborators Ilf and Petrov whose satiric novel, *The Little Golden*

Calf, is not only genuinely funny but so biting that when an English translation was published the then Commissar of Education provided a preface in which he danced on eggs in an effort both to praise and to explain it away.

A few years later, when the collaborators visited the United States and I met them at a party, Petrov (who spoke a very little English) delighted me by responding to my remark that, though a cat lover, I did not remember seeing a single cat in Moscow, by saying: "Oh, there are lots of cats there; but you won't see them in the street. They are all Soviet cats and hard at work catching mice." Nevertheless, the reins were by then being drawn tighter. While the authors were still in this country I wrote an article about them in *The Nation* and was therefore invited to a reception given by the Soviet Consul in New York. As I was leaving, the consul stopped me to say that the Messrs. Ilf and Petrov wanted him to thank me for the article and to say that though they had been in general most pleased they also wanted me to be told that one thing had hurt them. "What was that?" I asked, though I could guess easily enough. "You say that their satire is so amusing and so objective that it would be impossible to determine from internal evidence whether they were convinced Communists or not. They want me to tell you that they are very loyal Communists indeed."

Lunacharsky, the Commissar for Education who had apologized for Ilf and Petrov, had been a pre-revolutionary and he was so old, Louis Fischer explained, and he had brought so much of the past with him that he would be forever incapable of understanding the new spirit; and he did not, indeed, last very much longer as commissar. When I talked with him in his office he seemed to be more than anything else a "good European" of the old German socialist type. He professed to be anxious that

Soviet art should be a continuation of, and a logical development from, the art of the past. He said he had watched without enthusiasm the increasing tendency of the theater to devote itself to contemporary social problems to the exclusion of everything else. "I shall," he said, "be ready very soon to issue a protest against the growing neglect of the classics in the state theaters and against their tendency to produce no new plays except those which concern themselves with more or less minor details of social adjustment. What used to be called the 'eternal problems' were properly so called, and they are as important to the members of a Communist society as to those of any other. Sooner or later Russian art must return to a consideration of them.

"Of course," he continued, "I do not mean that I desire any return to 'art for art's sake.' From the standpoint of a Communist, art must have its social function, but that function is a broad one. It includes the widening of the intellectual horizon as well as the discussion of sociological problems, and it is particularly important in an industrial state. The life of the workman is inevitably narrow if his experience is confined to the factory alone. He more than anyone else has need of those aesthetic experiences which will expand his range of comprehensions and appreciations. It is for this reason that I am even more interested in the music drama than in the ordinary play. Unfortunately we have not at present any new composers equal to the task, but I look forward most eagerly to the time when some Russian shall arise who will express the hope of the Russian people in a form not dissimilar, perhaps, to that in which Wagner embodied his Schopenhauerian pessimism."

The "new ideas," on the other hand, I got in their most extreme form from Eisenstein, the maker of the famous films *Potemkin* and *Ten Days That Shook the World*—the English title of the latter being taken, of course, from the book by the American John Reed.

Eisenstein received me in his very modest lodgings littered with books and scraps of film. A large, heavy man, with a head of flying hair like that affected some years ago by the youth of Italy, his bearing and his conversation alike suggested very strongly the Italian Futurists with whom, as a matter of fact, he had been allied, and they prepared one for the fact that his communistic ideology was superimposed upon the Futurism which was at its full tide in Russia when the Revolution broke.

Like most people brought up in the Futurist school, Eisenstein began by sweeping nearly everything that *is* into the junk heap with one wave of the hand. The theater, of course, is dead and done for. Art should strike with the direct impact of a physical blow, and only the cinema can do that. The only good play in Moscow is *The Humming of the Rails,* and it is good only because it is killing the theater. In fact, its perfectly literal naturalism is not theater at all—it is merely inferior cinema. The people of the future will want only actualities and the movie is much more actual than the stage.

The legitimate function of art is a purely practical one; its purpose is solely to produce convictions and to lead to actions. During the Revolution, for example, its duty was to provoke revolutionary acts. People went from the theater or the cinema to the barricades. Now that the Revolution is accomplished it has, of course, other work to do. Religion, for example, has not been completely destroyed and for that reason the thing which he likes best in his new film *October* (shown in America as *Ten Days That Shook the World*) is the attack upon religion.

Since the purpose of art is purely practical there is no

such thing as a "permanent aesthetic value" and every work must be judged according to its usefulness at a given time in a given place. He himself is no longer interested in *Potemkin* which is more or less passé and not as purely cinematographical in its methods as he would like it to be. One can get an idea of what he wants to do from certain scenes in *October* where dynamic ideas are translated into pictures. The scene, for instance, in which the overweening Kerensky is shown, all alone, mounting up and up the successive flights of stairs in the imperial palace which lead to the throne room, or that in which the downfall of religion is suggested by a series of flashes beginning with a picture of the fully developed God on an icon and descending through a whole series of representations to the grotesque idol of a savage.

Warming to his theme, Eisenstein developed it to its simple logical conclusion. In the perfect state there will be no art. Bourgeois art is a vicarious fulfillment of unsatisfied desires; Communist art an instrument for social adjustment. But in the perfect state there will be no unsatisfied desires and no more social adjustments to be made. Art, therefore, will disappear. I reminded him that in *Reason and Art* Santayana suggests that this is exactly what Plato meant when he said that poets would be expelled from the perfect republic. But Eisenstein, as one might guess, was not much interested in either Plato or Santayana. Louis Fischer, who was acting as my interpreter, put in a word: "The theater is already dead. Then I suppose you consider it your function to kill the cinema." Eisenstein smiled. The idea pleased him.

To my mind, his films were more impressive than his theories and I realized that the latter represented "Futurism" at least as much as the more practical-minded Russian communism. He had been so long accustomed to *épater le bourgeois* that he was now inclined to *épater le prolétariat* instead, and in the last of three articles I sent from Moscow I concluded with two paragraphs which are sufficiently accurate and sufficiently inaccurate in their guess at the probable outcome of the conflict between the Lunacharskys and the Eisensteins to be (I hope) of some interest.

It is obvious that there can be no peace between the representatives of attitudes so opposed. To Eisenstein, Lunacharsky is only a half-assimilated bourgeois; to Lunacharsky, Eisenstein is only a new barbarian. From the standpoint of fanatical logic there is, of course, no doubt that Eisenstein would have the better of the argument. His theory is based upon one of the fundamental Communist postulates—that in a communistic state the ordinary processes of life will be all-sufficient in themselves—while Lunacharsky's assumption that the life of a factory worker is "narrow" does constitute a sort of heresy. I am told that once when he was explaining his theories at a public meeting some one rose to charge him with defending a kind of art which was, in effect, only another "opium of the people." That charge embodies the substance of a complaint often made against him. A cultivated man with a strong love of the past, he wept when he heard the false report that the Kremlin had been fired upon by the Bolsheviki, and he is less anxious to destroy what the old society created than he is to put the new masses into possession of whatever may be salvaged from it.

It is not, of course, worth while for an outsider to venture any opinion concerning the probable outcome of a conflict as fundamental as this one is, though it goes without saying that the ideas of Lunacharsky are far more easily comprehensible to such an outsider and must seem to him more reasonable, even if less simply logical, than those of his opponents. But like all that concerns contemporary Russian art, the question has connotations not purely artistic,

> and the conflict is only part of a much larger conflict upon the issue of which the future of the whole communistic experiment will depend. If communism is essentially only a new form of political and economic organization—if, that is to say, it is merely a logical continuation of the evolution from absolute monarchy through constitutional government and democracy—then its task is to rule a humanity not in itself radically different from the humanity we know, and Lunacharsky is right. But if, on the other hand, the coming of communism is, as to its more fanatical proponents it seems, a phenomenon of an entirely different sort—a reconstruction not merely of the social order but of human nature itself—then of course we who are as yet unreconstructed can know nothing of its future and can only conclude that whatever seems to us most incomprehensible is that which the future will probably choose.

What actually happened was, of course, that all eccentricities and indeed all experimentation soon came to be denounced as "cosmopolitan," "decadent," or "formulist." But Soviet literature and art, instead of merging with the main stream of Western culture as Lunacharsky had hoped, became "socialist realism" instead, and this meant in literature the flattest possible imitation of Nineteenth Century didactic naturalism; in the graphic arts something very much like the worst of English academicism at the middle of the same century. In 1928, on the other hand, the thing most frowned upon was not "experimental" forms, but whatever suggested a concern with the mere individual. Thus when I asked the directress of a theater which had recently produced O'Neill's *The Hairy Ape* if she planned to do his new *Strange Interlude* she replied with great condescension: "No. We have got far beyond interest in the psychological problems of the individual."

▲

When, after nearly a month, the time came in May to leave Moscow just as the ice was breaking up in the river and citizens sporting embroidered blouses, if they were lucky enough to have them, were beginning to sit coatless in the sun, I was not sorry to leave. For one thing, and though no one had been other than cordial to me, the shabbiness omnipresent except in the theaters was oppressive. For another I sensed (or perhaps only imagined) the watchful eye of the servants of a police state. Our passports had been taken away as soon as we registered at the Savoy and I could not know that they would be handed back without question when I applied for our exit visas. Getting mail from New York was a matter of friendly informality. I would call at the Foreign Office where a Mr. Podofsky, whose exact position I never learned, would rummage through his desk and either produce a letter or two or would say, "They are here somewhere but I can't seem to find them; you had better call again tomorrow." Was this merely amiable inefficiency or did it mean that the letters were being read somewhere? I never knew.

In any event, it was obvious enough that the Soviet citizens themselves were well aware both of spying eyes and of the necessity for obeying promptly whatever orders came down to them. A short time before, Leon Trotsky had been excommunicated. Every reference to him had been removed from *Ten Days That Shook the World*. Every one of the pictures and busts which, so I was told, were formerly to be seen everywhere, had disappeared overnight. Trotsky had played no part in the Revolution. When the young director of the English language library (on one of whose shelves, by the way, he had proudly pointed out my book on Poe, and who said he was not a member of the party) had occasion to make some reference to Trotsky, he dropped his voice and said "the unmentionable one."

Perhaps it was the result of mere timidity, but I confess that I sighed with relief when the train carried us across the Soviet border into Austria and that I was surprised when more than one Viennese apologized for the shabbiness and gloom of his city. To me it seemed, by contrast, very spruce and very gay. Even Marcelle, who likes nearly every place she has ever visited and had expressed some regret at leaving Moscow, was compelled to agree.

Neither here nor in Budapest was there much of interest in the theater (unless you count the translated *Abie's Irish Rose*), but a short stay in Budapest was a delightful interlude. We had brought letters of introduction to Rustem Vambery, son of a very famous Oriental scholar and himself dean of the law school in Budapest. A charming specimen of the Good European and an old friend of *The Nation,* he spoke English perfectly and was eager to introduce us into one of those delightful social circles which can exist only in communities where everybody, or rather (if this doesn't sound snobbish) everybody who *is* anybody, knows everybody else. There were luncheons in private houses and dinners at the famous restaurant on Margaret Island in the Danube. It was very different from Moscow and I find myself remembering with especial vividness a luncheon given by the wife of a liberal nobleman then serving a prison sentence for some incautious utterances, where the guests included, beside Vambery and his equally charming wife, a sadly genial poet, said to be the finest in Hungary though destined never to be known outside it because he was quite untranslatable, and Enrico Caruso's widow (the only foreigner except for ourselves) who was the daughter of New York's Park Benjamin. She told us affectionately some anecdotes of her late husband's intellectual childishness. He was, for example, so distressed by the time she wasted in reading books that he once brought her a stamp album in the hope that she might be diverted into philately as an activity less incomprehensible.

Our new friends were very much aware of the fact that Budapest was on the outer edge of Europe though not of the fact that this gave it what was to us, at least, one of its charms; and we were more than once assured that we mustn't think it was actually Balkan. When we came at last to leave regretfully for Paris the poet (who seemed to have become quite fond of us, as we were of him) remarked sadly: "Of course I shall never see you again. No one ever pays more than one visit to Budapest."

Neither I nor Marcelle have, it is true, ever returned. But this was not the last we were to see of the Vamberys. They were accustomed to spend part of their time on a property in what was by then Czechoslavakia where the situation was growing steadily worse. Presently they escaped with their son to the United States ahead of the German invasion. Here, he gave lectures at the New School for Social Research and the family lived in very straitened circumstances for some years until his death when Mrs. Vambery and their son Robert (by now American citizens) moved to California.

Half Jewish himself, Vambery had a touch of that humorous, self-accusing anti-Semitism not uncommon among members of the race. I remember especially the bitterness of his remark concerning some of the refugee intellectuals from Germany. "They combine," he said, "the modesty of the Jew with the charm of the Prussian."

When we reached Paris from Budapest, M. Gemier, director of the Odéon, expressed a current opinion. "So you have come from both New York and Moscow, the only two cities in the world today where the theater is interesting!" My obligations to *The Nation* were fulfilled when I sent one article from France and I had time left over for my own enterprises.

Of these the most important was the half-written *Modern Temper*. Hardly had I begun again to think a little about it when a telegram came from Harcourt, Brace and Co. They were anxious to publish the book in the spring of 1929. Could I deliver the manuscript by September—which was about the time I expected to reach New York?

Far from anticipating any such pressure I had only a very general idea how I was to go on from the point where I had broken off. But a publisher's request is a very stimulating thing to a young writer and I made a rapid calculation. Another thirty thousand words—approximately the same number as were already written—would be, I decided, about right, and there were just thirty days left until we were due to sail. A thousand words per day was the stint to which I had accustomed myself. If I could keep on schedule I should be able to finish just in time to catch our boat. At the moment, we were staying with Marcelle's sister in her apartment on the Boulevard St. Jacques near the Boulevard Raspail and the concierge volunteered that there was an unused maid's room under the roof. That solved one problem by providing what was precisely the traditional garret.

On the first morning I mounted to it, I plunged into the next chapter, the subject of which had somehow miraculously presented itself. Every morning thereafter, I climbed the stairs again and as I finished each section I found myself knowing what the next should be. As soon as a thousand words had been written I stopped where I was, descended to rejoin Marcelle, spent the afternoon either reading or walking the streets while thinking of entirely different things, and passed most of the evenings at the Dôme with the mixed company of Americans and Parisians gathered there. When I came to the end of the thirtieth session, the book was finished.

Only once since, when writing the first of my "nature" books, have I ever had the experience of going so regularly and steadily ahead with a discourse which I had not consciously thought through to the end and which, on the contrary, seemed merely to lead me on. No doubt the fact that I had a very definite deadline had something to do with the phenomenon in this first instance of it. But it was more important, I think, that in both cases I had been, without knowing it, long preparing what I had to say.

Ideas, convictions, and attitudes, which had previously found no adequate expression and of the interconnection between which I was not fully aware, suddenly crystallized into a coherent discourse. I listened to what I had been saying to myself for several years, without being quite aware of the fact, and I simply wrote it down as I listened. Here were the conclusions I had come to as I digested or reacted against all I had read, heard, or discussed from the freshman days at college down to the latest book I had reviewed and the latest conversation I had heard in *The Nation* office. For the first time I was prepared to say what I, at that moment, believed; just what, in my opinion, the "modern ideas" I had met came down to.

Marcelle shared my elation as we climbed the gangplank with the manuscript under my arm. During the crossing I read it over and the usual reaction set in. "Dull, dull, dull," I said to myself. "It won't do." Still it had to do; and Harcourt, Brace got it on time.

"Chacun," wrote Anatole France, "fait son salut comme il peut." And ever since I can remember, even far back into my childhood, I had practiced a private technique to save myself from the utter despair into which the anticipated failure of almost any enterprise I undertook would otherwise have precipitated me. It was simply to cultivate some side issue or hobby into which I could take refuge. The technique worked in Paris.

Since childhood I had had an interest in the sciences—some of them the very ones I had been charging with responsibility for our present plight. Among other things I had spent many hours with a microscope, and when I had passed through Germany on the way to Russia I had bought there a first-class instrument, far better than any I had ever owned before. If, I said to myself when I began to write in my garret, this book is a failure I will devote myself to microscopy as a hobby. During the afternoons when I was not promenading the boulevards I read what a bookseller recommended as the standard textbook of protozoology. And it turned out, as it frequently had in the past, that the hobby later supplied material which I could use professionally. Back in Cornwall I put the microscope to work and the experiences I had with it were to furnish one chapter each in two much later books of a kind I did not then dream I would ever write.

Part Two

9

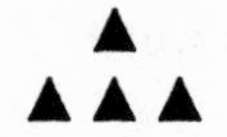

The Modern Temper was published on schedule in the spring of the fateful year 1929. It was widely and favorably reviewed, though no reviewer, I think, said he agreed with it fully. It was also much preached at from pulpits, and it brought more letters of protest and praise than anything else I have ever written, some of them suggesting what one asked in so many words, "Why don't you hang yourself?"

When in the late summer of 1926 I had submitted the first chapter to Ellery Sedgwick at *The Atlantic* he had replied as follows:

> God help you, for your creed never will! But in spite of all that, I will admit not only the close argument of your paper, but its ability and real interest. I was brought up

> in a pragmatic school, and my fundamental objection to your ideas is that they lead directly away from all the enthusiasms and ferments which are at the bases of the creeds that work.
>
> But what I think about your beliefs no whit affects my satisfaction at having so able a piece of work. I accept it with pleasure. Thank you very much.

Sedgwick's letter anticipated the tone of a good deal of the subsequent comment, but from the current paperback edition I have learned what I had ungratefully forgotten, namely that Irwin Edman called it "a terrifyingly honest book," and Bertrand Russell "Profoundly interesting and very penetrating." Also that Granville Hicks (with whom I was to quarrel in public a few years later over the emerging literary leftism) pronounced it "One of the crucial documents of this generation."

Thirty-five years add up to a period of time too great for me to bridge completely, and I cannot remember exactly the stages which had led to my complete rejection of the optimism which the Twenties had founded upon science and upon the rejection of what it regarded as all the errors, prejudices, superstitions, and fears of the past. But what I now undertook to demonstrate in my book was that this synthesis (which I myself had also been inclined to make) leads logically to despair rather than to hope. Sedgwick had said that my creed would not "work." My criticism of the modern temper and the premises which generated it was precisely the same: it wouldn't work—because it left man too bleakly and hopelessly alone in an alien universe.

I had, in other words, returned to a rock bottom of skepticism and, to use the now fashionable word, alienation. Most of my subsequent intellectual history—if that is not too pompous a phrase—has been an attempt to climb out of the pit into which I had led myself, and, speaking only of my own present temper, I can say that though I am still to a considerable extent "alienated" from the beliefs, aims, and pursuits of contemporary society I no longer feel myself alienated from man or the universe.

A defrocked Catholic priest who was one of the early reviewers remarked sarcastically that the motto on the second title page should have been, not the quatrain from Mark Van Doren which it was, but an exclamatory question from *Lamentations*. "Is any sorrow equal to my sorrow?" But though the sorrow was intellectually quite genuine a false impression would be created if I did not add here that it did not prevent me from enjoying some of the superficial pleasures of life. When, a few months after the book was published, I went on a cross-continent lecture tour and was to be met in Detroit by the president of a woman's club she approached me only after every other descending passenger had left the platform. "Are *you* Mr. Krutch?" "I am." Her face fell. "But you do not look as, as—*depressed* as I expected!"

In the preface I wrote: "The book is at once a study and a confession—a study of various tendencies in contemporary thought and a confession of the mood which the submission to these tendencies has engendered. Insofar as it states what these tendencies are it is, I believe, objective; insofar as it treats of the emotional states which these tendencies produced, it is, of necessity, colored by an individual personality, and yet the effort has been, even where these are concerned to deal only with those emotional attitudes, which bear a strong family resemblance to those which are common to many. Here are, at least, no private adventures, no purely individual experiences, but only the thoughts engendered by the contemplation of the facts and theories familiar to every reading person and stated in a form as detached as I was capable of achieving . . . I have been compelled to make reference to many facts or supposed facts in biology, psychology, and anthropology. Obviously no person is qualified to assert them all with authority and, obviously, I am much less qualified than many others, but when I do so I state them not as facts but simply as commonplaces which we have been taught to believe . . . I am responsible not for Truth but for the convictions, scientific or otherwise which I and my contemporaries have been led to hold."

The first chapter began: "It is one of Freud's quaint conceits that the child in his mother's womb is the happiest of living creatures. Into his consciousness no conflict has yet entered and the universe is as he wishes it to be." My thesis was that just as the infant suffers a birth trauma when he first discovers that he has exchanged the world of the womb in which he is omnipotent and perfectly adjusted for a reality far otherwise, so man has suffered a series of similar traumas as he has learned that he is not the inhabitant of the universe he had imagined in which his importance is ultimate and which corresponds in some general way to his image of what a universe should be, but that he is instead an accident somehow endowed or cursed with needs, hopes, and values to which nothing outside himself corresponds.

Hence, I went on, the universe revealed by modern knowledge and modern deductions from it is one in which the human spirit cannot be comfortably at home. That spirit breathes freely only in a universe where Value Judgments are of supreme importance. It needs to believe, for instance, that Right and Wrong are important and enduring realities, that Love is more than a biological function, that the human mind is capable of reason rather than merely of rationalization, and that it has the power to will and choose instead of being compelled to react in a fashion predetermined by its conditioning. Since the sciences and quasi sciences of psychology and biology as well as of anthropology have tended increasingly to convince us that none of these beliefs is more than an illusion, we will be compelled either to surrender what we have been accustomed to call "our humanity" by adjusting to the real but alien world, or to live some sort of tragic existence in a universe alien to the deepest needs of our nature.

Irwin Edman was to tell me later of a little adventure of his own while he was waiting in Rome for an interview with Santayana. A secretary told him he might like to pass the time by looking at his own new book which Mr. Santayana had recently read and in which he had made some marginal notes. Opposite a sentence where Edman had made some reference to "the disillusion characteristic of modern writers" the skeptical philosopher had written: "Such as Ecclesiastes and Heraclitus."

In my own argument I had perhaps not taken sufficient note that some of the "modern" doubts about man's hopes and pretentions were not exclusively modern. As for man's lack of free will, had I not myself tried to shock my freshman teacher by reciting "With earth's first clay they did the last man knead/ And there of the last harvest sowed the seed./The first morning of Creation wrote/ What the last dawn of reckoning shall read"? The fact still remains, however, that what had been unusual and blasphemous heresies were tending to become the commonplaces of the intellectual, and I suppose that my position might have been called Existentialist if the word had then been known to any except theologians.

In one chapter called "The Paradox of Humanism" I

wrote: "To those who study her, this Nature reveals herself as extraordinarily fertile and ingenious in devising *means,* but she has no *ends* which the human mind has been able to discover or comprehend. Perhaps, indeed, the very conception of an end or ultimate purpose is exclusively human." In another chapter, "The Disillusion with the Laboratory," I find, looking through it again: "We went to science in search of light, not merely upon the nature of matter, but upon the nature of man as well and though that which we have received may be light of a sort it is not adapted to our eyes and is not anything by which we can see . . . We had been assured that many troublesome shadows would flee away, that superstitious fears, irrational repugnances, and all manner of bad dreams would disappear. And so in truth many have. But we never supposed that most of the things we cherished would prove equally insubstantial, that all the aims we thought we vaguely perceived, all the values we pursued, and all the principles we clung to were but similar shadows, and that either the light of science is somehow deceptive or the universe, emotionally and spiritually, a vast emptiness."

One chapter, "Love—or the Life and Death of a Value" Sedgwick had feared was rather too gamy for *Atlantic* readers and he suggested that we skip it. He reconsidered when I agreed but added that I would send it to *Harper*'s which had asked for something from the book. As it turned out, this chapter, together with "The Tragic Fallacy," was the most discussed and (especially the second) the most often reprinted in anthologies and collections for college reading.

The chapter on Love was devoted to the simple thesis that the tendency of science to concern itself with origins, and often to equate everything with these origins, had reduced what had once been either a sin, a sacred mystery, or an aesthetic game to a mere biological function; and that while one might live for love either as a mystery or as a game, one could not very well live for it as merely nature's device for securing the survival of the species.

(In a parenthesis I would like to add now that the prevalent attitude of today which frowns upon as "immature" the tendency of the Twenties to get freely as much as it could of the devaluated biological impulse has, in my opinion, done little to reestablish Love as a central human experience. Who wants merely "a satisfactory"—and of course "mature"—"marital adjustment?" Who does not want ecstasy instead?)

"The Tragic Fallacy" argued that the greatest tragic drama—witness that of Greece and that of Elizabethan England—had been always associated with ages of confidence and a strong conviction of the essential, indestructible greatness of man. In order to produce its tonic effect it must exclaim when it contemplates his refusal to be utterly defeated "How like a God!" and it must find a new world "brave" because it "hath such creatures in it." But man, having become merely an animal like the other animals and inhabiting a universe ignorant of his aspirations and his values, had now accepted an ultimate defeat and was henceforth destined to be, even in art, merely pitiful rather than tragic.

In the last chapter (written, of course, after I had returned from the Soviet Union) I brought the Russians into the picture. Since it is not by thought but by unthinking animal faith that men live, societies have been saved in the past, not by their thinkers, but by the unthinking barbarians who moved in to destroy their more complex civilizations. The new Russians seem young in the only possible sense of the word when applied to any part of the human family every member of which is presumably as old as any other. They are, in other words, full of energy and little disposed to ask ultimate questions.

"There has already developed in Russia a new philosophy of life, which, in spite of the fact that it has taken a form influenced by modern industrial conditions, is easily recognizable as being essentially primitive in its simplicity. Sweeping aside the intellectual and emotional problems of Europe, refusing even in art to concern itself with the psychology of the individual soul, communism assumes that nothing is really important except those things upon which the welfare of the race depends, and in assuming that it is assuming exactly what a primitive society always assumes. Its drama and its poetry celebrate the machine exactly as the literature of a primitive people celebrates the processes of hunting or of agriculture, and they do so for exactly the same reason, for the reason, that is to say, that agriculture on the one hand and industry on the other are the two fundamental processes by which the life of the people is sustained."

Within a few years after this was written many American intellectuals were describing the Russian phenomenon in less pejorative terms, but were in fact outlining it in much the same way. They were bidding us accept for ourselves also this wave of the future and to hail the dawn of a new age. Such was not however the conclusion I drew, either later or in the concluding paragraphs of *The Modern Temper*. We had indeed, I said, strayed far from the animal faith proper to the healthy animal. Nature may offer rejuvenation at a certain price. We might embrace some new illusion before it is too late, "But we prefer rather to fail in our own way than to succeed in hers [Nature's]. Our human world may have no existence outside our own desires, but those are more imperious than anything else we know, and we will cling to our own lost cause, choosing always to know rather than to be . . . If death for us and our kind is the inevitable result of our stubbornness then we can only say 'So be it.' Ours is a lost cause and there is no place for us in the natural universe, but we are not, for all that, sorry to be human. We should rather die as men than live as animals."

If all of this does somewhat suggest Existentialism (especially in the contention that man creates his own values) I refused to go so far as some of the present day who, if I interpret them aright, have combined Sartre with Baudelaire to arrive at the conclusion that in a wicked world the best way to praise virtue is to illustrate its opposite vice. Having no Jean Genêt (to take only one example) to whom I might refer, I went back to the Manichaeans who elevated Judas to sainthood because, without him, there would have been no crucifixion, and Jesus would have been without power to save. The logic, I said, was admirable but we live in a world where many things work better in social practice than logic does. "It is rather difficult to carry on trade with a man who may be planning to revivify your Idea of Justice by cheating you unmercifully, and rather difficult successfully to bring up a family when the father illustrates benevolence indirectly by beating the children or when the mother sets out to secure a clear idea of Purity by prostituting all her daughters."

Inevitably I was offered salvation by various well-wishers who had accepted various creeds. One such offer came in a letter from the prophetess Mabel Dodge Luhan, now best remembered because she had "willed" D. H. Lawrence to come to her at Taos and he came. Because she is a figure in recent cultural history, her letter is worth printing—with the possibly unnecessary explanation that the Mr.

Orage she mentions was the American exponent of the mystical philosophy of Gurdjieff in whose French retreat Katherine Mansfield spent her last days.

Taos, New Mexico
November 27

My dear Mr. Krutch—

Your article, "The Paradox of Humanism," is very interesting. It shows how you have thought this recurrent plight of ours out to the very end: You have just about fully explored your prison, and that is, you know, the point that all previous civilizations reached when they toppled. When people became really self-conscious so that they were ready to observe themselves (not others, as the behaviorists do) then, apparently they didn't know what to do about it, or why they should be obliged to do anything about it, so they didn't. They had reached a point where all the impressions they could receive were carried in their consciousness—the saturation point of experience—and also they had exhausted the diversities of Nature. Nothing remained to them, or so it seemed, but to repeat, and when experience becomes recurrent in the same individual, the civilization of which he is a part is at an end—so down it goes.

Now I am about to make a suggestion to you that, when it is made to me, is ignored, but I do hope something will come of it in your case. I want you and Mr. Orage to meet and have a talk. It is a tiresome suggestion I feel sure. People generally dislike having others shoving them towards strangers. I do. I never pay any attention to these attentions on the part of assiduous well-wishers—yet I do feel it would perhaps open a window if you and Orage hit it off. Unless, perhaps, you have already had a bite off him and rejected it? Well—he is telling the truth about a certain principle that is open to one to at least try as a means of getting out of the explored prison. You—with your extremely honest and individual habit of thought will be one to appreciate what Orage says about all this if you happen to get along alright with him—not intellectually—but chemically. And also if you are not predisposed to avoid him through prejudice against his associations. I think I will ask Herbert Croly to bring you together in case you haven't the initiative. (I suppose you know Croly?) And I will send Orage your article which is sure to interest him for you are so essentially on the brink!

And forgive my attempting this at all.

Sincerely yours,
Mabel Dodge Luhan

Mr. Croly forwarded to me the letter she wrote to him and I attended the luncheon. Fortunately or unfortunately, I made no sense out of what was imparted to me. Help in escaping from the prison had to come from elsewhere.

When the time comes I shall have something to say about how I did finally escape but at this point it is more appropriate to remark that it was unfortunate for me that my book was published only about six months before the Wall Street crash wrote finis to the roaring Twenties. My skepticism and what many regarded as gloom (I would have called it a "tragic sense" rather than gloom) were a reaction against the libertarian optimism of the decade just passed but they in no way anticipated what was about to happen. The dilemmas the book propounded were abstract, intellectual, and metaphysical. It assumed, as the Twenties had been assuming, that peace, prosperity, and what we now call a High Standard of Living were all more or less permanent and it asked only "So what?" "The sorrows of our proud and angry dust are from eternity and shall not fail."

For a few months I found myself in the position of an important new thinker. To my own gratified surprise I was invited to contribute to the volume called *Living Philosophies* (1930) where I found myself in the astonishing company of Einstein, Bertrand Russell, John Dewey H. G. Wells, J. S. B. Haldane, and Dean Inge. But the American intellectual and his readers were suddenly plunged into a new world. The problem seemed now to be, not the Good Life, but Survival. Political Science, Sociology, and Marxian propaganda occupied most of the time left over from debate concerning the immediate practical steps to be taken in a society which seemed about to collapse.

One minor aspect of the change is amusingly illustrated by a little adventure or misadventure of my own. A month or two before the crash, the editor of *Redbook,* then one of the most successful of the "slick" magazines, asked me to write an article setting forth briefly the thesis of *The Modern Temper.* He paid me for it the largest sum I had ever been paid for a single article and, as a matter of fact, the largest I was ever to be paid until many years later. But the crash intervened and the article was never published. When I asked him, (not really for information) more than a year after it had been accepted why it had not appeared, he replied jokingly: "You are asking me! I'll be glad to trade it back to you for another piece a good deal different in tone." In August 1929 even the mass public would have been willing to hear something about the ideas of a philosophical pessimist. After the end of September of the same year it was in no mood for such abstractions.

For the moment at least I, on the other hand, was not prepared to change radically the trend of my thinking. Since I had said all I then had to say on the condition of man in an alien universe and had no special interest in political or economic problems, I turned again to literature of which I had just written in the chapter of *The Modern Temper* called "Life, Art and Peace":

> In one sense the aim of the scientist and the aim of the artist are the same since both are in pursuit of what they call Truth; but the difference between them is this, that while for science there is only one Truth, for the artist there are many. The scientist, that is to say, is in search of truths which owe their name to the fact that they correspond to something in the world outside himself, while the artist is in search of those which need to be true only in the sense that they seem true to him and that they hold good within the artificial universe which is enclosed within the frame of the work of art he is creating.

This, so it seemed to me, might be one of the things to be illustrated in a book which was ultimately called *Five Masters: A Study in the Mutations of the Novel.* The five masters turned out to be Boccaccio, Cervantes, Samuel Richardson, Stendhal, and Proust. I rapidly learned just barely enough Italian and Spanish to make sense of untranslated works by or about Boccaccio and Cervantes. Proust was just then appearing in English but fortunately French happened to be the only foreign language in which I was reasonably at home and I could read the untranslated volumes in his own words.

During the winter of 1929 and through the spring of 1930 I was busy reading; and during the following summer in Cornwall I began to write. Sedgwick took for the *Atlantic* a section or two but before the whole book was finished Abraham Flexner who, with his associate Raymond Fosdick, had been interested in *The Modern Temper,* suggested that I apply to the Guggenheim Foundation for a grant to enable me to go to Europe, finish *Five Masters,* and write still another book I had by then in mind. The grant was the godsend it has been to so many writers and others.

Marcelle and I sailed in the spring of 1930, went directly to Paris where I could find in the Bibliothèque St. Geneviève the comparatively little which had been written about Proust. Then we spent some weeks in the little border town, Hendaye, where Marcelle had been born, after which we went to Antibes where I began to lose weight so alarmingly (my nearly six feet weighed only 129 pounds fully clothed) that I left Marcelle there, spent five weeks in bed at the Johns Hopkins hospital in Baltimore, and returned to live in a cottage she had rented about halfway between the Cap d'Antibes and Juan-les-Pins.

By this time *Five Masters* had been finished and it was published in late 1930. It was given a pleasant but rather mild reception, was reprinted once during the next year, and came out also in a London edition. Then it quietly disappeared until, many years later, it was reissued in the still current paperback. I was considerably disappointed after the stir created by *The Modern Temper* but was free now to begin on the little treatise called *Experience and Art* which had been the excuse for the Guggenheim grant.

I have always prided myself on the fact that if I have something to write I can write it almost anywhere there is a table and a typewriter, but I have seldom found it so difficult to work as I did in the relaxed atmosphere, physical and spiritual, of this pleasant coast. Neither Antibes nor Juan-les-Pins had yet become the noisy, crowded resorts which both, especially Juan-les-Pins, have now become. They were, however, already much favored by permanent or temporary expatriates many of whom did not even pretend to be "creative workers" but were frankly pleased with a place where you could be idle quite cheaply. All day they sat on the beach-facing terrace of the Caravelle café; every night they congregated in the little casino to lose at boule the few francs (all they had left from more prosperous times) they would lament next day at the café. Some lived on small boats permanently anchored at the jetty and spent their days cleaning or scrubbing, their evenings dressed in their best at the casino. Most were hoping that the depression would soon be over and on the terrace they would interrupt their lamentations over falling dividends and their gloomy thoughts concerning dwindling capital to raise an arm and call out: "Garçon! Une autre fine."

I remember especially one young man, a would-be cartoonist, who was, like me, living on a Guggenheim grant and who confessed that since his arrival many months before he had not so much as put paper on a drawing board. One afternoon he was in the depths. "Last night," he said, "I lost at boule again. I *don't* know why I do it; I can't afford to lose. Now I am absolutely broke and I don't know what is going to become of me." He was cheerfully advised by my table companions that suicide seemed the best solution but instead of following this advice he cabled his parents for passage money home, received it, and then promptly lost it again in the casino. One of our female companions, daughter of a partner in one of the best known American textbook publishers, saw a copy of *Five Masters* and complained that Boccaccio was the only one of the masters whose name she had ever heard. Of another of our companions, one who claimed to be "Pretender to the throne of Peru," she remarked in all innocence that she had no use for him. "There are too many pretenders around here."

The most intimate friends we made in Antibes were Morgan and Dorothy Worthy of whom we were later to see much in New York. They told us one anecdote concerning Gerald Murphy which I have ever since delighted to tell Bostonians. Murphy (son of the then proprietor of the Mark Cross shop in the United States and brother of Esther Murphy whose New York salon was famous in the Thirties) had a large Villa America on the Cap. He was not in residence during our stay but some time earlier he had taken a Christmas package to the local post office. The postmaster looked dubiously at the address "Boston, Massachusetts" and reached for the postal guide. Running his finger down a column he read off a list. "Boston, Alabama; Boston, Georgia; Boston, New York; Boston, Ohio," and so down the list checking each entry by a glance at the parcel. Finally he shut the guide with a bang and announced with reproachful finality: "Non, monsieur. Boston Mas-a-chu-settes n'existe pas."

Despite all these distractions I finished my small book by early summer and we set out on a holiday, spent principally in Italy and Switzerland, before returning home in early fall to resume my job at *The Nation*. *Experience and Art* was published that winter and fell flat. None of my other books had been or, to date, was to be, so little (and often so tepidly) reviewed. It sold little. It soon went out of print, and was never reprinted until the paperback edition of 1962. It is often missing in libraries which have everything else.

All this was a discouraging experience since I had begun to believe that my books would, almost as a matter of course, attract at least modestly favorable notice. I took what comfort I could in telling myself that it had been published at the worst possible moment.

By now everybody was writing about politics and economics—even those who still pretended that their novels, plays, and poems were either belles lettres or, if not, then the "social criticism" in fictional terms which was henceforth to take the place of the discredited art forms. I, on the other hand, had stubbornly disregarded this new wave by continuing the line of thought begun in *Edgar Allan Poe* and hinted at it in *The Modern Temper.* I was defending, though perhaps not at the moment conscious of the fact, that "bourgeois art" which Eisenstein had defined for me in Moscow when he called it "the satisfaction in imagination of unfulfilled desires."

My thesis attempted a logical if seemingly improbable reconciliation of Freud, Marx, and Eisenstein by accepting the latter's description of "bourgeois art" but then interpreting it in such a way as to make it support a theory of the function of such art which would make "bourgeois art" by no means the trivial thing either popular Marxism or popular Freudianism tended to make it.

To those who followed the line so clearly stated by Eisenstein all literature which was not "a weapon" was merely an escape; hence, like religion, an "opium of the people" who live in a debilitating dream of that Good Life which capitalism has denied them. To oversimple Freudians this same literature was often reduced to a similar dream in which readers identified themselves with the Cinderella who married a prince or with the Oedipus whose incest they did not dare imitate in real life. Nursery tales and nursemaid novels (the soap opera had not yet been invented) certainly did owe at least part of their charm to the fact that they provided such dreams. But the most important "unfulfilled desires" of mature and intelligent people were not, I argued, so simple or so trivial. The deepest, and most fundamental, of these desires is the desire that the universe be comprehensible, meaningful, and not wholly indifferent to the value judgments which the human being cannot help but make.

I was still thinking of *The Modern Temper* as an account of what this universe actually is, or at least of what we had come to believe it to be. I thought of this new book as a sort of companion description of the World of Art which man has made in his own image. Hence in the first chapter I wrote:

> The world of art is a mimic world, superficially resembling the natural one but fundamentally quite different. For even when it seems most literally imitative, even when it is most determinedly realistic, it is conceived in accordance with the laws and limitations of the human mind. In it the emphasis is the emphasis of an unescapable human prejudice; the very order of events is an order logical according to the system of human logic; and the meaning is a meaning humanly comprehensible instead of being, as the meaning of Nature may very well be, quite beyond the understanding of man, who is only one of Nature's innumerable children. Nor can even the most desperately "naturalistic" art escape the fact for it is, at its most literal, nature passed through a human mind, nature probably distorted by desire, and nature certainly modified to whatever extent is necessary in order that it may be comprehended by reason which can operate only within its own limitations. Philosophers may dispute concerning the extent to which the actual universe is a *thinkable* one, but the distinguishing feature of the Universe of Art is just the fact that it is perfectly and readily thinkable—for the very reason that it came into existence by being thought; that it is everywhere molded by the human mind.

I shall not attempt to indicate the ways in which I tried to use this central thesis as the basis for a commentary upon the various styles which artists have adopted and upon current tendencies in painting as well as in literature. Perhaps the lack of interest which the reading public manifested in it was justified. I myself am more a pluralist than I then was, and I am no longer sure that the universe is as alien as I then believed it to be. But for me if for no one else it was important that I should write this book. It said that man's answer to a meaningless universe is the creation of another one which does have meaning, and I still believe both that it is the artist who is most likely to find the elusive meaning if it exists and that if, perchance, it does not exist, then it is he who can create an "as if" by which we can live. Or, as I put it in the last chapter of *Experience and Art* where I commented upon the notion recently popularized by Havelock Ellis that to say "Life is an Art" gives us a faith to live by and that Aesthetics can thus take the place left vacant by Religion and Morality:

> If Love and Honor and Duty can be salvaged, then someone must write about them in a fashion which carries conviction. If we are to get along without them, then someone must describe a world from which they are absent in a fashion which makes that world seem worth having. And it is just the failure to do either of these things quite adequately which reveals the weakness of contemporary literature.

10

Perhaps my sixteen months' stay in Europe had been in part at least an "escape" and I had some not very lively hope that by the end of it the United States would have returned to "normalcy."

Many of our economic pundits had predicted as much. I remember, for instance, seeing cruelly revived some years later a newsreel which concluded by saying: "In short, then, my prediction is that 1930 will be a very good year." In spite of 1929 we still believe the new generation of wise men who tell us that though permanent prosperity is not the automatic thing the Twenties assumed it had become it can still be assured by "planning."

Whatever hopes I may have had of returning to the world I knew were soon shattered. By the fall of 1931 the economic effects of the depression were becoming more gravely evident and, of more immediate importance to me, was the great swing of intellectuals and artists toward the left that had already begun. Soon reviews of "proletarian" novels were almost monopolizing the literary supplements and "proletarian" plays almost monopolizing the stage. Some critics and commentators formed an alliance more or less close with the Communist party and even many of those who made no such commitment nevertheless agreed that the left-wing writing was now the most significant. If art was not exactly that "weapon" which the extremists called it, it should at least have "a social function"—which meant that it should include a criticism of the prevailing political and economic situation and, preferably, suggest remedies for all the evils.

For various reasons, including, I suppose, the new problems and new attitudes, Mr. Villard no longer wanted responsibility for *The Nation.* He sold it to an investment banker, the late Maurice Wertheim, who had been one of the founders of the Theater Guild and for long a friend of mine and of Miss Kirchwey. Villard was to remain as Contributing Editor and to have a signed page in every issue, but the management and control was, in January 1933, turned over to a sort of soviet composed originally of Henry Hazlitt, Ernest Gruening, Miss Kirchwey, and myself. Gruening soon left to enter government service (he was governor of Alaska for many years) and there were other changes from time to time in the top staff, which was joined by Max Lerner and Raymond Gram Swing. For the next four years, however, the plan of operation remained the same. Though it was never very rigid, the general understanding was that each member of the editorial board might say what he pleased in signed articles but that unsigned editorials must be approved by at least a majority. All this meant that I was more active in the operation of the paper than I had ever been before and for a time I contributed a signed page three times a month in addition to the play and book reviews.

Nevertheless, I still thought my position as Drama Critic the most important, and it was in the theater that I first became acutely aware of the changed atmosphere of the decade.

Even the established playwrights of the Twenties responded to some extent by changing their themes and their styles. Sidney Howard, who had always thought of himself as a teller of stories not at all tendentious, came up with *Yellow Jack* (1934), an improving tale of the conquest of yellow fever which he wrote more or less in the manner of *The Living Newspaper* which the WPA theater (often very far left in its implications) especially favored. Elmer Rice offered *We the People* (1933), a sort of pageant of the depression, and even S. N. Behrman, the most suave and "uncommitted" of our writers of high comedy, felt compelled, without actually taking sides, to introduce the theme of "social criticism" into such plays as *Rain from Heaven* (1934) and *End of Summer* (1936).

Much more attention was attracted by a whole new school of playwrights and by at least four new theatrical groups—the Theater Union, the Group Theater, The New Playwrights Theater, and the Federal Theater Project (WPA)—all of which, except the second, were almost exclusively devoted to left-wing drama. Few of those now too young to have been aware of these events are likely to realize how much was made of writers and plays now almost totally forgotten. In manner these plays ranged all the way from such ostensibly realistic if didactic melodramas as *Stevedore* (1934) by Paul Peters and George Sklar and *Black Pit* (1935) by Albert Bein through *The Living Newspaper* presentations of such dramatic reportages as *One Third of a Nation* (1938) and on to such wildly "expressionistic" (but also clearly left-oriented) plays as John Dos Passos' *The Moon Is a Gong,* presented at the New Playwrights Theater in Greenwich Village. Most of the New Playwrights' productions imitated what I had seen at Piscators Theater in Berlin and the Vakhtangov in Moscow where the wild incoherence of the text is complicated by such devices as having the characters make their entrances via moving belts or on slides like those found in playgrounds.

Many rich men, including even financiers, were moved to support such enterprises either because they believed they represented the art of the future or, perhaps, just in order that "comes the revolution" they might have something to point to in extenuation of their careers. Among these men was Otto Kahn who gave generously to the New Playwrights Theater; and I think the best comment upon the fact was made by Alexander Woollcott who wrote in his review of one of its antic exhibitions in the course of which girls dressed as monkeys rushed down the aisle to present lollipops to members of the audience: "As I went out into the alley I tossed my confection to a waiting urchin and walked away, reflecting that the greatest all-day-sucker of them all was Mr. Kahn."

Toward this newest "new drama" I was far less sympathetic than I had been to that of the Twenties. Neither its aims, its methods, nor its explicit doctrines appealed to my own convictions or sensibilities. Nevertheless, and while making this fact clear, I did my best to judge its effectiveness in the terms of its intentions, judging melodrama by the degree of excitement it engendered and asking of propaganda how likely it seemed to change or activate convictions. If "art is a weapon" and if, as Eisenstein had told me, its only legitimate function is to lead to action, then how likely were *Stevedore* and *Black Pit* to inflame sufficiently those who saw them? Would they, as Eisenstein said the Russian audiences had, "go from the theater to the barricades"—or at least to the picket line and the protest meeting?

By this test I found *Stevedore* one of the most successful, and of it I wrote:

> The subject is a race riot in Louisiana; the method frank but skilfully cumulative melodrama and the whole reaches a really smashing climax 'on the barricades.' If *Stevedore* is uncommonly effective both as melodrama and as propaganda, the reason probably is that it sticks with uncommon persistence to a single purpose—which is to inflame the passions of its audience and to sweep the audience forward on a wave of fighting hate. Most authors of such plays seem a little uncertain just what it is that they are trying to do. They explain a little, they debate a little, and they plead a little. The result is usually as dispiriting as a protest meeting and gets just as far. But those responsible for *Stevedore* adopted a different method. They assumed—safely enough—that their audience knew the arguments already and that its sympathy was with them. Their business, like the business of any mob leaders, is to get the crowd going somewhere and *Stevedore* becomes an incitement to riot of the very first order.
>
> The spectator at *Peace on Earth,* the play which preceded it at the same theater, might reasonably be expected to emerge from the auditorium and join an organization for the promotion of something or other. The spectator at *They Shall Not Die* probably felt like writing a letter to the *Times* about conditions in Georgia. But a goodly percentage of those who saw *Stevedore* were probably ready to seize the nearest club and crack someone over the head. Most books and plays offered as proof that "art is a weapon" remind one of wooden swords, but this particular play is

really a bomb—homemade, perhaps, but full of power and quite capable of going off. Such a contraption may have seemed a bit odd in the hands of an organization which was so recently pleading for peace on earth, but that organization was not the first to conclude that a good deal ought to be blown up before we settle down to living in brotherly love with the survivors—if any.

This was certainly praise of a sort—rather too much perhaps since as a reviewer often realizes after the passage of time, he is very likely to rate moderately good works too high and the best ones not, by comparison, high enough. But I also made it clear in the case of this and similar plays that I neither sympathized with the point of view nor thought that such excellence as I conceded they achieved was of a very high kind. I am pleased to remember that the only one of the left-wing playwrights of the decade to whom I granted more—namely Clifford Odets—is also the only one still often remembered.

Waiting for Lefty, the first of his works to be produced, seemed to accept completely both the thesis that art is a weapon as well as most of what was sane in the unconventional methods of staging sometimes associated with this thesis. It took place on a nearly bare stage supposed to represent the platform in a union hall; the audience was assumed to be the listening members. The Lefty for whom all were waiting, and who (like Godot) never came, was a "worker" involved in a proposed taxicab strike which is voted as the play ends. Judged as a *tour de force* it was more completely successful than any other attempt to produce a similar effect and its success led to the production of Odets' first full-length play which had, it appears, been written earlier, before he had definitely espoused the cause of left-wing action. *Awake and Sing* (1935) has a tacked-on ending in which, without adequate preparation, a principal character declares his intention to devote the rest of his life to the cause of "the worker." But the play as a whole is much richer than its merely didactic conclusion and is perhaps the best of Odets' work.

Several of the other "art-is-a-weapon" writers later fled to Hollywood as, indeed, did Odets himself, though he emerged some years later with *The Big Knife* (1948). This was an attack upon the industry in which he had become involved, and it charged corruption of the creative writer. I was moved, I remember, to remark that Mr. Odets was biting the hand which had overfed him.

If Odets and the lesser members of his school could be easily accounted for on the theory that art is both a product and a reflection of the ideology created by economic conditions, the only other new American playwright definitely to emerge during the Thirties (he was at the very end of them) was a severe test of such theories—unless indeed one accepts the convenient explanation that while some react *to* "conditions" and "conditioning" others react *against* them. This new playwright was, of course, William Saroyan, who came exuberantly out of Fresno, California, to proclaim that people are beautiful and that life is wonderful if only you will relax, inhale, and exhale. Like Odets he first attracted attention with a short piece, *My Heart's in the Highlands* (1939) which was a gay, engaging and imaginatively absurd fantasy which he never quite equaled again though *The Time of Your Life* achieved a considerable success and was given the Critics Prize for the same year. If, on the whole, his subsequent writing for the theater has been less and less successful that is perhaps because he abandoned himself more and more to the romantic theory that writers should simply let themselves go and say whatever happens to come into their heads. Nevertheless, he was—and for all I know may still be, though I have not seen him in years—an engaging if occasionally exasperating person and he was very welcome to some of us in a decade which had forgotten how to enjoy what one could still find to be enjoyed.

Boastful of his egotism and frankly proclaiming his great talents he was, however, that rather uncommon type of egotist who is content to exalt himself without depreciating others. He admired nearly all plays and heartily proclaimed the talent of their authors. In any company he was likely to express amazement that such a galaxy of talent should be assembled in one place. "Here we are," he would seem to imply, "all geniuses. I, to be sure, am the greatest, but you, and you, and you, and you are all geniuses too." His naïveté was, of course, part pose; but it was partly genuine also, and I know nothing which would better illustrate his character and behavior than a little anecdote in which I figure as a spectator.

He, George Jean Nathan, and I had gone after the theater to a Village night club to see the performance of some young lady of whose talents Nathan was convinced. Presently two women, obviously suburban and, in appearance, startlingly like characters in one of the Helen Hokinson cartoons then so popular in *The New Yorker,* approached our table. "You are Mr. Saroyan, are you not?" Nathan, always lordly toward Philistines, spoke up: "No! No! Go away." For some reason I joined in. "He does look like Mr. Saroyan," I said, "but he isn't." The ladies apologized and had started to move away when the object of their interest raised a commanding hand. "Come back here," he said. "I *am* Saroyan, too, and I can prove it." Out of his pocket he took a telegram addressed to himself and waved it in front of them. They were obviously not quite sure who was trying to play a joke but the waver of the telegram clinched the matter by exclaiming: "And what is more, if you think I am not Saroyan because I am so anxious to prove that I am, *that just shows how little you know me.*"

11

▲
▲▲▲

Shortly after my return from Europe I had written for *Harper's Magazine* an essay called "Communism and the Old Pagan." For the first time, I said, I had begun to understand something of what a cultivated Greek or Roman must have felt when he discovered with amazement that his most intimate friends were turning one by one to a strange new delusion called Christianity. They had for years read the same books and exchanged the same ideas. When they met their conversation began where it had left off and they understood one another in a fashion possible only to those whose vocabularies coincided both as to meaning and connotation. But suddenly everything was changed. A new vocabulary and a new set of ideas had taken possession of them, and a new Truth had suddenly emerged. Almost everything which had once seemed the mark of the intellectual—tolerance, skepticism, and individuality—had become abhorrent and Faith the supreme virtue. Those who only yesterday had believed in Freedom more than they believed in anything else now gave their highest praise to dictatorship. I, so I concluded, was left in the small company of surviving Old Pagans amazed by the way in which the new faith had rendered unrecognizable minds which I thought I knew so well. *Harper's* printed this essay and another called "Jam Tomorrow." Still another—"Jingoism and the Class War"—was rejected in a letter by a subeditor which seemed strongly to suggest that he too had undergone conversion.

The first of these essays was no extravagant fancy. Reviewing plays with which I was fundamentally out of sympathy had not been especially pleasurable but *The Nation* staff never made any protest against what I wrote about the theater. I was having my say. Nevertheless, the growing coolness of various friends and acquaintances was another matter, and increasingly over the next few years I was startled to discover from the conversation in various groups that all its members were now taking for granted attitudes which would, a short time before, have shocked them as much as they were now shocked to discover that I did not share them.

For a short time I assumed that all the staff members of *The Nation* were still loyal to the libertarian principles it had defended ever since my first connection with it. In all innocence I wrote an occasional editorial or editorial paragraph defending what I thought was its position only to discover that, though still usually published, they were met, first with cold silence and then with angry protest from certain members of the staff not in a position to deny me the right to express my opinions. Open war was finally declared when my editorial "Class Justice" appeared in the issue for May 3, 1933.

The occasion was that trial and condemnation of a group of Russian engineers which was one of the first practical demonstrations that the new regime had definitely rejected the whole concept of "fair play" which I was still naïve enough to believe American sympathizers still cherished. Of the trial I wrote:

> It is difficult to see how liberals who have always protested against the effect of class prejudice in other famous cases . . . can logically acquiesce in the methods of Russia just because they happen to sympathize somewhat with the basic aspirations of the Russian people. The prosecutor himself boasted that it was not an impartial trial and declared that its purpose was to administer "class justice." The prisoners were long held incommunicado under conditions which certainly gave ample opportunity for a third degree and they were allowed no counsel except that which was appointed for them and which, presumably therefore, did not really want them acquitted. They were definitely presumed guilty unless proved innocent and now that they have been sentenced it is impossible to determine from any of the long dispatches what specific acts they were declared guilty of. We shall not stop to remind our readers that one of the outrages of the first Scottsboro trial was the fact that the defendants were represented only by lawyers appointed by a prejudiced court but we shall point out that the engineers in Russia were apparently convicted for reasons resembling those for which Sacco, Vanzetti, and Tom Mooney were convicted in this country—because, that is to say, the court was convinced that no matter what specific charge could or could not be proved against them they were in general enemies of the social order which the court defended. No one ever denied that either the victims of Massachusetts or the victim of California were guilty of being radical. More-

over, in the case of Mooney at least, it was pretty generally recognized that he was by no means incapable of employing dynamite. But most of the defenders of all three insisted that the question was not whether the accused were radicals, that it was not even, primarily, a question of whether or not they were guilty of the specific acts charged against them; but that it was, on the contrary, essentially a question of whether or not they had enjoyed the benefits of a fair trial upon the specific charges.

Now we know very well what the reply of the Communist is. An impartial trial and a classless justice are, he says, impossible. He wants quite frankly therefore a justice prejudiced in his favor and an opportunity to prejudge his enemies as he believes that his enemies have always prejudged him. But though that position is perfectly logical it is not the position which the liberal has always maintained, and he is destroying himself if he accepts it, as he has recently shown some disposition to do when his sympathies happen to be engaged. Nor is it sufficient to say that the situation is entirely changed by the fact that the American system pretends to afford an impartial trial while the Russian does not and, unlike the United States, partly recognizes the political nature of the alleged offense. The fact remains that liberals have never said that they demand only that the American government should acknowledge the "unfairness" of its system. They have insisted upon the individual's right to an abstract justice, and they cannot logically change their attitude for Russia without changing it for America also.

The historical position of *The Nation* is the liberal one. It has not changed. We still advocate a classless impartiality. We refuse to be satisfied merely to have prejudice change sides, and to forget all the dangers of a medieval method of trial just because that method happens for the moment to be working in the interests of a revolutionary government whose basic aim is to secure greater economic liberty.

What I did not, of course, realize were some simple facts: first, that though I had at least the qualified support of a majority of the governing board, some other members of the staff were now quite openly determined that what I had called the "historical position" of the paper ought to be changed; second, that the new Communist and Communist sympathizing readers to whom I was pointing out what I regarded as deadly parallels would actually regard them as irrelevant, since they had already either openly or secretly taken the position that "fair play," "impartial justice," "free speech," and the rest of the liberal principles were notions to be defended only by minorities whom they would advantage and to be scorned as soon as they were themselves in a position to disregard them.

I was not, however, yet ready to give up. Beginning in May 1934 I published in *The Nation* a series of four longish articles under the general title "Was Europe a Success?" The thesis was that however much the political and economic systems of the western world might now appear to many as worse than merely defective, European civilization had been a success insofar as it had produced what I considered mankind's most precious achievements in science, philosophical thought, and art, whereas the proposed Communist remedy for the alleged defects of our political and economic institutions would certainly deprive the human mind of both the liberties and the standard of values which had made them culturally a success.

After the series was finished *The Nation* printed in three pages long letters of comment from five prominent intellectuals of whom four expressed complete or qualified approval while the fifth and last undertook a formal rebuttal. They constitute, I think, an interesting cross section of opinion.

Albert Einstein wrote in part: "Your articles . . . must make a great impression on thoughtful people. The humanitarian ideal of Europe appears indeed to be unalterably bound up with the free expression of opinion, to some extent with the free will of the individual, with the effort toward objectivity in thought without consideration of mere utility, and with the encouragement of differences in the realm of mind and taste . . . You ask if it is justifiable to set aside for a time the principles of individual freedom in deference to the high endeavor to improve economic organization . . . No purpose is so high that unworthy methods in serving it can be justified in my eyes. Violence sometimes may have cleared away obstructions quickly, but it never has proved itself creative."

Aldous Huxley, briefest of the five, began: "I should like to take this opportunity of saying how admirable I think these articles are. For condensed statement and judicious commentary they could not be bettered." He then went on to add that to him a great and neglected need of the moment was that, along with social planning, should go "individual psychological planning, for the investigation and systemization of old and the discovery of new techniques for getting the most out of the individual spirit."

H. L. Mencken contributed (in part) this somewhat oblique but certainly characteristic comment:

"The average man enjoys being foolish, for God hath made him so, and he glories in being incompetent for the same reason, but he is always greatly upset when he has to face the natural consequences. At such times he is prone to assume that his discomforts are the work of wicked men who have taken advantage of him, and to demand that the government protect him against them.

The reasoning has some holes in it, but it undoubtedly seems convincing to those who resort to it. And in cherishing it they are always supported by large synods of eloquent charlatans, each with something to sell.

"At the moment such charlatans hold the stage, and for the moment their triumph seems almost complete . . . But that they are in for a long reign is by no means sure. They had been wiser if they had been less eager to seize power. As it is, they are in the dangerous position, for all their high and mightiness, of the poor fish who essays to be his own man. Sooner or later their gaudy imbecilities will come home to roost, and having tasted the sweet music of the mob's hurrahs they will have to face the dreadful hazards of its ire. Each of these inspired and consecrated men has but one throat to cut. There has been some hemorrhage already, and there may be plenty more anon."

Bertrand Russell hedged somewhat. He doubted that European civilization had been superior to some others in art or philosophy and believed that it was rather in knowledge and power that it was preeminent. "I do not disagree with Mr. Krutch as to what I like and dislike. I disagree only as not regarding the disagreeable features of communism and fascism as any serious departure from the European tradition. Would either of us have found Sparta any pleasanter than Soviet Russia? Should we have liked to live in societies which put men to death for not believing in witchcraft? . . . It is possible to admire Europe for the creation of scientific knowledge, and for conferring upon man a mastery over his environment such as no other continent had the intelligence to achieve. More organization and less personal initiative is necessary if the new power is not to bring disaster . . . We must not judge the society of the future by considering whether *we* should like to live in it; the question is whether those who have grown up in it will be happier than those who have grown up in our society or in those of the past."

That Russell had made some points I could not but agree, though it seemed to me then (as it does now) that to judge of the desirability of a future society exclusively on the basis of what we assume others will come to like is a very dangerous method.

After beginning with soft words James Burnham, then emerging as an ardent defender of radical political theory (but not of the current regime in Russia) and some years later to attract wide attention with *The Managerial Revolution,* gave an unequivocal defense of the Revolutionary ideals:

"The charm of Mr. Krutch's manner must not be allowed to hide the danger of his ideas. His recent series . . . is in effect a moral attack on the revolutionary movement, an attack all the more persuasive because written with such absence of bitterness, such a striving for impartiality, such evident sincerity . . . It is not my purpose here to question the particular values in terms of which Mr. Krutch defines the European man. I shall grant that Mr. Krutch's values are roughly descriptive of what gives meaning to life for the European man and reply: Not only does the socialist revolution not threaten to destroy these values; it is the revolution alone that gives any promise of preserving what of them is worth preserving . . .

"The writings and agitation of many Marxists themselves make the revolution appear the enemy of civilization. This may readily be explained. It is partly because the practical tasks of the revolution often make all other problems sink into the background. (Ezra Pound once said that we do not argue over free will in the midst of a shipwreck.) Partly it is that the working class is the carrier of the revolution and since the workers have never shared in what freedom, individuality, personality and detachment capitalist civilization has allowed, they are not so worried about preserving them. Partly, too, it is because of the corruption that has entered into Marxism under the leadership of the present regime in the Soviet Union, which includes an intellectual and philosophical degeneration that must indeed be resisted. Such resistance is worse than futile from the enemies of the revolution. It can come effectively only from its active friends . . . The side of Mr. Krutch's values, the side of civilization is the side of the workers revolution."

Late in the same year my articles were published as a small volume in which several other essays on related themes were included. Among the latter were the two pieces from *Harper's* of which one, "Jam Tomorrow," was an anticipatory reply to those of my critics who insisted upon judging "the Communist experiment" only in terms of its theoretical future. The volume was well reviewed, attracted a little flurry of attention—in England also where the *Times Literary Supplement* thought it wise, despite a foolish title—but soon disappeared and has remained unreprinted.

One reason that it was not more widely read at the time may have been simply that sympathy was running too strong in the contrary direction. If it has not been reprinted perhaps its arguments, though somewhat novel then, were soon to become familiar to all those likely to be sympathetic to them. But I take what I hope is a pardonable satisfaction in the realization that I had so early and so unequivocally made a stand. Mr. Burnham's contention that the preservation of the values he and I both professed to cherish would be saved by the revolution despite the fact that the latter had already been corrupted by those who had seized power does not, to date, seem to have been justified by events.

The severest review of "Was Europe a Success?"—and I suppose the most damaging in the eyes of many—was written by Lincoln Steffens who was generally regarded as one of the ablest of those who had devoted their lives to a crusade for the rights of what in his youth had been called "the laboring man" but was now known always as "the worker." He denounced and dismissed me as one of the unfortunately surviving old fogies who are simply incapable of understanding the new world about to come into being. He had cried out in 1919 on his return from a visit to Russia: "I have been over into the future, and it works!"

Just how far organizations which still called themselves "liberal" had already gone in accepting double standards, and also double talk, is illustrated by an exchange of letters which *The Nation* permitted me to print in the issue for Jan. 23, 1935. Note that the editorial comment describes as an "interesting, if casual, commentary" what seemed to me a clear revelation of glaring inconsistency:

A CORRESPONDENCE ON LIBERTY

The Nation *reproduces the following five letters between Mr. Krutch and representatives of the American Civil Liberties Union as an interesting, if casual, commentary on a problem of immediate importance in a period of social unrest.*

Joseph Wood Krutch to Elmer Rice

Dear Rice:

I am enclosing a check and membership card to the American Civil Liberties Union. I must say frankly, however, that

I would be happier if I were convinced that the majority of members really believed in civil liberties as such. I wonder if Roger Baldwin does?

New York, December 13 Joseph Wood Krutch

Roger Baldwin to Mr. Krutch

Dear Mr. Krutch:

Elmer Rice has sent me your letter of December 13 with a copy of his reply. I see that you raise some question as to whether I really believe in civil liberties as such. I think the best practical answer to that is that I do believe in applying without discrimination the right to carry on any propaganda whatever without interference, regardless of the political or economic philosophy involved. On that point I am in entire agreement with my fellow-members of the Civil Liberties Union, who represent, however, quite diverse elements from the point of view of their politics and economics.

On the economic front my views are left. I can support for that reason the Soviet dictatorship, which tolerates no civil liberties. I do so because, though I oppose dictatorship in principle, the Soviet Union has already achieved economic liberties far greater than exist elsewhere in the world. In the long run the only ground on which liberty can be securely based is economic. The workers democracy, despite the limitations of dictatorship, is the nearest approach to freedom that workers have ever achieved—and they constitute all but a small minority.

New York, December 19 Roger Baldwin

Mr. Krutch Replies

Dear Mr. Baldwin:

Thanks for your letter. I know that the American Civil Liberties Union has more important things to do than to carry on a controversy like this, but I am going to answer your letter anyway. My original question was prompted by the book you wrote a year or two ago about Russia. I am well aware that the union makes a practice of defending the civil liberties of all sorts of people, but I assume that this is merely because you believe that in a democracy it is only by such tactics that you can effectively fight for the civil liberties of the particular kinds of persons you are interested in. It does seem to me, however, that it all comes down to this: I believe in civil liberties as long as my side is in the minority and can enjoy liberty only by granting it to others, but of course if my minority should become the majority it would promptly deny to others the liberties which it now claims for itself.

I feel that free criticism is the only thing which could possibly prevent any dictatorship or bureaucracy from becoming completely corrupt. The article you inclose says that when the power of the working class has been achieved, you are for maintaining it by any means whatsoever. The only way it can maintain itself is by securing the right of criticism.

New York, December 31 Joseph Wood Krutch

From Mr. Baldwin

Dear Mr. Krutch:

I have to add a postscript to our correspondence in the light of yours of the thirty-first, to say that I entirely agree that the right of criticism is indispensable to the successful conduct of any government. In the Soviet Union they have sought to achieve that by what they call self-criticism in the Communist Party—a quite limited right I agree—and the development of the so-called workers-and-peasants correspondents all over the Soviet Union, who are encouraged to register complaints and kicks with the authorities.

I know this does not take the place of a political opposition, but I concur in the view that this is quite impracticable in a period such as that through which Soviet Russia is going. For a political opposition would strike at the very framework of a socialist state. I say all this, deploring, as

I know you do, the terrorism and highly concentrated political power of the present regime in Russia. I can tolerate it only as preferable to the concentrations of power in capitalist countries.

New York, January 2 Roger Baldwin*

From Mr. Krutch

Dear Mr. Baldwin:

You say that political opposition is quite impracticable in Russia today. Now I am constantly being assured by Communists that while capitalism is obviously collapsing, communism is inevitable. If this is true, then is it not obvious that a communist state is in a better position than a capitalist one to permit opposition?

New York, January 9 Joseph Wood Krutch

Not long after these letters were printed I made at the office and in the presence of an old staff member some remarks about the inconsistency of Communist sympathizers in their attitude toward free speech. My one time friend who had been most noted for his almost Quakerlike gentleness but who had nevertheless coldly disapproved of the "Class Justice" editorial, turned on me with a fury of which I would not have believed him capable and shouted: "What you do not understand is that *we Communists* believe in free speech only until five minutes after the revolution." This was the first time he had admitted, at least in

* Many years later, in December, 1961, when granting permission to use these letters in this book, Mr. Baldwin wrote:

"Both events and experience long ago brought me to reject the views I expressed in these letters in 1934. They were the product in part of fears aroused by the rise of the Nazis, in part by Marxist notions of working-class forces as the base for greater freedom, and wishful thinking about the Russian revolution and the Soviet dictatorship.

Events have proved that Mr. Krutch was right and I was wrong. Liberty cannot be served by yielding its principles to any economic system or choosing between one dictatorship and another."

my presence, that he had gone over completely to the enemy and it illustrated perfectly how those who had taken this stand not only confessed to, but gloried in, hypocrisy as a political technique. Never again did I suppose that it was worthwhile to point out such aspects of the Communist doctrine as I had assumed all decent men would find repellent. I felt like an "Old Pagan" indeed.

Never before had I found myself so nearly surrounded by colleagues whom I knew to be enemies or, at least, not certainly to be trusted. In the past I had been glad to be in what was, so far as the total population was concerned, a minority. I was pleased that not only *The Modern Temper* but many of the articles I had written—from that on prohibition in the undergraduate magazine through those on the Dayton trial—would be disapproved of by many. But most of the members of my own circle and most of the readers with whom I identified myself were on my side. Now my former friends had, many of them at least, gone over to the enemy. As a present-day sociologist might say, my in-group had become an out-group; and to be disapproved of by those upon whom one had counted for support is quite different from meeting disapproval where one has actually hoped for it.

I remember especially one evening at the home of a successful radio producer where I astonished everyone by refusing to agree that Franklin Roosevelt would go down in history as the great betrayer of the oppressed because his economic concessions had postponed the revolution.

About this same time a close acquaintance took Marcelle aside to say that he had discussed me with nearly all my friends—how many he actually spoke for I do not know—and that they had all agreed: I had, at one time, shown promise as a writer and thinker but obviously I now had no future as either.

Neither the Civil Liberties Union nor Roger Baldwin would now defend the position the latter took in his letters to *The Nation*. The friend who broke to my wife the news that I had no future apologized to me not many years later, and a considerable number of those who were at the time avowed Communists or strong Communist sympathizers have since swung far to the right—much, much further indeed than I can imagine myself ever going. But that is not really surprising because what was constant in them was the tendency to go to extremes, and those with such a tendency very often find it easy to switch from one extreme to another. They believe at one time that communism is the answer to everything, at another that an equally complete answer is given by unregulated competition and the social Darwinian's "survival of the fittest." The rest of us have never believed that any system or doctrine is the complete solution of any problem.

Once when I happened to be sitting next to Arthur Train, the lawyer-author of the popular "Mr. Tutt" stories, and when the policies of *The Nation* came under discussion, he turned to me and asked: "By the way, what are *your* political opinions?" "Well," I replied, "some of my colleagues think I am a rank reactionary." He paused for a moment obviously unsatisfied and then said: "That *still* leaves you a lot of latitude"—as indeed it did.

Those who ardently championed communism in their youth but have since rejected it are often excused or even praised by some formula analagous to the old chestnut which maintains that "A young man who is not a socialist has no heart; an old man who is still a socialist has no head." After all, it is said, the early enthusiasts had no way of knowing how the "experiment" was going to turn out. They could not have been expected to see even what

Mr. Burnham was already aware of. Perhaps. Nevertheless, to me it seems that in even the professed aims of the early Communist leaders there were things which should have alienated any thoughtful man. They not only accepted but seemed to glory in evil and brutal means. Lenin was often quoted as having said that in politics there is no such thing as morality. They were proud of ruthlessness and of hypocrisy, vehement in their scorn of anything which smacked of intellectual honesty or fair play—as my former friend had been when he boasted that he would deny others the freedom he was then claiming for himself. How could those who had the "heart" which is supposed to have misled them accept doctrines, attitudes, and actions which should have been, so it seems to me, repellent to any "good heart"?

13

▲
▲▲▲

For obvious reasons I found myself as time went on less and less comfortable at *The Nation*. From Miss Kirchwey I could expect support even though we did not always see eye to eye. The same might be said of Raymond Swing while he continued a member of the board. With Max Lerner, who soon joined it, the situation was somewhat different, both because he tended further to the left and also because he simply did not regard the literary section, of which I was by then officially the editor, of much importance. A similar attitude was taken by Heywood Broun who was a staff contributor and Alvin Johnson who had been drawn in as a consultant.

Broun, formerly an almost Menckenesque libertarian and later to become a Roman Catholic under the guidance of Father Sheen, was then in his revolutionist period, and he liked to make remarks like one I remember when Union violence during a strike was under discussion. "Well," he said, "I wouldn't myself like to beat up a fellow worker who crossed the picket line but I realize that it has to be done." He and Alvin Johnson were inclined to believe that the literature and arts section might well be dropped to make space for more political articles, and though Wertheim would never have consented, my position was obviously not very comfortable when, for instance, Johnson, in the course of the detailed comment he made on every new issue, would simply pass my article by with a "Humph" and go on to the next.

In 1936 Marcelle and I left for another short stay in Europe in the course of which (though not this time sponsored by *The Nation*) I wrote some articles based on interviews with Bertrand Russell, André Malraux, T. S. Eliot, and others, all of which were concerned with the status and future of old-fashioned liberal ideas. Malraux was then in his Communist period and the attitude of Russell (by then Lord Russell) was so complicated that what I remember best from our several cordial talks is a little interchange which illustrates so perfectly the lingering sense of class even in those of the English who profess to despise it that I hope he will forgive me for reporting it.

He had been kind enough to come to my hotel for a late afternoon chat and at about six he suggested that if I would permit him to change into a dinner jacket in my room we would have just that much more time for talk. Opening his bag to take out the black-tie outfit he grumbled: "I hate to get into these things. We will never be civilized as long as we put up with them. That's one of the reasons I hate to come to the United States; always having to put on this ridiculous uniform." "But," I protested, "I thought this was more usual in England than in my country." "Used to be," he insisted, "isn't any more." Then: "Know why I have to do it? It's because I am having dinner with *Wells* and Wells is so anxious to prove that he is a gentleman . . . Of course if he were one he would know it's not necessary."

Shortly before we sailed on this little trip which took us only to London and Paris, Columbia University had invited me to return with the rank of Professor. When I told Wertheim privately that I had decided to accept and would therefore leave *The Nation* in the fall of 1937 he said he was much relieved. He was dissatisfied with the way things were going but had not wanted to bow out as long as I, to whom he felt a certain obligation, was willing to accept the *status quo*. It was soon arranged that the paper should be sold to Miss Kirchwey who then became Editor and Publisher. She invited me to continue as Drama Critic which I was very glad to do until 1952 when I left the New York area. But I never again had any editorial responsibility on *The Nation*.

How I came to be invited back to Columbia is a little story in itself which I got from Hunter Wright, by then head of the English Department, after the whole affair was settled.

Three years earlier President Nicholas Murray Butler had sent word to Professor Wright that he would like to see appointed a new faculty member who might represent the Man of Letters rather than the specialist scholar of the type now holding most of the professorships; and he asked for a suggestion. The committee (there is always a committee) took my name to the President but he shook his head. "I think *The Modern Temper* is an evil book. We don't want him." Decision was then postponed for another year when a new request came in and my name was again presented—to meet the same response in almost exactly the same words. Thoroughly discouraged, the committee decided the year thereafter to propose some other names. Butler listened rather impatiently and then said, "How about that man Krutch?" Whether he had forgotten his previous objections or merely, after the fashion of executives, wanted the suggestion to come from him, I do not know. But everybody was now in agreement and I became officially a Man of Letters.

With the aging President himself I had always the most amicable, if necessarily somewhat distant, relations. Despite the fact that he was a really great college president who enormously increased Columbia's prestige and had the special gift of knowing just who was really competent in any field whether it was atomic physics or Semitic Languages, he had long been (and for sufficiently obvious if irrelevant reasons) a figure of fun in the public press—the pattern of the academic stuffed shirt. He lived and breathed only for Columbia University and for himself as the head of it, and he seemed to live a life so completely public that one could not but wonder whether, should he ever by any chance be alone in a room, he would not, like the character in a Henry James story, simply disappear.

How he acquired the real and useful knowledge which he had of men and affairs is hard to understand for though he talked, he seemed never to listen. Go to see him in his office and your business would be either settled in a moment or brushed aside. Then a monologue would follow in the course of which you would hear some anecdote about what Lloyd George or President Wilson had said to him when he happened to be present on some historical occasion; and you got the impression that, like Upton Sinclair's Lanny Budd, he had always managed somehow to be on hand when any news had reached the very world figure whose reaction to it would be the crucial one.

Of David Starr Jordan, the eminent ichthyologist who became President of Stanford University, a pleasant story is told. He had so prodigious a memory that he compiled his catalogue of American fishes without referring to any works of reference because if *he* didn't know the Latin binomial attached to anything with fins nobody else would know it. When he became Stanford's president he thought the least he could do would be to remember the names of students. "But I soon had to give that up. Every time I remembered a student I forgot a fish."

Columbia was so enormous an institution that President Butler could not hope to remember the names of even the faculty members unless they were especially eminent, but he tried to keep in some sort of touch by establishing a routine which provided that every full professor would be invited once every two years to dinner at his home (if so public a place could be called that) and there were usually present also one or two distinguished outsiders, usually European. These dinners were white-tie affairs and since most college professors do not have many occasions for such a costume many of us kept tails and an opera hat in mothballs from which they emerged regularly only every two years.

What took place at these dinners was not unlike what took place tête-à-tête in President Butler's office. He would tell one anecdote after another (play one of his records, the cynical said) while even the distinguished outsiders usually did little except listen. In the drawing room afterwards there was more of the same until the guests left and the faculty members departed to put away their gala costume for another two years.

Irwin Edman is responsible for the anecdote which I think best catches the atmosphere of these occasions. When he was very young and very new to the professorial dignity, and was attending his first of these affairs, it happened that the outsider was some high dignitary of the Church of England. After dinner, President Butler suddenly boomed to him across the considerable expanse of the drawing room: "And how is Canterbury?" "I thought," said Edman, "he was referring to the cathedral." But the dignitary replied, "Oh, he is very well, very well indeed." "Good," said Butler, "I knew him when he was only York."

Every year *everybody,* from the greenest new instructor to the most distinguished professor on the brink of retirement, was invited to a huge reception. It was generally understood that if each of us would attend every third year this would fill the rooms to capacity and satisfactorily discharge our individual responsibility. The President stood at the top of a rather formidable flight of stairs shaking the hand of each new arrival but at the same time moving his arm in the direction of the interior in such a way that the newcomer could not possibly pause. Each departing guest got a similar handshake accompanied by a tug in the direction of the exit so irresistible that many felt they were not so much being said good-by to as being thrown down the stairs. Actually, all this was quite as it should be. Nobody wanted to stay any longer than necessary and any pause in either arriving or departing would have interfered with the steady operation of the moving belt which ran with perfect efficiency.

It would be grossly unfair not to pay a tribute to the way in which Mrs. Butler aided (and endured) these affairs. A robust, friendly, no-nonsense woman, she often mitigated slightly the stuffiness of the atmosphere by speaking her mind. And I never forgot my gratitude to her when, after my first dinner and when I was under slight suspicion as the author of an evil book as well as under rather graver suspicion as an ex-member of the staff of a dangerously radical paper, she spoke, almost shouted, to me across the room so that everyone present would be sure to hear: "*The Nation* is one of the few magazines I think worth reading." I am sure that she protected her husband if (which I doubt) there was ever an occasion when he felt the need of protection, but she also understood him well enough to reply at one of the receptions when a polite guest remarked that the President must find all this handshaking very fatiguing: "Oh, don't worry about him. He is like a horse. He rests standing up." Probably the only time he could not rest was when he was alone.

I think the most interesting man I ever met at one of these dinners (or at least the most interesting I was ever given an opportunity to talk much with) was the late Enrico Fermi, one of the several fathers of the atom bomb. He was a man of gentle manners as well as of wide interests and he was also the subject of one of Butler's favorite anecdotes. Some years before the war he had been in effect a prisoner in Mussolini's Italy when Butler, exercising his somewhat mysterious gift, realized that Fermi was a great man probably destined to be even greater. Somehow or other Mussolini's suspicions were lulled; Fermi was permitted to accept an invitation to give some lecture or other at Columbia; and then he simply did not return. Whether or not there was poetry as well as truth in this anecdote I do not know. No doubt the secrets of controlled atomic fission would have been discovered sooner or later without him, but it is at least possible that Butler's stratagem changed radically the course of events.

How many times Mrs. Butler had heard the favorite records played and how she took them I do not know. But perhaps she had a resource like that of Mrs. Bernard Shaw, which I heard about from Lawrence Langner, one of the directors of the Theater Guild and hence the producer of all of Shaw's later plays.

He and Mrs. Langner were dining with the Shaws in London. G. B. S., so Langner said, put on a dazzling performance. Anecdotes, epigrams, and opinions flowed, or rather burst, like a continual succession of skyrockets. Never had he heard so remarkable a performance. Meanwhile Mrs. Shaw was quietly knitting, and Mrs. Langner leaned over to whisper, "What are you making?" "To tell the truth," came the reply, "I am not making anything; but I have heard THE GENIUS tell these stories so often that I should go mad if I did not have some occupation." The great, I fear, are more often heroes to their valets than to their wives. Perhaps I should add here that, though I three times went to England with letters of introduction to Shaw and though I did once see him surrounded by admirers on the Riviera, I never presented any of the letters. I did not know what on earth I could say to him and was quite sure there was nothing he would want to say to me.

I am, however, proud in the knowledge that at least once and for a moment Shaw was aware of my existence. When the Theater Guild undertook the world premier of one of his later plays (I think it was *The Simpleton of the Unexpected Isles,* though I am not sure) I reviewed it rather flippantly in *The Nation.* The author, I said, had once interpreted Wagner's *Ring* as an allegory of the Collapse of Capitalism and would, therefore, no doubt be capable of finding some equally improbable significance in this amusing but completely disorganized comedy. I myself did not think it meant anything at all except that the playboy in Shaw was having a good time. When this piece was later performed at the Malvern Festival in England, my review was reprinted in the souvenir program together with a retort by Shaw. In a rather long essay he went on, as I had prophesied that he would, to say that this was actually the most serious, meaningful, and minatory of all his dramatic works. It was indeed his revelation to the world of the horrors which threatened it. "The trouble with Mr. Krutch is," he concluded, "that he has insufficient respect for the Apocalypse." This I have always cherished almost equally with Mencken's remark on my failure to "come all the way from Tennessee to civilization in one generation." To be insulted by the great constitutes a kind of compliment.

But to return to Columbia. For me it was, of course, a return home, or at least a return to one of the places where I had felt most at home. I had never completely lost touch with the academic world either in the persons of my friends there or even more directly. For several years during the Twenties I had given one course in the School of Journalism, and for several years during the early Thirties one course in the writing of criticism at Vassar College which I visited once a week. I gave also, once or twice, a series of literary lectures at the New School for Social Research on Twelfth Street.

Moreover, Columbia had remembered me to the extent of inviting me one year to give five special lectures at the Summer School on what I somewhat grandly called "The Aesthetics of Literature." Summer School audiences were composed mostly of teachers in middle age or beyond, and

I have always remembered one little incident which illustrates an attitude into which the chronic takers of "courses" tend to fall. After my fifth and last lecture I invited questions and one mature lady rose hesitantly, stammered, and finally, after much encouragement, managed to blurt out: "What I really want to know is this. Did *you* take a course in this somewhere or did you just kinda figure it out yourself?" What the poor thing wanted to find out was whether what she had heard had previously passed through a sufficient number of notebooks to be established as gospel or whether she might consider herself entitled to take it or leave it.

At the time of these quasi-academic performances, and even after I had become again a regularly accredited professor, I enjoyed the benefits of a certain paradoxical attitude on the part of writers and journalists toward professors, and of professors toward journalists and writers. Each ostensibly scorns the other. But at the same time each has a certain curiosity and a certain sneaking respect. Just how, wonders the writer, do you get certified as academically learned enough to teach in a university? Do professors really know a lot of things we do not? The professor, on the other hand, wonders what special talents you need to be acceptable to the general reader. He is sure that he knows more about his subject than anyone who touches upon it in nonacademic publications. Still, these journalists must have something he hasn't. Being neither wholly fish nor wholly fowl gives one a rather peculiar, and not always unenviable, position.

The Columbia to which I returned had grown somewhat larger, and of course the faculty was not wholly the same. But no such transformation as was to take place immediately following the Second World War had yet occurred and the whole atmosphere was familiar to me.

Professor Thorndike, who had been head of the department while I was student and instructor, had died and so had Professor Trent who had been in charge of my doctoral thesis. But the new head of the department, Ernest Wright, I had known in the old days and a number of my own contemporaries—Neff, Weaver, Clark, and various others, including of course Mark Van Doren—were still there, as well as certain of my elders such as the rather indolently brilliant Harry Morgan Ayres, the philologist, and Jefferson Butler Fletcher, the specialist in the Renaissance.

The Brander Matthews Chair of Dramatic Literature (to which I was to be appointed a few years later) was occupied by Matthews' immediate successor, George Dinsmore Odell, already deeply immersed in his huge, seemingly endless *Annals of the New York Stage,* each successive volume of which, as he said somewhat ruefully, was regularly and rather ominously called by reviewers "monumental" and which, as a matter of fact, he did leave as a still unfinished monument in the form of fifteen large, encyclopedia-sized volumes.

I had known Professor Odell in my days as an instructor when he was in charge of Freshman English in Columbia College and already very much a "character" on the campus. His brother had once been Governor of New York State and he himself, a rather crochety bachelor, was very much the old-time New Yorker of the proper genteel sort. He also had a consuming passion for everything concerning the theater of the great days of his youth before it had been spoiled by the intrusion of such dubious and dubiously respectable characters as Ibsen and, he was inclined to suspect, Bernard Shaw. While I was serving my term as student instructor for freshmen I had asked his permission to put *Ghosts* on my reading list. He replied with resigned tolerance: "Yes, yes. By all means have them read *Ghosts,* if you think it will make them any happier . . . Though I can't for the life of me see why it should." At the time I was deeply shocked; but though I still think students should read *Ghosts* I see his point better now than I did then.

Even at this early date there were countless anecdotes illustrating his weary tolerance of the vagaries of freshmen and there was one with which I especially sympathized. Daily themes were the rule and one of the requirements was that they should be written on a standard-size sheet. One day when Odell's assistant handed him the latest stack of callow effusions, one paper stuck out three inches beyond the rest. Regarding it with distaste he tore off the offending projection and then wrote at the top in pedagogic red ink: "Your discourse lacks connection."

When I returned to Columbia in 1937 and, among other chores, took over his undergraduate course in modern drama I am sure that he regarded me with considerable suspicion, for even if he had known that *The Nation* regarded me as little better than a reactionary he would have felt, like Arthur Train, that this allowed me far too much latitude. But from the beginning he treated me with old-fashioned courtesy, and when the time came a few years later for his retirement I think he was satisfied that I would be no more unworthy of his chair than any other product of degenerate times was sure to be.

Once, after some new production of *Hamlet,* he turned aside from a discussion of it to say, "Of course you are too young to have seen Forbes Robertson" and when I protested that I had indeed seen that actor in what was called "the best performance of *Hamlet* ever given by a Professor of English Literature" he retreated to his second line of defense. "Oh, well, the best performance I ever saw was

Booth's." Nor was this any idle boast, and he used to astonish students (quite deliberately I am sure) by casual reference to intimate details of the theatrical history of still remoter times, as when, for example, he interrupted a candidate's defense of a thesis on a Nineteenth Century Boston stock company. "You call Mrs. So-and-so a distinguished actress. I wouldn't say she was actually a 'distinguished' performer. She couldn't very well have been. The poor thing drank too much, you know."

He still attended the theater quite frequently but he seldom expected to be pleased and he had long ago given up all personal contact with those actively concerned in it. Nevertheless, he was delighted when I invited him to go with me to one of the dinners of the New York Drama Critics Circle of which I was that year the president. During the preliminary cocktail period he asked me to point out the notables. When I said, "That is Brooks Atkinson," or "Richard Watts," or "Burns Mantle," he would reply, "Oh, yes, I am glad to see him; I am familiar with his writing." But presently he asked, "And who is that gentleman over there?" "That is Walter Winchell." Long pause. "And who is Mr. Winchell?" It was not, I am sure, that he didn't know; he merely wished to indicate that he would prefer not to admit the fact.

A little later I saw him lending a polite but somewhat distant ear to a very well-known actress who, though of more or less distinguished family background, had long ago aggressively abandoned the manners of what Odell would have called "a lady." "This," I said to myself, "will be good," and I joined the duo. The actress was explaining her difficulty with her role in a current great success. It was the first time she had appeared in a "period piece"—one, that is to say, where what she was required to be was precisely "a lady." She did not know what to do with her hands. She couldn't smoke a cigarette and she couldn't hold a cocktail. Once she had caught herself just in time as she was about to cross her legs. "I felt as though I had done something awful—like dropping my drawers, you know." Odell maintained his composure. "Quite so, Miss B—. Yes, yes, I understand." Next day when I met him on the campus he thanked me for having taken him to the dinner. "They were very interesting people," he said. "I liked them all." Pause. "That is, all except Miss B—. I can't say that I cared much for her." The subject was closed.

Since it occurred later the same evening this is perhaps the best time to mention a little incident which will illustrate how it sometimes happens that prudence is the better part of gentlemanliness as well as of valor. Somehow or other—whether because we had volunteered or because we had been appointed I do not remember—George Jean Nathan and I were to escort to their apartments this same Miss B—and the woman playwright who was the author of the successful "period piece." The two ladies sat in the middle of the taxi, George and I beside the doors. Both ladies were in a rather elevated state and a quarrel soon broke out. "Just for that," said the author, "you can't be in my play any more." Whereupon the actress hauled off and gave her a resounding blow on the face.

At the moment the taxi was stationary before a red light. Without even exchanging glances, George and I came to the same conclusion. We opened our respective doors, stepped into the street, and slammed the doors shut again. The light changed; the taxi moved away, and though we have both since agreed that we were sorry never to have learned how the evening ended, we agreed also that knowledge would probably have come too high.

At this time Odell had already published I do not remember how many volumes of his "monumental" *Annals of the New York Stage* and was devoting most of his time to it. The work was planned on the grandest scale and for him it was, I am sure, a delightful *recherche du temps perdu* in the course of which the past he had experienced was only barely distinguished from that in which he had thoroughly soaked himself. Compiled largely from newspapers, the record began at the very beginning, defined New York as the whole metropolitan area, and "theater" in the broadest possible terms so as to include amateur as well as professional performances of anything which, by any stretch, could be called theatrical. It gave dates, casts of characters, etc., for every new play, for every revival, and for every change of cast during the run of either. Perhaps the best way to suggest its fearsome completeness is to say that once when I had occasion to introduce the author at a dinner I said: "I shall now pass on a piece of information which probably no one except Professor Odell and I are masters of and of which, as a matter of fact, even I was ignorant until an hour or two ago." Then I quoted. "On such and such a day, a strawberry festival, preceded by a Punch and Judy Show, was held at St. Mary's Church, Staten Island."

Near the end of his life when I saw Professor Odell for the last time he was seated nearly helpless on a chair in the hotel suite where he had long lived alone and was surrounded by all the paraphernalia necessary for compiling the index to the most recently finished volume. "How long does it take you to make one of these indexes?" "About three months." "Working how many hours a day?" "Working *all* day." "Couldn't you get someone else to make them?" "No, no, that would not be possible. Here is an illustration right here. See these two John Smiths?" (This was probably not the real name but it was something hardly more memorable.) "They were contemporaries and both were variety-hall performers. I am the only person in the world who could keep those two John Smiths separate." It had never occurred to him to doubt that keeping them separate was important. And perhaps he was right—at least if you believe in scholarship at all.

Among faculty members of approximately my own age the two of whom I saw most (always excepting, of course, Mark Van Doren) were Emery Neff and Raymond Weaver, both of whom I had known intimately during my early days as instructor in Columbia College. Weaver had then come from a year or two of teaching in Japan. We soon were intimates, and had continued some association during my years on *The Nation*. Now I saw him almost daily until he became one of the closest (and often the most exasperating) of my friends.

I mention him and Neff together because, though each was an extremely effective teacher, two men could hardly have been more different in temperament or method. Neff was (though not devoid of eccentricity) essentially an intensely serious, very hard working, deeply learned, and almost painfully conscientious man. As a director of doctoral theses he was superb, perhaps almost too demanding, but also tirelessly helpful, and he was responsible for several very solid pieces of scholarship which established immediately the academic reputation of the students who had labored long and hard on them. Weaver, on the other hand, was first of all a personality and a performer who intrigued and baffled undergraduates so fruitfully that they often developed intellectual interests of which otherwise they would never have believed themselves capable. If I discuss him at some length it will not, I hope, give the impression that either all or the most successful members of the Columbia faculty were "characters" like him and

Odell. But it is usually the personalities who make the best copy.

Gravely aloof in manner but also somewhat flamboyant and given for a day or two at a time to sporting a large ring, wearing a special tie, or tucking a conspicuous handkerchief into his outside coat pocket, he came closer than any of his colleagues to suggesting the aesthete. It was characteristic that he had never taken his Ph.D. (he could never have endured the humiliation of being questioned as the rest of us had been) and he was not especially learned in any of the more conventional literary subjects. Yet the fact remains that he had struck out for himself and published commercially the first modern book on Herman Melville and was probably more responsible than any other one man for the rediscovery of *Moby Dick*—a financial failure which had attracted almost no attention when originally published and was almost forgotten. Later he edited a standard edition of Melville's complete works, but it was to the creation of his legend as it grew during many collegiate generations that he devoted most of his time and his reputation was in full flower when he died suddenly while he and I were still members of the faculty. I think he first attracted my attention as someone worth watching when, while we were both new instructors, I heard from a bewildered freshman about the quiz he had just given. The first question written on the blackboard was, "Which of the required readings in this course did you find least interesting?" Then, after members of the class had had ten minutes in which to expatiate on what was certainly to many a congenial topic, he wrote the second question: "To what defect in yourself do you attribute this lack of interest?"

Though he was not, as I have already said, likely to know very much about anything the rest of us knew as a matter of academic course, he would take up some esoteric subject and soon know at least enough about it to dazzle undergraduates and to lead any of his colleagues beyond their depth if they undertook to dispute it with him. At one time the subject might be the traditions of Courtly Love and at another the mystical visions of St. Theresa, but he would expound and expostulate with students who soon came to wonder how they could have remained so profoundly ignorant concerning a subject so essential to any comprehension of the intellectual, aesthetic, or philosophical life. At the same time his own personal convictions remained a mystery which he would deliberately deepen by sometimes striking a pose of almost unctuous piety and at others uttering what seemed dangerously close to blasphemies. A faint odor of the sulphurous was seldom absent for long. The rumor would often go about that Weaver had been or was about to be received into the Catholic Church. Then again it would appear that he was rather closer to Diabolism than orthodoxy and more likely to attend a Black Mass than a white one. The truth was that it was all nine-tenths theater, though he would sometimes try the experiment of attempting to take in his colleagues as well as his students.

Many times when he tried the trick on me I attempted to puncture him, but I rarely succeeded as I did on one occasion which I remember just because I felt that for this once he had been deflated. Seating himself opposite me at a Faculty Club lunch table he announced without preliminary and in his grandest manner, "Joseph," (for he alone always gave me the dignity of an unabbreviated first name), "Joseph, it is too bad that I am not a Cardinal." "Too bad for *whom?*" I asked and the subject was dropped.

Usually, however, his friends were let in on the joke and he would tip them a wink if they happened to be present when he was putting on a show for the benefit of some undergraduate, as he did on an occasion I happen to remember. One of his duties was to participate in the seminars which made up an honors program to which only the best students were admitted and only after a personal interview. A few days before one of these interviews was to take place I happened to mention that I thought a moderately obscure baroque poem by the second-rate English comic dramatist, Mrs. Aphra Behn, was striking amid the general mediocrity of her writing. He said that he too happened to know it and agreed with me. When I entered his office near the end of the interview he was asking in his best episcopal voice, "Are you interested in poetry?" The student hastily professed that he was. Then, catching sight of me, Weaver asked, "Do you know Mrs. Behn's 'Love in fantastic triumph sat'?" Already alarmed, the poor student admitted that he did not. "What!!! You pretend to be interested in poetry and you do not know Mrs. Behn's 'Love in fantastic triumph sat'!"

Charlatanry? Perhaps; but conscious and deliberate. The student departed convinced, as students should be, of his vast ignorance, impressed by the learning of his mentor, and almost certain to seek out Mrs. Behn of whom it is very unlikely he had ever heard before.

Columbia is one of the least cloistered of the great American universities. The members of its faculty are part of the metropolitan community. They are not thrown willy-nilly into one another's company; they may, if they like, have all their social life off-campus and associate with their professional colleagues only insofar as a friendship develops just as it would had they met elsewhere.

Partly, perhaps, for that reason, the atmosphere in the department to which I belonged was singularly free from the irritations, tensions, and even open quarrels which, so I have both read and heard, are common in the academic world where it sometimes happens (as at one time it did in one great American university) that certain members of the English Department stop speaking to one another and even come to blows. Another reason for the pleasant atmosphere was no doubt the wise and generous attitude of the successive executives. Ultimately I divided my time almost equally between the Graduate School of English and Comparative Literature and Columbia College which is the undergraduate Liberal Arts unit of the University. During my fifteen years, the Chairmanship of the first passed from Hunter Wright, to O. J. Campbell, and then to Miss Margery Nicolson; that of the College English Department from Harrison Steeves to Charles Everett. Some of my colleagues I saw much of, including, during the latter part of the period, the Shakespeare specialist Alfred Harbage, now at Harvard. Of others I saw little. But if there was any ill feeling anywhere I was not aware of it, and there was certainly never even a minor or momentary flare-up of temper. If any of us lacked repect for any other member of the faculty the fact was concealed.

Marcelle and I had, since 1932, been spending our summers and frequent week ends in an old house in Redding, Connecticut, which we had bought the year following our return from our winter at Antibes. Now, thanks to the fact that I could arrange my academic schedule to suit my convenience, we came more and more to think of it as home, of New York City as the place where duty called me. Things finally worked out so that I would go into town either Tuesday night or Wednesday morning and return Friday afternoon which meant that I spent more than half my time in Redding. It was a rather sharply divided existence and the mid-week stretch in the city was frantically busy with seven lectures (three of them to audiences which gradually grew until one of them numbered two hundred and fifty) as well as evenings in the theater to catch at least the more important of the plays I was still reviewing for *The Nation.* I should not want to follow such a schedule now, but I found it then a good if strenuous life though I was coming to cherish more and more my half-week of country living.

Since one of my courses was in the modern drama from Ibsen to the present day a good deal of the playgoing would have been necessary quite aside from the reviewing, both because I was treating the theater as a still-going institution and because students, sharing that curiosity concerning the nonacademic which I mentioned once before as characteristic of even the more completely academic of faculty members, found an additional interest in their course because their teacher was also a practicing journalistic critic and could bring them fresh news of the latest opening.

Especially during the first three or four years I was kept pretty busy "working up" in Redding the lectures I would give at the University. I confess that I never practiced the heroic procedure which some in my position have adopted; I never, that is to say, threw away the notes I had prepared in order to start afresh each year. But I did always revise them drastically and did always say to myself that this subject or that would have to be better presented than it had been the year before.

Even if my persistent tendency to think that I did almost everything I undertook rather badly had not made it impossible for me simply to repeat a canned discourse over and over again as some very eminent professors have done, I would probably have been frightened out of this time-saving procedure by a story Harry Morgan Ayres told of a certain professor of geography in a well-known institution who had done just this, and who lisped besides. For twenty years he had read the same lectures, and when he came around for the twentieth time to the point where he announced: "'Fo inthstance the Mithithippi wiver depothith *a hundred thouthand* of thilt at the delta ev'y day" something unexpected happened. For the very first time in all his career a student raised a hand at this point. "Just a moment, Professor; is that a hundred thousand tons or a hundred thousand cubic yards?" The startled geographer looked down again at the manuscript and exclaimed with reproachful amazement: "It doethn't *thay!*"

During my four months of summer vacation (a blessing which now descends upon fewer college teachers than formerly) I usually took four or six weeks for some sort of vacation trip and spent the remainder working on some book to which I could devote little or no time during the college session. The first product of these summers was *The American Drama Since 1918* which covered the period during which I had been continuously acquainted with the theatrical activities of New York. It came out in 1939 and, though I wrote for the new edition of 1957 a supplimentary chapter on the most important developments since the year of original publication, it remains primarily a rather detailed discussion of the playwrights who seemed important in 1939 though not all of them seem so now.

The year of publication was, of course, the beginning of that new era of war and postwar changes which have made our lives vastly different from what, even during the decade of the depression, we still rather hoped they might some day be again. Marcelle and I were returning home via Montana from an automobile trip through the Southwest and the West when we bought in a tiny village a local newssheet (it had no wire service) announcing the beginning of a European war. By the time we arrived home something of the magnitude of the catastrophe was already apparent.

Ever since the fall of 1933 I had kept (and still keep) a sort of skeleton diary—no thoughts or reflections, simply a bare record of where we were and what we did. One volume is open before me as I write and it is strange to see how the trivial and the immeasurably important events are noted side by side. Under the date Dec. 7, 1941, I read: "When we returned about 3:30 this afternoon from a circular walk through the woods with Ossie, Pepper and Hodge" (all cats) "Larry" (our hired man) "told us that he had heard that Japan had attacked Hawaii and the Philippine Islands."

The first great war had passed over me while I served in a safe noncombatant company. I was by now too old to be called up, but Marcelle and I were aware that, at best, the shadow of what had just begun would probably hang more or less deeply over the rest of our lives. Nevertheless, we suffered no more than anxiety and inconvenience. Getting back and forth to Columbia was more difficult since I could no longer drive; and when we had to give up the *pied à terre* we had kept in the Village, my problem was to find a hotel that would take me in for the few days I was in town—and I stayed in some pretty dismal ones.

Marcelle served on the Redding ration committee; I went once a week to the office of the War Writers Board; we both kept watch, sometimes from midnight to dawn, in the plane-spotting station on a cold hillside in Connecticut. But, whether I should apologize or not, I must confess that except for these trivial things I went on as best I could with my own life and work. Nevertheless, those who were then not yet born, or were too young to understand what was happening, probably do not realize how distressing the early months were as a series of calamities, major and minor, came over the radio during the nerve-racking "news on the hour every hour." I was in New York when the *Normandie* burned and rolled over on her side and I remember a little later walking the streets alone just after we had heard of our first great defeat in the Pacific. One could not help wondering about something we could not more than half believe possible. Suppose Germany and Japan should triumph? Marcelle's sister, her husband, and two sons were later to be caught in the invasion of Paris and then to escape to us. Their stories helped us to realize dimly what defeat means.

I remember very well the first class I met after the attack on Pearl Harbor. It happened to be undergraduate and it seemed impossible to go on with whatever we had been talking about. One student challenged me: "If we fight this war," he asked, "can you assure us that we will then have a better world?" "No," I replied, "I cannot. But there is one thing I *can* say. If we don't fight it we will have a much worse one." And I still think that was a sensible answer.

The University was, of course, soon and progressively disrupted. The undergraduate body melted quickly away and there was left only a residue of those too young or physically too unfit for the armed forces. Even in the Graduate School women as well as men drifted off into wartime occupations. Classes became mere shadows of their former selves. In the College I found myself trying not very successfully to carry on a discussion with three or four young men who were perhaps on the point of being called away or whose minds were in any event elsewhere.

In the Graduate School I might lecture to a group no larger. When, after four or five years, many of those who had disappeared turned up again one thing particularly impressed me. Some of them had been through experiences which I could hardly imagine, and they themselves would never be quite the same again. Yet the scars were so deeply hidden that one often could not know without putting the question whether they had been shot down over Germany, wounded on some Pacific Island, or, like me twenty-five years before, passed their time peaceably in some home-based camp.

I did not know that some of the early experiments which were to lead to Hiroshima were conducted in the basement of Philosophy Hall, just under the large lecture room where I, perhaps at the very moment, was lecturing to four or five students on the Drama of the Restoration and Eighteenth Century. My elder brother Charlie was then working in the public relations department of the expanding and various activities of the Tennessee Valley Authority, and some time in 1944 he flew up to New York on business in the TVA airplane. Marcelle and I returned with him to Knoxville and flew around the perimeter of the forbidden area occupied by the mysterious plant at Oak Ridge, just about twenty-five miles from Knoxville.

The whole region was buzzing with curiosity and speculation. Some thought, so my brother told me, that what was going on there had something to do with the disintegration of the atom. "That," I said, "is a very wild, improbable guess. I know just enough about the subject to be sure anything of the kind is at least a long way off."

Then, not long after I had returned to New York, I happened to sit at table in the Faculty Club with Dean Peagram, the physicist who was also dean of the Faculty of

Philosophy and Pure Science. I told him about my visit to the Knoxville area and asked if he knew what all the activity at Oak Ridge was about. "No," he said, "I have heard that something is going on there but I have no idea what it is." I was completely convinced, and when I learned after the secret was out that Peagram had been the one who had accompanied Fermi and the others to vouch for their competence at an interview with President Roosevelt, my first thought was, What a poker player Peagram would make.

Early in the morning of Monday, Aug. 6, 1945, I was still asleep in Redding when Marcelle waked me to say that the radio had just announced the dropping of an atom bomb on Japan. "What does that mean?" she asked. Still not quite awake I said, "It means that I am scared to death." If my dismissal of the rumor that Oak Ridge was preparing to disintegrate the atom on a large scale was as wrong as possible, this reaction to the news that the feat had been accomplished was right enough to redeem me.

14

▲
▲▲▲

I am somewhat ashamed to say that so far as my own work is concerned the most significant effect of the war was that it enabled me to complete my most laborious book a good deal sooner than I would otherwise have found possible.

As far back as my graduate student days I had been fascinated by the personality, opinions, and genius of Samuel Johnson. Boswell was a favorite bedside book and Boswell had led me to Johnson's own writing and to the eighteen volumes (then supposed to be all we would ever have) of that most astonishing of literary finds, Boswell's own private journal, and also, of course, to some of the many books about Boswell, Johnson, and the other members of his circle. Even so I had never even remotely supposed that all this would ever be more than a hobby until my old mentor Professor W. P. Trent wrote me a letter praising the essay on Samuel Richardson in *Five Masters* and added that he hoped I would some day do a similar piece on Johnson. I do not think I took the suggestion very seriously at the time, but a seed was planted and all during the next decade I occasionally remarked when I happened to be in an expansive mood that *someday* I was going to write about Johnson. I also continued to read, though more as a recreation than with any serious purpose in mind.

One day shortly after the war had begun Mark Van Doren (again playing a crucial role) said to me: "You have been talking about Johnson too long. I mentioned you and your long-delayed project to Bill Sloane (then chief editor at Henry Holt) and he is all worked up. Tomorrow I am going to take you to his office and you are going to sign a contract." Cornered I said, "O.K.," and the contract was duly signed.

I knew that in a few years I would be due my first Sabbatical leave from Columbia and that the "year," counting the two summers, would actually be of nearly seventeen months. Marcelle and I had long agreed that when these seventeen months finally arrived we would take a complete vacation and realize one of my romantic dreams. We would go to Africa where we could see the spectacular zoo animals without bars. Obviously, the war made this out of the question. Perhaps I had best spend the time on Johnson. Accordingly the intervening summers, as well as such time as I could spare from classes and the theater during the winters, were spent in organizing as well as extending my information and even in getting a little down on paper. Then when I came back to Redding after my last class and last doctoral examination in May 1943 I plunged in to emerge with the MS. complete before the Sabbatical was quite over.

Shortly after it was published in 1945 I (to anticipate just a bit) participated in a radio panel called, I believe, "Meet the Critics," which that evening was devoted to a discussion of a new novel by Jerome Weidman. I remarked that I thought it too long. Weidman interrupted vehemently: "You have your nerve, when you have just published six hundred pages about, of all things, Samuel Johnson!" I was able to reply: "Your facts are wrong. It is not six hundred pages long. It is only five hundred and ninety-nine."

Since Boswell's biography is conventionally regarded as the finest ever written about a man of letters, to write another one might seem at first sight both impudent and unnecessary. The fact is, however, that the almost fanatical assiduity of the many "Johnsonians" and the even more numerous "Boswellians" had accumulated many relevant facts which Boswell—or sometimes, for that matter, Johnson himself—did not know. "Except for Shakespeare," so I wrote in the first chapter, "no English author has been the center of a more eager band of scholarly devotees, and even within the past two decades the antiquarian skill plus the almost incredible industry of scholars has established dates which remained vague to all previous biographers and discovered facts about persons more or less remotely connected with Johnson which would have been news to the Doctor himself. What he spent for food at Oxford, when he stopped being charged for food there and when, by inference, he departed from the University without his degree can now be easily ascertained by anyone who cares to know. So, too, for instance, can the name of the first wife of the husband of his wet nurse, Mrs. John Marklew, nee Joan Winckley."

Except to the passionately dedicated some of these facts are of less than overwhelming interest but there are also many which do add significant touches to the picture. And because, despite the innumerable books of various kinds, including a number of short biographies, no attempt had been made since the Eighteenth Century to tell the whole story in one volume, I hoped that it would be worthwhile to draw upon every known fact in order to present in one substantial volume a more complete account of Johnson's life, character, and works than could be found elsewhere within a manageable number of pages.

An even more important reason was my hope to help rescue Johnson from a conventional view which has prevailed in at least the popular mind since shortly after his death. In this view, which goes back to Macaulay's famous essay, Johnson appears as a crotchety, wrong headed, eccentric and dull writer of whom Boswell created an image sufficiently amusing to be remembered though no one any more reads Johnson's own works and though he would by now be forgotten were it not for Boswell. No view could be more wrong. Instead of being created by Boswell, he was described by other contemporaries in a similar and quite as admiring a manner, though none of them had Boswell's special talent for portraiture. It was Johnson who made Boswell's reputation, not Boswell who made his. As for the neglect of Johnson's own literary works though this was, unfortunately, true, the fault is not his but that of those who have never attempted to read him sympathetically. The conventional view of him is no more than a parody of the real man.

That he was crotchety, sometimes stubbornly intolerant, and, at least by now prevailing opinions, quite wrong in some of his opinions and attitudes is obvious enough. But that such crotchets, intolerances, and wrong judgments should be taken to sum him up is simply preposterous. His was a powerful mind and a powerful gift for expression—sometimes witty, sometimes magnificently somber. Everybody knows a dozen of his sayings which hit a nail on the head so accurately that they are too familiar to be cited. But quite aside from these tidbits there are extended passages of exposition or description which in their own way are hardly surpassed in all literature. He was a profoundly wise man even though, like all men, he was not always wise.

It would be out of place to illustrate this fact here by lengthy quotations but I will cite one of his *obiter dicta* not quite so well known as some of the others. "All censure of a man's self is oblique praise. It is in order to show how much he can spare." That alone is sufficient to demonstrate that he was a psychologist as penetrating as, say, La Rochefoucauld, and it is also something the writer of an autobiography ought to remember when he thinks he is being modest.

Another thing which undoubtedly attracted me was the presence in Johnson of an underlying somberness of temperament, accompanied by a keen delight in those pleasures which existence nevertheless offers us. The first sentence of my book is: "Samuel Johnson was a pessimist with an enormous zest for living." The next paragraph begins: "Of his many categorical judgments none is better known than that which he puts into the mouth of Imlac the philosopher in *Rasselas:* 'Human life is everywhere a state, in which much is to be endured, and little to be enjoyed.' Yet even Imlac is not made to say that life has no pleasures; only that its pains outnumber them. And Johnson had a wholehearted relish for such of the former as came within his reach." His estimate of the possibilities of human life is darker than any I would want to make at this moment but the drift of it I can at least understand.

I do not think I had read *Rasselas*—at least not with

close attention—before I wrote *The Modern Temper* but when I did come to consider it carefully I was amazed to discover that, for all the difference which changing patterns of thought make, there is a certain fundamental similarity in the two theses. Consider this passage:

" 'What,' said he, 'makes the difference between man and all the rest of the animal creation?' Every beast, that strays beside me, has the same corporeal necessities with myself: he is hungry and crops the grass, he is thirsty and drinks the stream, his thirst and his hunger are appeased, he is satisfied and he sleeps: he rises again and is hungry, he is again fed, and he is at rest. I am hungry and thirsty like him, but when thirst and hunger cease, I am not at rest; I am, like him, pained by want, but am not, like him, satisfied by fullness. The intermediate hours are tedious and gloomy; I long again to be hungry, that I may again quicken my attention. The birds peck the berries, or the corn, and fly away to the groves, where they sit, in seeming happiness, on the branches, and waste their lives in tuning one unvaried series of sounds. I likewise, can call the lutanist and the singer, but the sounds, that pleased me yesterday, weary me today, and will grow yet more wearisome to-morrow. I can discover within me no power of perception, which is not glutted with its proper pleasure, yet I do not feel myself delighted. Man surely has some latent sense, for which this place affords no gratification; or he has some desires, distinct from sense, which must be satisfied, before he can be happy." As a later poet was to say, "The sorrows of our proud and angry dust/Are from eternity and shall not fail."

What then I hoped to do was both write a full biography which took advantage of the more significant parts of the knowledge which has accumulated since Boswell's time, and revise as far as possible the popular notion of

Johnson as hardly more than the convenient subject of Boswell's amusing portrait. I certainly cannot claim to have originated the tendency of present-day students to make precisely this revision of Johnson's reputation, but I may have helped somewhat and the tendency has continued. One sign of it is that the last collected edition of Johnson's works had been published in 1825. Now an elaborate edition with the full panoply of modern scholarship has begun to appear volume by volume.

I confess that I suffered a good deal of apprehension. I was definitely not a member of the sizable group of "Johnson specialists" who had made him the principal interest of their lives. Few of them even knew that I was interested in him and there was the danger that they would regard me as a rash intruder. Hence I simply could not afford to be guilty of many errors of fact. It would require a lifetime to read absolutely everything which has been written about Johnson, even during the last fifty years. James L. Clifford's bibliography *Johnsonia Studies. 1887-1950* not published until 1951) lists 2078 items. I could only hope that I had not overlooked anything important and to avoid minor errors I spent two months going over my MS. line by line, checking every date and quotation and, so far as possible, questioning every statement.

Then I wrote Clifford (whom I had never met) and he generously read my work, made a few suggestions, and in general approved. Another difficulty now arose. I wished to make some quotations from the privately printed and carefully protected *Private Papers of James Boswell.* The last of the two editors of these eighteen volumes was hesitant. He would not give permission unless he too could approve of the MS. But after I had sent it on to him he kindly consented. As a result of my care (greater I confess than I had ever taken before or have ever exercised since) I know of only two flat errors. One was pointed out to me by the expert descriptive bibliographer Allen Tracy Hazen. The page from Johnson's dictionary which I reproduce and call simply "from the first edition" is actually from a second printing. The other error I discovered for myself too late but it occurs, unfortunately, on the very first page where I say that Johnson once remarked "I hate a *cui bono* man" when, as a matter of fact, it was Boswell who said that Johnson would have agreed with a certain person of Boswell's acquaintance who remarked "I hate etc." That there are other errors I do not doubt, but so far as I know I have not been called publicly to account for them.

One embarrassing error I was saved from just in the nick of time. For some reason publishers do not usually submit proof of the jacket, or even the text on the jacket, to the author. Shortly before the book appeared I was told that its jacket was to be adorned by a fine color picture drawn for the purpose. When I saw it I was in despair. It showed Boswell and Johnson seated at the window of an inn outside of which the sign read "The Cheshire Cheese." Now though this particular restaurant thrives on the carefully cultivated legend that Johnson frequented the establishment, though indeed it is quite possible that he may have sometime eaten there, there is not a shred of evidence that he ever did. I took my head in my hands. Any reasonably well-informed person interested in Johnson who saw that picture would conclude that the author of the book was not very familiar with the better sources of information. The publisher responded sympathetically to my anguish. All the jackets prepared for the first printing were run back through the press and the terrible words "The Cheshire Cheese" were obliterated by cross hatchings. On some of the copies printed near the end of the run you can still make out, if you study it very closely, the offending legend.

I had assumed that publishing a big book on Johnson would be largely a self-indulgence but it turned out to my amazement that it sold more copies than any of my other books before or since, at least in their hard-cover editions.

The second and third great find of Boswell papers were made after my book appeared; but though they add much to our knowledge of Boswell, those so far made public do not, I think, require any correction of anything I wrote about Johnson himself. They did, on the other hand, lead to some friendship with that eccentric literary explorer, the late Colonel Ralph Isham, whose shrewdness, persistence, and diplomacy enabled him to make the astonishing finds—perhaps the most spectacular in the history of modern literature. It will be years yet before they all appear in the series of volumes now being issued one by one.

I remember very vividly a little scrap of paper which Colonel Isham showed me. It was dated six weeks after Johnson's death and it read (as well as I can remember for it has not yet been printed): "Last night I dreamed that I was talking with Dr. Johnson. I knew that he was dead but it did not seem strange that we should be talking. 'To die,' he said, 'is a terrible thing.' 'Yes,' I replied, 'but that is where you have the advantage of me; for you, Sir, have got it over with.' " No doubt Colonel Isham had showed it to a few others, but on no other occasion have I ever had so strong a sense of a long dead voice speaking to me.

Shortly after the Johnson biography was published William Sloane left the Henry Holt Company to found his own publishing firm which was later to be absorbed by William Morrow and Company, though the Sloane imprint is still used. One of Sloane's first undertakings was "The American Men of Letters Series" to be composed of moderate-sized volumes devoted to biographical-critical studies. He asked Margaret Marshall, Lionel Trilling, Mark Van Doren, and me to be the editors and to contribute one volume each to the series. We all agreed, I on the condition that I should take Thoreau as my subject. Mark chose Hawthorne and my volume (1948) was the first to appear, Mark's the third, with an *Edwin Arlington Robinson* by my Columbia colleague, Emery Neff, coming in between.

My choice of Thoreau was not at random because he had been, except for Johnson, the writer most in my mind for a number of years. I remember very well that I first read *Walden* in 1930 during the long train journey back from Los Angeles after the end of a cross-country lecture tour on which I expounded the modern temper to a variety of audiences ranging from little companies of knitting ladies to college groups and a Mormon Lyceum in Salt Lake City. The other incident of the tour that I remember best is a remark made to me by the gentleman in charge of the weekly noontime lectures in the assembly hall of the California Institute of Technology. We were on the platform when the noisy crowd of students pushed in to fill the room and line up along its walls. Obviously they came weekly not knowing (probably also not much caring) what to expect, and I wondered if they would quiet down. The reply of my companion to the question struck me as very significant. "Oh," he said, "they will be a docile audience if, one, you stop by twelve-fifty so that they can get their lunches and, two, are very careful not to say anything in favor of either religion or morality."

The reading of *Walden* on that train trip made a tremendous impression and I still have the little flexible leather volume on a back flyleaf of which I scribbled some still legible notes. That the Great Depression was just revealing itself as a good deal more than a mere temporary setback was no doubt responsible for the fact that the only sentence I copied out in full was the one which sums up his quasi-Marxian criticism of our economic system. "The principal object is not that men should be well and honestly clad but that corporations may be enriched." But I was also (for a reason presently to appear) even more interested in resolving the paradox of his exaltation of the primitive. My observations are obvious enough, but I will copy out one or two of them just because, obvious as the commentary is, those who dismiss Thoreau as a mere crank seldom take the trouble to make them.

> Thoreau mentions the Laps with admiration but he would not want to be one. Natural man does not philosophize about nature and that is what Thoreau wants to do. He requires the civilized background and civilized training which he despises. The fallacy of the noble savage is everywhere evident. [Actually Thoreau never falls into it.]
>
> The true moral of the book and perhaps one which Thoreau would have accepted is not that men should do as he did and society attempt to compose itself of Thoreaus but that every man should try to lead the kind of life which seems best to him.
>
> Thoreau took a humorous and extravagant way of calling attention to the fact that men have lost their way. That they lead lives of quiet desperation. Return to essentials. A rediscovery of what we really want.

More important perhaps was the flat sentence, "Man must be reformed first." This is, of course, precisely what most of the modern social reformers, even those like members of the early British Labor Party, who acknowledge a great debt to Thoreau, refuse to believe. They insist that "the system" must be changed first, that society makes men and not, as Thoreau insisted, that men make society.

It was not until years later that I first came across his seemingly brutal comment on a minor depression of his own day. If, he said, thousands are now unemployed that proves that they were never well employed. Had I known it I should probably have at least half agreed. Moreover, I was drawn to *Walden* no more by its criticism of the social system than by the way in which it illuminated my own growing interest in the world of nature as spectacle, refuge, and teacher of lessons.

During my first ten years in New York I had never left the city without regret except to go from it to the cities of Europe. Then, as I have mentioned before, Marcelle and I spent a number of summers in Cornwall, Connecticut, and in 1932 bought the old house in Redding which we came more and more to think of as home. With increasing insistence I escaped to it at every opportunity, at first merely because of what I wanted to get away from, then more and more because I realized that there was something I wanted to escape *into* as well as something I wanted to escape from.

What was it? Some of my New York friends understood, as of course Mark Van Doren did. Others twitted me more or less good-humoredly. Professor O. J. Campbell, who was completely urban, could not imagine why anyone should leave theaters, concert halls, and social gatherings to retire into the country which he regarded as what Sidney Smith called "a kind of healthy grave." He often teased me. "What on earth do you *do* there?" he would ask. "What you call contemplation, I call merely 'presiding over a vacuum.' " And if he had known Johnson as well as I did he would no doubt have quoted Johnson's "those who live in the country *deserve* to live in the country" or his rebuke to Mrs. Thrale, "You feed your chickens and starve your mind."

Raymond Weaver was even more vehement. He came a few times to spend a week end with us but on the last occasion he exploded as he stepped down from the train: "I *hate* the country." A few years later I took my revenge by describing him (without mentioning his name) in an essay.

> He has never spoken, as another friend sometimes does, of his eagerness to get back to "God's concrete," but I know that he feels it. Even as he steps off the train at our rather bustling little station, he looks about warily as though half expecting to see hostile Indians, and by the time our automobile has stopped in front of my garage, he is definitely alarmed. He knows that I am not going to ask him to clear the forest or, for that matter, go for a walk. But the surroundings suggest the theoretical possibility of such things and they make him uneasy.
>
> Outdoors in summertime he tolerates my small lawn and mildly approves the few flowers carefully confined to their beds. They are like caged animals in a zoo, put on exhibition to satisfy a public curiosity and therefore well enough in their way. But why, just beyond the confines of this lawn, are all those other trees and shrubs and herbs allowed, as it were, to run around loose? I do not think that he anticipates any definable danger from a bit of wild laurel or even from a squirrel, but they are obviously out of place. My modest little woodland, mostly unimpressive second growth, carries the threat, vague but disturbing, of the immemorial forest pushing in to surround him.
>
> My friend has, in other words, got used to the assumption that Nature has been tamed, that even plants are things that grow when, and only when, they are tended in pots on a

window-sill or a penthouse terrace. They are, in their way, as safe as pekinese or poodles. But out here they are actually growing on their own. I do not water them; the rain does. They do not even ask my permission to grow. They have a will and a competent self-reliance of their own. To what may such a state of affairs possibly lead? Just how safe are we against the possibility of a sort of revolt of the Helots? If Nature looks as though she might be capable of seizing a favorable opportunity to take over, then he would prefer to be somewhere else. New York City might have time to prepare her defense while Connecticut was being engulfed.

To put it more simply, he was distressed by that "wildness" which so haunted the imagination of Thoreau and was beginning to fascinate me.

When later I came to write what are called "nature books" I was often asked if I had simply agreed to write a book about Thoreau and become converted in the process. Actually I chose Thoreau as a subject because I was already interested both in him and in nature. A different question cannot be answered so simply. "How," I have been asked again and again in one way or another, "can you possibly admire greatly both Thoreau and Johnson?" Actually they have in common a good deal more than strong, self-reliant personalities and great wit. I once tried to illustrate some of the differences and similarities in an imaginary conversation which was published in *The Saturday Review* for July 21, 1951. Some of the remarks attributed to each are direct quotations, some are modified to fit the occasions and some are pure inventions which seemed to me in character. I hoped that it would not be too evident which were which. In any case I think it explains better than anything else could why I admire both men almost equally.

The most obvious of the contrasts between the two

was, of course, that the one was a lover of nature and wildness, the other of cities and civilization. But there are others almost as absolute. In religion Johnson was orthodox, though somewhat uneasily so, and he would have been almost as much shocked by Thoreau's "One world at a time" as by his even more resounding blasphemy in proclaiming that he and God had never quarreled. One believed that mankind had almost always been wrong in its beliefs, judgments, and values, the other distrusted all novel opinions because he held to the typical Eighteenth Century conviction that what most men at most times had believed was most likely to be true. Thoreau sought new truths; Johnson reasserted and rephrased the old.

Yet the similarities are equally striking and perhaps more fundamental. Both were sturdy individualists and both had the gift for the pungent phrase. Both believed that "the mass of men lead lives of quiet desperation" though Thoreau was sure they need not do so while Johnson believed that no one could escape what was an essential part of being a man. Neither was, in the usual sense of the word, a puritan since even the pessimistic Johnson insisted that the pleasures of life were not only real but legitimate and permissible. Neither believed that we need be a mere slave to duty, and Thoreau's "God did not send me into the world without some spending money" is a more picturesque way of reiterating Johnson's angry reply to the suggestion that he should write more, "No man is compelled to do as much as he can." Had they met they would have clashed but they would have ended (as they do in my dialogue) with mutual if grudging respect.

One winter night shortly after I had finished *Thoreau* I was reading a "nature essay" which pleased me greatly and it suddenly occurred to me for the first time to wonder if I could do something of the sort. I cast about for a subject and decided on the most conventional of all, namely Spring.

It couldn't be far behind, as both Shelley and the calendar assured me. Those little frogs known to all New Englanders as the spring peepers would soon be making their premature announcement and it was something for which I had long been accustomed to wait. This "Day of the Peepers" I considered as my spring festival and rather more meaningful as such than Easter (which moves back and forth too widely to have great meteorological significance) while the voice of the frogs has a definite meaning: the temperature has been above freezing often enough and for long enough periods to bring them to life. As a subject it would do.

Style and tone was another problem. All of my books had been serious and rather more solemn than I would have liked them to be. I wanted something lighter and more definitely in the manner of the now generally despised "familiar essay." I wrote half a dozen first paragraphs before I hit upon one which seemed to me reasonably satisfactory and then went on to finish the first essay without thinking beyond it. It concluded:

> Surely one day a year might be set aside on which to celebrate our ancient loyalties and to remember our ancient origins. And I know of none more suitable for that purpose than the Day of the Peepers. "Spring is come!" I say when I hear them and: "The most ancient of Christs has risen!" But I also add something which, for me at least, is even more important. "Don't forget," I whisper to the peepers, "we are all in this together."

This last sentence was important to me because it stated for the first time a conviction and an attitude which had come to mean more to me than I realized and, indeed, summed up a kind of pantheism which was gradually coming to be an essential part of the faith—if you can call it that—which would form the basis of an escape from the pessimism of *The Modern Temper* upon which I had turned my back without ever having conquered it. From another standpoint this paragraph was unfortunate because when the publisher of the book to which my experiment soon led sent the first chapter to a leading literary monthly the editor replied that his magazine "could not possibly publish an essay which spoke disrespectfully of Easter."

Having finished that essay I started another called "A Question for Meloe," the lady referred to being a blister beetle which has one of the most extraordinary of life histories even among the insects which are remarkable for the strange complications of their lives. The survival of Meloe depends upon a series of accidents so improbable that the vast majority of her offspring inevitably perish somewhere along the line before they reach maturity and it is a wonder that any ever survive. Pressure of college work led me to abandon this essay after only a few paragraphs had been written and it lay neglected until summer when I decided to try to finish it.

Then something happened very much like what had happened in the case of *The Modern Temper* but never, since then, has happened again. By the time I had finished this essay I knew what the next would be and I completed the short book of twelve chapters in about thirty days. Since each chapter was assigned to a month Mark Van Doren suggested that I call it *The Twelve Seasons* and I submitted them very hesitantly to Bill Sloane. He and his assistant editor, Helen Stewart, were enthusiastic and the book was published in 1949, when it had a good reception and modestly good sales.

Charles Poore wrote in the *New York Times* daily book column an amiably flippant review in which (thinking also no doubt of his colleague Brooks Atkinson) he called me "another Broadwayite doubling as Connecticut Yankee." But he had the thing the wrong way around. I had found a new subject and for the next few years I was to be a literary naturalist doubling as Broadwayite.

Doubling (or tripling) as Broadwayite, college teacher, and Connecticut Yankee had not become as much easier as I had hoped it might with the ending of the war. Transportation was simpler and so was finding a night's lodging in town. But the huge influx of students into the University placed an unprecedented burden even upon those who did not attempt to lead more than one professional life. My graduate courses swelled to such proportions that I had to give one of them in the MacMillan Theater auditorium. Candidates for the Doctorate multiplied to such unheard-of numbers that theses piled high on our desks and oral examinations were scheduled twice a week (sometimes oftener) throughout the year. Margery Nicolson, by now chairman of the department and the victim of a Scotch conscience, was the wonder of us all even though we also were more harassed than we would have believed it possible to be and survive. There was no longer time for the chats I had so much valued with my special friends like Clifford, Harbage, or even, for that matter, with Mark.

One day there appeared at my office an unusually pretty girl. When she asked rather timidly if she might see me for a moment I invited her in with more than usual cordiality. *"What,"* I asked hopefully, "can I do for you?" "Well," she replied, "I am writing a paper in American literature at——university. And I have been told that . . . well, that *you* were *alive* during the F. Scott Fitzgerald period." Perhaps that had something to do with my growing conviction that it was time for me to retire from the world.

Meanwhile, the theater which I had found somewhat distasteful during the Thirties came to life again with the appearance of two new figures. Every decade has seemed to produce some new phenomena and the Forties brought into notice, first Tennessee Williams with *The Glass Menagerie* (1945), then Arthur Miller with *All My Sons* (1947). Each announced definitely a new gifted writer and whatever else one may say of the two authors there is no doubt that they brought into the theater the most striking talents to appear since Eugene O'Neill. Neither was "like" O'Neill except in the very general sense that they attacked seriously the dramatic problem of the darker aspects of human life. They were also rather less like one another than the mere fact of their outstanding reputation makes us sometimes assume. Miller (as his first successful play makes clear) "took off" from the Thirties and "social criticism." Williams is, superficially at least, far more subjective and at times points in the direction of the very latest "new wave" of existentialist unreason and despair.

From the standpoint of what is important to this autobiography rather than to the history of dramatic literature the most significant fact is the extent to which both belong to a spiritual generation later than mine and the fact that, for all the power and originality which I recognize in them, I cannot feel the same sympathy, the same sense that they are to some degree speaking for me, which I felt sometimes when seeing a new O'Neill play; or, for that matter, works far less imposing than either his or theirs but, nevertheless, contemporary with my own youthful convictions and hopes.

Many members of the present-day audiences still able to applaud the revivals of O'Neill are in an exactly opposite situation. They were born too late ever to have known the times in which he wrote. His is a voice from the past even though they recognize it as an arresting one and possibly not only of "the past" but also of "the permanent past." Yet, to many of them it must seem that his disillusion and his "alienation" are of so innocently old-fashioned a kind that he barely escapes being that most contemptible of creatures, a "square." This is hardly to be wondered at if they have come to take for granted, not only Williams, but also such others of the present generation as Anouilh, Beckett and Ionesco, to whom man is not merely egotistic, treacherous, and cruel but also so "absurd" that he cannot be rationally presented and can be truly revealed only as a figure in a surrealist nightmare. O'Neill was waiting for God: his successors are sure that no God (not even a Godot) will ever come.

In those Nineteen-twenties which now seem by comparison so innocent, O'Neill was sometimes accused of being "obsessed with sex," especially in its more tortured and least respectable aspects. But he is innocent almost to the point of naïveté by comparison with Williams—to say nothing of that even more advanced exponent of the abnormal, Jean Genet—both of whom give the impression that normal sexual love, no matter how defiant of the conventional rules of either manners or morals, is mere pap for babes and that sex is not even interesting unless it is somehow perverse—either sadistic or at least homosexual.

Is this psychologizing at greater depth, or is it merely a form of decadence, the need of the jaded for madder music and for stronger wine? I will not attempt to pronounce, but I cannot help being reminded of what happened when the Elizabethan tragedy became the Jacobean as blood and violence and perversity became, seemingly for their own sakes, more and more the subject. If O'Neill was "a banshee Shakespeare" perhaps Williams and some of the others are analogous to Webster and Ford.

Miller is perhaps closer to O'Neill than Williams because, even in a play superficially as close to mere "social criticism" as *Death of a Salesman,* one senses an underlying concern with the essentially tragic situation of man. I am not unaware that Williams also has hinted, in one way or another, that he too is really on the side of the angels, and what I have been saying here is not intended to deny that perhaps he and the others actually are. It is merely to suggest why, when I came presently to turn my back upon Broadway and its theater, it was less regretfully than might be expected in the case of one who had for so long devoted a major part of his life to it.

During all this time anyone familiar enough with any of my work to "place" me would probably have said "Drama Critic"; and I had considered as well as met all the various conflicting attitudes toward those of my profession—from that of the frivolous who thought it must be a delightful profession because it involved being entertained almost nightly, to that of the "serious critics" who asked contemptuously how anyone with any pretense to taste could consent to spend his life thus. Also from that of managers who accused us critics of being impossible to please to that of friends who berated us for praising so indiscriminately that we persuaded them to waste their time and their dollars upon what bored them so intolerably that they were inclined to demand (as Irwin Edman once actually did) money back from the author of the review that had deluded them. When in the mid-Thirties I published a book about the American drama since 1918 the review of it in one of the better-known quarterlies began with the statement that a critical work which took O'Neill seriously would obviously be of no interest to the readers of this particular magazine.

Though I did and still do "take O'Neill seriously" I readily recognize the fact that reviewing is not the same as criticism; that most of it, whether of books or plays, does not aspire to more than ephemeral interest; and that the drama critic works under conditions less favorable than the book reviewer because his professional responsibility is to the whole of an institution defined by the physical fact that it centers in a theater, rather than by any degree of artistic or intellectual pretention. Most book reviews (aside from those written by regular columnists) are composed by persons who address themselves to books of one special kind or degree of seriousness. They do not appraise Thomas Mann one day and Zane Grey the next. But a drama critic attends a revival of *Hamlet* one night and a machine-made farce the next. And he is not doing the job he is supposed to do unless he honestly attempts to assess each in terms of its intentions and pretentions.

It is now nearly ten years since I have seen the curtain rise on a new Broadway production, and since I shall have little more to say on the subject I shall take a farewell to it by reprinting here some excerpts (not elsewhere available) of an essay I wrote for *Theater Annual* in 1943 and which sums up my "Defense of the Professional Reviewer." It is the best defense I can make for myself and the best method I can find of explaining why I regarded my long practice of this particular journalistic job as respectable, though only occasionally "significant," work.

If the man from Mars should ever actually make his long expected visit to our earth, nothing would puzzle him more than the continued toleration accorded to various occupations and institutions which seem to be universally condemned. Very few things—and almost no "good things"—have ever been said in favor of marriage or the professions of law and medicine. Yet century after century men continue to get married and doctors and lawyers are not only permitted to exist but actually are paid—rather well, at that—by the very people who have exposed their essentially pernicious activity.

The existence of professional critics of literature and the theater affords, as the Man from Mars would discover, a minor but very extreme example of the same paradox. In the English-speaking world, literary criticism has been a paying trade for about two hundred and fifty years; play reviewing for a somewhat shorter period—for though "the critics" begin to be contemptuously referred to toward the end of the Seventeenth Century, the reference then was to amateurs, and plays were not regularly reviewed in periodicals until about a century later. Yet, during all this time, few words have been said in favor of critics of any kind. As nearly everyone knows, Dryden first embodied in words one standard reproach against them when he defined a critic as something generated out of the corruption of a poet. The friends of Samuel Johnson were already questioning the right of any man who could not compose tragedy to presume to criticize one, and the play reviewer had no sooner appeared than playwright, producer and spectator agreed in referring to him in terms of bottomless contempt. Nevertheless, the play reviewer persisted and flourished . . .

Various charges are perenially leveled against him. Nowadays he is seldom accused of being open to bribery, but he is periodically denounced as too blasé to recognize merit when he sees it, too frivolous to appreciate anything except light entertainment, and so anxious to show off that he gladly sacrifices fairness to epigram. Yet these charges, grave as they are, are not the most fundamental. A good play reviewer might, in theory at least, avoid all of them. Fundamentally, most protesters imply a doubt that there is any such thing as a good critic of plays. His trade, so it seems to them, involves a double impertinence. He tells his betters (the authors and the actors) what they should do and he tells his equals (the spectators) what they should like. Why, they unite in asking, should they stand for it? If critics do not like a certain play and a certain production why don't the critics write a better one and act in it themselves?

Yet it is these same people who enable the critic to continue to draw pay for his impertinence. The managers send him tickets. The spectators buy the papers in which his "worthless opinions" are set forth. After an opening night, most of those concerned with the new production sit up until dawn waiting for the first editions, and if the "worthless opinion" happens to be favorable, it reappears within a few hours in the form of a gigantic photographic enlargement outside the lobby of the theater in which the play was produced.

One must begin by assuming that criticism, in the highest sense of the term, is bound to constitute, at best, only a small portion of all the writing which any professional critic publishes. If by such criticism we mean profound generalizations concerning works of permanent artistic value, then no man ever lived who was capable of producing it in sufficient quantity to earn himself a livelihood as a working journalist; and if such a hitherto unparalleled genius were to appear, he would not find in the course of the best theatrical seasons very many opportunities to exhibit his powers. If, even, within the limits of any drama critic's ability, he were to attempt to try each new offering by the highest artistic standards; if he were to resolve to view everything from the aspect of eternity; to call nothing good which was not absolutely so; then, masterpieces being rare as they are, it is obvious that he might pass his whole professional life without once deviating from an invariable judgment which would read "By the standards which Sophocles, Shakespeare and Molière have established—even by the standards set by Ibsen and Shaw—this play is a failure."

That he does nothing of the sort and that not one of his readers expects him to is evidence enough that a tacit understanding exists. "Good," "bad," even "great," are used relatively. The reviewer means, and is understood to mean, "relative to the standards set by the prevailing level of the dramatic and theatrical art." If he is a good reviewer, he occasionally reminds his readers and himself that this tacit understanding does exist and he makes some attempt to estimate just how low or how high the assumed standards are; but this is the material for an occasional essay, not something which needs to be or could be repeated every time an interesting drama or an amusing comedy makes its appearance . . .

To say this, is not, however, to imply that reviewing is merely irresponsible criticism. The so-called drama critic is, most of the time, a reviewer rather than a critic; and it is only as a reviewer that he can, as a rule, usefully employ his talents, however great they may be. The real justification for his existence lies in a proper understanding of the nature of reviewing rather than in any consideration of criticism in the more exalted and formal sense. That a reviewer may occasionally write such criticism is beside the point. Others may write it also, and at best the professional reviewer will not and cannot write it often enough to make it the activity for which his magazine or newspaper pays him a living wage. But he can and often does make of reviewing a useful and difficult art with aims and principles of its own. And it is as reviewer that he finds a public large enough to give him his important place on the staff of the publication which employs him.

What, then, is good reviewing and what is the task to

which a good reviewer sets himself? Extremists have sometimes maintained that good reviewing is merely good reporting. On occasion they have gone so far as to deny the reviewer the right to any opinions or judgments of his own and have urged him to limit himself to a detached account of what happens in the play plus a report on the reaction of the audience. That, of course, would be a preposterous program, but a new play *is* new, it *is* something which most of the reviewer's readers know nothing about when they begin to read his piece and that fact, by making it necessary for him to be a reporter among other things, establishes immediately one of the fundamental differences between the good review and the good critical essay. The latter normally assumes that the reader is familiar with the work about to be criticized, that he is in possession of all the obvious facts, and that the critic's judgments or interpretations can begin at the level where he is aware of insights not assumed to be necessarily shared by every ordinarily competent reader. The reviewer, on the other hand, can assume nothing of the sort. He cannot pass a convincing judgment nor undertake any sort of criticism, properly so called, until he has given the reader a working equivalent of the experience which is to be interpreted and judged. In all, he will have for his review a thousand, or fifteen hundred words at most and of these he will have available for any kind of criticism only those left over after he has told the reader what it is that he is criticizing.

Obviously the preliminary task is formidable. In a few hundred words the reviewer must manage to convey the effect of a play lasting two hours and a half. The reader will expect no less since he turns to the review first of all, not because he will accept without question the "yes" or "no" of the reviewer, but because he expects to judge for himself, on the basis of the account, whether or not the play is one which he wants to see. The reviewer can aim at no less, not only because he must give the reader what the reader expects, but also because, if the reader is to pass an intelligent judgment, he must be in possession of something which will take the place of a direct experience with the play being reviewed.

No mere summary of the plot or statement of the theme will do. A fair summary of *Hamlet* can, as Voltaire proved, make it seem like one of the most preposterous dramatic compositions ever offered any public. Not an account, but an equivalent, of the spectator's experience must be presented, and to do that the reviewer must practice, not reporting, but the art of re-creating in descriptive terms the effect of a narrative. That particular art is essentially the one used and abused by certain Nineteenth Century writers who undertook to present "the adventures of the soul among the masterpieces."

It has more recently fallen into disrepute as a method of criticism and has been described by T. S. Eliot, in his lofty way, as the result, not of a genuinely critical impulse, but of a "weak creative impulse." Perhaps Mr. Eliot is right. But however unacceptable as a method of criticism in the most exalted sense of the term, it is a *sine qua non* of really good reviewing since the reviewer, though not merely a reporter of the external circumstances of a new play and of its reception by the public, must nevertheless be first of all a reporter of aesthetic experiences. In so far as every such experience is personal and not identical with the experience of any other spectator, the reporter is also an interpreter and a champion of the justness of his own reactions. But only in so far as he is convincing, only in so far as he succeeds in making the reader assume that he would have reacted in substantially the same manner, will the reviewer either be accepted as a guide or become capable of rendering significant any genuinely critical observations which he may finally get around to making . . .

That the professional reviewer wields an enormous immediate and practical influence is plain enough from the growing tendency of managers to close, at once, any production which has received generally unfavorable notices. To what extent reviewers have influenced for good or ill the general development of playwriting during the last decade or so, it would be difficult to judge. Comparatively few have made themselves crusaders, as Shaw did in the Eighteen Nineties, and their influence has for the most part been hard to measure. None has evolved a *Hamburgische Dramaturgie* in the course of his reviewing; many have set an example of intelligent and enlightened commentary which has probably imperceptibly molded the taste of the average theater goer to a considerably greater extent than he is aware. And it ought to be remembered that the narrowly crusading critic, however important the function he may perform, is a bad reviewer—as Shaw frankly admitted himself to be in the preface to his *Dramatic Opinions and Essays.*

I prefer to rest the defense of my colleagues and of myself on our practice of the art of reviewing as I have attempted to describe that art. I doubt that we have actually done much to assist our leading playwrights to find themselves. On the other hand, our record has, I think, been pretty good so far as our ability to recognize and applaud important talents as they have appeared is concerned. And by giving the theatergoing public reviews which it found interesting, I think we have probably helped to find an audience for those playwrights whom we have not called into being and probably not greatly aided in the solution of their own artistic problems.

By the late Forties various influences had begun to converge upon me, all tending in the same direction. A time had come to make the most drastic change in my life since the day, some thirty-five years past, when I had said goodby to Knoxville.

The fact that I was beginning to feel that my interest in the theater had passed its crest had something to do with it. So too did my increasing interest in the country, not merely as an escape from the city but also for what positive pleasures it had to offer. But health was the decisive factor without which mere inertia would probably have persuaded me to continue in the way I had been going. Because other people's maladies are a very dull subject I shall say only the minimum necessary.

Ever since adolescence I had been afflicted with violent colds and before I had reached middle age they had got into the habit of turning into asthmatic attacks of such increasing seriousness that I was completely incapacitated two or three times every year for a period of a week or ten days. My allergist (and I boasted to friends that to be able to say "my allergist" was really more up to date and smart than "my psychoanalyst") finally said to me: "What we call infectional asthma is a kind for which there is no effective remedy. You will probably get worse as you get older. What you really ought to do is to live in Arizona. But I suppose that, like most of my patients, you will say 'I'd rather die here among my friends than bury myself there.' "

Happily I was able to reply: "On the contrary, to have a really good excuse for living in Arizona is just what I have been unconsciously waiting for. In fact, if I had not developed this affliction long before I knew anything about the Southwest I might suspect that my benevolent Id (or should it be Super-Ego?) had invented the asthma to provide me with an excuse."

This to him unexpected reaction is because twelve years before, in 1937, Marcelle and I had made the first of four automobile trips during four successive summers through New Mexico, Arizona, and Utah. If the war had not intervened, we should probably have continued them. Marcelle, who had first taken me unwillingly to Connecticut and seems on several important occasions to have known better than I did what would please me, was responsible for the first of the western expeditions. I consented to it only because, having taken up photography as a hobby, I thought I might see something to take a picture of. While I was doing a week-long series of special lectures at the Columbia Summer School she drove to Lamy, New Mexico, alone and I joined her there. No sooner were we speeding along the roller-coaster road which leads across the undulating desert towards Albuquerque than I felt a sudden lifting of the heart. It seemed almost as though I had lived there in some happier previous existence and was coming back home. I was like a fish returned to water or, more accurately perhaps, like some mammal returned to air. That I might actually make my home in some such region certainly did not occur to me then, but the seed was planted.

I suppose that the mere physical effect of the dry air had something to do with it. My physiology was changed and with it my spirits. After we had made several such trips Marcelle said to several of our friends: "You wouldn't know Joe out there. He is an entirely different person." And I thought rather unkind the usual response: "Isn't that nice!" But it was not all physiological. The strangeness was a strangeness which made an immediate appeal both aesthetically and intellectually. The austere beauty of the desert and desert mountains excited me as it does many, though assuredly not all, since I have known those whose first reaction was almost of terror and whose first exclamation was either, "How can I get out of here as quickly as possible," or, as I later heard a plane passenger exclaim as she looked out of the window, "Just hundreds and hundreds of miles of nothing at all."

Another reason for my interest was that the unfamiliarity of every shrub, tree, animal, and bird stimulated enormously my desire to learn more about the natural world. Still a third reason was probably that I had lost my taste for crowds. Thoreau struck a sympathetic chord in me when I read his comment on the New York of his quieter day. "The city is large enough now, and they intend it shall be larger still . . . When will the world learn that a million men are of no importance compared with *one* man."

Gertrude Stein remarked in one of the few of her sentences I have ever been able to understand: "In the United States there is more space where nobody is than where anybody is." And at the risk of alienating many readers I will add that the fact that this is becoming less and less conspicuously true is one of the things which distress me most in our current civilization. I do not think that the life of the hermit or even of the frontiersman is the best life. But as Aristotle pointed out, "Most people believe that a city must be large in order to be happy," and most people today not only continue in this error but compound it. They think that a city to be happy must be getting larger by leaps and bounds.

Since I was due my second Sabbatical leave in 1950-51 it is not surprising that, instead of reviving the African dream, we rented our Connecticut house for sixteen months, piled our car high with all that could be imposed upon it, and set out, not with any definite resting place in mind, but feeling like Adam and Eve:

The world was all before them, where to choose
Their place of rest, and Providence their guide.

We were already nearly sure that we would not return to New York for more than the eight months of another college year.

Bill Sloane gave me a letter to his sister-in-law who was the widow of General Leonard Wood's son and was living in the tiny village of La Luz, high in the hills above the White Sands in New Mexico, by then the famous rocket testing field. We were delighted with La Luz and thought of stopping right there but decided to look about a bit first. Traveling westward across southern Arizona we met a truck transporting an army barracks and learned that Fort Huachuca, in the mountains about a hundred miles east of Tucson, was being dismantled but that a few officers' houses would be left and could be rented. We drove up to the deserted Post, examined a few of the houses, but decided not to make a decision yet—which was fortunate since only a month later the army decided to reactivate the Post, replaced the barracks which had been sold as surplus, and ousted the few families which had rented the officers' houses.

Mrs. Wood, in her turn, had given us a letter to Mrs. Ada McCormick, a well-known Tucson citizen and sister of the painter, Waldo Pierce. She knew of a house on Ina Road, some ten miles north of the city and in a then sparsely inhabited region, which would be available for the summer. We snatched it at once because it was in the middle of precisely the kind of desert I had hoped to observe. Just before leaving New York I had agreed with Bill Sloane to do a book reporting the experiences of a newcomer whose innocence and ignorance might give a special tone to his discovery of the desert and desert life. I had also two weeks' work still to do on the introduction to a volume of selections from the letters of Thomas Gray. But as soon as that was finished I started to set down my earliest impression in the first chapter of what was to be called *The Desert Year* and was published a year and a half later.

Before fall came and we would be compelled to vacate the house on Ina Road we had met another prominent Tucson citizen, Mrs. Helen d'Autremont, who was known for innumerable kindnesses of various sorts and who offered us for the rest of our stay one of her two guest houses, both of which had in the past been temporarily occupied by various writers and artists ranging from E. E. Cummings to Hugh Lofting, the author of the enormously popular Dr. Doolittle books for children. During our stay there we had the pleasure of having as neighbors in the other cottage Elliott Carter and his wife, Helen. Elliott was already known as a promising composer but it was during this year that he wrote the string quartet which was to win the prize in an international contest and to clinch his reputation as perhaps the most talented of the American composers in an avant-garde style. We have seen Elliott and Helen only rarely since then but we still consider them very valued friends.

Before the sixteen months of the Sabbatical were over and we were obliged to return to Columbia, *The Desert Year* was finished and, what is more important, we knew that we would make a radical break with our past life. When I announced the decision to Marjorie Nicolson shortly after the new term had begun, she expressed polite dismay and suggested that I might spend alternate years at the University. But we realized that this would mean being settled nowhere, and if there were any lingering doubts they were dispelled when we both went down in midwinter with a severe case of 'flu complicated by a touch of pneumonia. It was evident that the New York climate was not for me, though Marcelle could no doubt have endured it with no more than the normally expected difficulties.

Most of our friends were amazed to the point of incredulity. "You don't mean that you are actually going to give up New York and all its opportunities to live 'way out there'?" "Why not?" "Well, for one thing it is so far away." And they were not convinced by my protest that they reminded me of the famous story of the headline in the London *Times:* "Storm Over the Channel; Continent Isolated." It all depends on your point of view. What is it you want to be close to? Neither Marcelle nor I have ever regretted for a moment the move. The ten years since we came to Tucson have been the most contented (and often the happiest) of our lives, and never since adolescence have I been physically so well.

Before I came I was already convinced that the natural as opposed to the wholly man-made world had become, for me at least, a necessary part of the context of a Good Life. A necessary *part* I say for I was never a romantic primitive, never doubted that Man, "placed on this isthmus of a middle state" needs both the nature of which he is a part and that world of human values and human culture of which, at most, no more than the beginnings are to be found outside man, or even outside civilized man. Just before we made the decision I wrote a series of essays (already quoted previously) setting forth this conviction and they were published as a volume, after we had definitely settled in Tucson, with the suggestive title *The Best of Two Worlds* (1953). In it I confessed that I had "met few men or women wholly country bred and completely without experience of life in cities, with whom I felt entirely at home." But I had already passed most of my mature life to date in cities and I felt that I knew too little of the other world.

I had traveled far since the days of my adolescence when merely to get to New York had been an ambition even stronger than that to learn something about English Literature. But the journey is a logical one. Thoreau himself, who is too often regarded as a simple primitivist, had said that "decayed literature makes the best soil." Or, to put the same thing in flat prose, it is a *return* to nature which is the most rewarding.

This paradox is as old as civilization itself for man had hardly built the first cities before he began to try to get away from them. In ancient Greece poets idealized the shepherd's life and in imperial Rome the literary cult of "the simple life" had already reached the point where satirists ridiculed it. In our modern world the engineer, the industrialist, and the builder of skyscrapers moves his family to a country house or the suburbs. He plants trees and cultivates a garden. He acquires animals as pets and perhaps he takes up bird watching—all of which reveal his unwillingness to let go of what in theory, perhaps, he no longer values. He may tell himself that he does these things only because they help him do next day a more efficient job in his serious occupation, but this is not the whole truth, and if he does do his work more efficiently that is a testimony to the refreshing health-giving effect of his brief contact with Nature.

The paradox of Man, who is part of nature yet can become what he is only by being also something unique, is so desperate that it never has been, perhaps never can be, resolved, and it is likely to lead those who ponder it from one foolish extreme to another. Wordsworth notwithstanding, Nature is quite capable of betraying the heart that loves her. But if she is not dependably the Kind Mother neither is she (as Tennyson was already calling her in pre-Darwinian days) always "red in tooth and claw." By our standards she is sometimes the one; sometimes the other. Her processes do not correspond exactly to any set of values we formulate. We must say of her only that she is what she is, sometimes what we wish her to be, sometimes repugnant to us. We both admire and are repelled. We co-operate and we resist. We dare not follow her blindly. But neither can we afford not to learn from her. She is magnificent and inscrutable. We are what Pope called us two centuries and a half ago, "The glory, jest and riddle of the world." We face back toward our primitive ancestors, perhaps even to the ape; we also look forward to we know not what. Ambiguous creatures that we are we can neither be satisfied with nature nor happy unless we achieve some compromise with her. And so, if I may be permitted to repeat, I felt that the time had come when I should take a closer look at that part of my universe which neither I nor my fellows had made. Surely the best place to do so would be one where she had not yet been wholly subdued to man's uses.

When the University term came to its end in the spring of 1952 Marcelle and I offered our Connecticut house for sale, packed up again, shipped by truck such of our belongings as we wished to preserve, and set out again. This time we knew where we were going because Mrs. d'Autremont had offered to let us have a modest tract of land not far from her own home where we were to build a modest house with an unobstructed view of the nine-thousand-foot Catalina mountains some ten miles away.

I think that our eastern friends, still incredulous, expected to see us soon back for good and, inevitably, when I have seen them since they have asked the same questions: "Don't you miss the theater, the University and all the rest of the stimulating life of New York?"

The simplest and the truest short answer is simply "No," though I should certainly add that if I do not too much miss my former life I am very glad indeed to have had it. Why I did not really miss the theater I have already explained: I had seen a great deal of it and I felt that it was paying diminishing returns. As for the academic world the situation is less simple. I certainly regret having lost (except for occasional letters and even less frequent and very brief visits East) the contacts with academic friends who gave me great pleasure. I have also had sporadic contacts with various universities which I shall later mention and I am very grateful to Columbia University for the opportunities which it gave me and proud of the fact that it thought enough of me to confer, after I had resigned my position, an honorary degree during the celebration of its bicentenary in 1954. I think that I can say both that I was a popular lecturer and that I often enjoyed lecturing—once I had launched myself into a discourse. But I am not, I am afraid, what is called "a born teacher." I dreaded the first weeks of every new term when I would have to establish a rapport with a new group and at the end of a session I was more often than not oppressed by a sense that I had not done as well as I should have.

One day as I was approaching the door of a lecture hall I met the late Burdette Kinne, a witty and unconventional teacher of elementary French in the College who had also taken on a section of the Freshman Humanities course. "You look depressed," he said. "Don't you look forward to this hour?" "No," I said, "I am afraid I don't." "Well," he replied, "that is something I can't understand. *I* never approach the door of a classroom without a lifting of the heart. Thank God, I say to myself, *I've got an audience.*"

The difference between us was not modesty on my part or lack of it on his. I would certainly not have written as much as I have if I, too, did not want an audience. But I think what I have always wanted was an audience of readers not of hearers, and that I am rather frightened of audiences that are present and visible. Applause at a distance is sweetest to me though I confess that I cannot read without embarrassment the explanation once offered by my old friend H. L. Mencken who accounted for the fact that writers stick to their painful profession by calling them vainer than most. "His overpowering impulse is to gyrate before his fellow men, flapping his wings and emitting defiant yells. This being forbidden by the police of all civilized countries, he takes it out by putting his yells on paper. Such is the thing called self-expression."

Another if minor reason for my determination to resign was my age, for I knew well enough that college professors often long outstay their welcome. A few years before I took the final step I had said one day to Mark Van Doren that I thought I would retire early. "Oh, I won't," he replied, "I'm going to stick until they throw me out." "But what are you going to do when the time comes that you can no longer conceal even from yourself the fact that your students think you a tiresome old fool?" He had a good reply. "It is a kind provision of nature," he said, "that such a time never comes." Fortunately or unfortunately this is very often true. But Mark, I should add, did not wait to be thrown out. In fact he was implored, almost desperately, to remain a few years longer than he did.

Drastic as I knew the break with my past life would be I had no intention of merely—in Professor Campbell's phrase—"presiding over a vacuum." I was running away from something, of course, but I firmly intended to run into something else, and as it turned out I found more than I had hoped for to say about what I did and saw, learned and thought, in the unfamiliar country I was trying to make my own.

Nevertheless this was not all I had come for. I hoped also, in Thoreau's incomparable phrase, "to meet myself face to face," to be compelled, indeed, to do so. In the busy life I had been leading it was too easy to think only of immediate tasks and to solve only immediate intellectual problems. I knew that *The Modern Temper* no longer summed up, as it once had, what I thought about the universe and man's place in it. But I did not know precisely what I did think. Perhaps I would now be able, not necessarily to reach final conclusions, but at least to bring up to date my hitherto somewhat unfocused ideas.

I did not believe then, and I do not believe now, that "a return to nature" would solve all the problems. Some of them are, to be sure, created by the complexity and artificiality of present-day society. Upon them the individual can turn his back and he can face what remains more directly than amid distractions. But Man is too much more than merely one among many other animals to be content with only what seems, superficially at least, to be Nature's values and methods. Samuel Johnson had written at the conclusion of the passage from *Rasselas* previously quoted: "Man surely has some latent sense for which this place affords no gratification; or he has some desires, distinct from sense, which must be satisfied, before he can be happy." Does this mean, as Johnson assumed, that there is some realm, some future life perhaps, which transcends nature and from which man is temporarily exiled? Or does it mean that this very universe we do inhabit is something more than what the modern scientists have found in it, that when we seem to be longing to transcend it we are simply refusing to recognize what we alone are capable of recognizing but which has, nevertheless, been struggling since the beginning of time to manifest itself clearly in us?

If this second alternative should be the true one then should we not seek for this something instead of either denying that it exists at all or insisting, after the Existentialist's fashion, that it is something which we have invented and thus, as it were, lifted ourselves by our own bootstraps? For myself I was already at least half convinced that since we are as "natural" as any other living creature, yet do have desires, values, and concepts which appear to be unique, then they cannot actually be such. Our minds like our bodies must have "evolved"; and to evolve means to grow as part of a continuity, not to be discontinuous with our origins. Fortunately, Hiram Haydn, then chief editor of the Bobbs-Merrill Company, had suggested independently that I might write some sort of "Modern Temper Twenty Years Later" and before Marcelle and I came back to Tuscon in the spring of 1952 I had this in mind as a major project to be undertaken at the same time as my investigation of external nature in the Southwest.

Before I was quite sure that I would make a definite break with the east I had accepted an invitation from Cornell University to deliver its series of five "Messenger Lectures" in the fall of 1952 and my first job on arriving back in Tucson was to write them. Then I flew to Ithaca, delivered the lectures, and got back to find the little house we were building well advanced. *"Modernism" in Modern Drama,* as published a little later by the Cornell Press, was not wholly irrelevant to the subject most on my mind since it dealt with the intellectual background of the leading modern playwrights and undertook to demonstrate that they, like so many modern writers, were leading us down a blind alley. Soon after we moved into our new home I sat down to begin a more general survey of my thoughts about that creature "placed on this isthmus of a middle state" and, because of his predicament, "the glory, jest and riddle of the world." The result was published in 1954 as *The Measure of Man.*

When, two years later, I was asked to write a brief preface to the paperback edition of *The Modern Temper* I first summarized more briefly than I did earlier in this book its thesis and then wrote: "More than a quarter of a century later I find myself asking three questions: (1) Do educated people continue to believe that science has exposed as delusions those convictions and standards upon which Western civilization was founded? (2) Is the ultimate cause of the catastrophe with which that civilization is threatened this loss of faith in humanity itself? (3) Is it really true, as I once believed, that there is no escaping the scientific demonstration that religion, morality, and the human being's power to make free choices are all merely figments of the imagination?

To the first two of these questions the answer still seems to me to be "Yes." Despite the so-called revival of popular religion which amounts to little more than the acceptance of the church as a social institution; despite also a perhaps increasingly strong undercurrent of pyschological and sociological protest against determinism and relativism, the most prevalent educated opinion is still that men are animals and that animals are machines. One kind of intellectual may respond to this conviction by embracing the creed of atheistical Existentialism which is the tragic solution proposed in *The Modern Temper.* A larger group turns optimistically toward experimental psychology, the techniques for sociological conditioning, and the methods of indoctrination developed by the manipulators of the media of mass communication, and hopes from them for the creation of a

Robot Utopia whose well-adjusted citizens will have comfortably forgotten that their forefathers believed themselves to be Men.

But neither the one group nor the other rejects the assumption that Western man, traditionally endowed with reason, will, and a valid sense of value, is an exploded myth. And because this conviction still prevails among educated men I still believe it true that it poses the most serious of all threats to our civilization and is, indeed, the ultimate source of most of our specific dilemmas—as it is, for instance of our dilemma in the face of communism which embodies the really logical conclusion to be drawn from the premises which so many nominally anticommunists share with their formal opponents.

The modern temper itself has developed somewhat, especially in the direction of that attempted "adjustment" to dismal assumptions which makes Social Engineering rather than Existentialist resignation the dominant religion of today. But the description which I gave of the origins of this temper, and the consequences likely to follow from it, seem to me as valid as they ever were. It is only my own attitude toward it which is different. What I described and shared in I still describe but I no longer accept it. Hence the situation which *The Modern Temper* presents as hopeless does not now seem to me entirely so, though by the diagnosis I will still stand.

How I arrived at this conclusion in writing *The Measure of Man* is something which can hardly be described in a few words, but its leading ideas are so important a part of myself that an autobiography would be very incomplete if it did not indicate briefly what their trend is. I began the discussion with that Loss of Confidence which has made our age so desperately uncertain and afraid despite the fact that it seems to be the richest and most powerful that has ever existed. If, I argued, this is to be attributed to the physical dangers we are exposed to, the fact remains nevertheless that our own activities have created them and that we doubt our ability to control those natural forces which it is, paradoxically, our great boast to have "conquered" and controlled.

The most important confidence we have lost is in man himself as more than the helpless victim of circumstance. The three most influential thinkers of the century just past were Darwin, Marx, and Freud, all three of whom (at least as popularly interpreted) rob man of his self-respect—the first by making him the accidental result of blind accident, the other two by calling him so little the captain of his soul that all his acts, choices, preferences, and thoughts are simply the product of either "the dialectic of matter" or the psychological accidents, influences, and traumas to which he has been subject. Hence he is neither capable of real choice nor responsible for the choices he seems to make. Therefore it is useless to urge him to think or to resolve. The best that can be hoped for is the development of those "behavioral sciences" by means of which he can be manipulated and "conditioned" into "socially useful" (there are no "true" or "right") patterns of behavior.

That there is a solid core of partial truth in these dismal theories I could not deny. We shall never again describe ourselves as a creature "how like a god." But are we *merely* machines? We are lost, I said, unless we can believe in what I called a Minimal Man, defined as a creature endowed with the following characteristics: (1) the capacity to be at least sometimes "a thinking animal" who can, on occasion, reason rather than merely rationalize; (2) the ability sometimes to exercise some sort of will and choice which enables him on these occasions to resist conditions, traumas, and "the dialectic of matter"; (3)

the power of making value judgments which are not always, inevitably, and no more than, a rationalization of the *mores* of his society. Or, to sum it all up, a man who cannot think as well as "react" is not a man at all.

Only extremists—such as, for example, the Johns Hopkins physicist, George Gamow, and the Harvard psychologist, B. F. Skinner—go out of their way to deny categorically the reality of even a Minimal Man. But they are less influential than the psychologists, the sociologists, the economists, and the criminologists who tend to disregard the existence of the Minimal Man; who assume, if they do not actually declare, that only the mechanical, the predictable, and therefore the manipulatable man plays a large enough part in making a society or a civilization to be considered for practical purposes. It is they who convince him that he himself is primarily a thing rather than a person; that he is the product of his society, and the victim of his wrongs; that he should be "conditioned" or "adjusted" rather than educated or taught to think and to choose.

But how sound and how complete is the biologist's evidence that we are "explained" in merely mechanical and chemical terms? What I called "The Stubborn Fact of Consciousness" remains; and it is unfortunate that in the great Nineteenth Century debate between the mechanists and their opponents the latter should have rested their case upon the existence of a "soul." "The soul" is indeed a vague conception and the reality of the thing to which it refers cannot be demonstrated. But consciousness is the most self-evident of all facts and neither any machine nor any mere chemical process can be shown to possess it. The physiologists are very fond of comparing the network of our cerebral nerves with a telephone system but they overlook the significant fact that a telephone system does not function *until someone talks over it.* The brain does not create thought (Sir Julian Huxley has recently pointed out this fact); it is an instrument which thought finds useful. Biologists have sometimes referred to the origin of life as "an improbable chemical accident." But is not the assumption of an "improbable chemical accident" which results ultimately in something capable of discussing the nature of "improbable chemical accidents" a staggering one? Is it not indeed preposterous? Is it not far easier to believe that thought in some potential form must be as primary as matter itself?

The orthodox "sciences of man" are actually far behind the times. They are based upon an analogy with Newtonian physics in which every atom in the universe behaves like every other atom, is therefore determined and at least theoretically predictable. But every present-day physicist knows that Newton's hypothesis is demonstrably false. His "laws" are only statistically true. Individual atoms are not predictable; and to assume that so highly organized a creature as man is more completely determined and predictable than dead matter is absurd. It may possibly be, so I went on to suggest, that the never yet defined difference between living and dead matter may be something like this: Dead matter is matter organized in such a way that the unpredictability of the individual particles is statistically canceled out so that Newtonian physics "works" in connection with every large aggregate. But living matter *may* be matter so organized that the individuality of the component atoms is pooled and, hence, instead of being canceled out, is cumulative. If this should be true, then that minimal but basic unpredictability of the living creature which is most conspicuously evident in man constitutes, in fact, the reality behind the concept of free will. Granted this, then the Minimal Man is something to be reckoned with. He is at least as mysterious as uranium. If matter can, as is now universally admitted, cease to be matter and become energy, why should it not also become thought?

A famous Nineteenth Century scientist once said that he did not believe in "the soul" because he could not find it in his test tube. But surely, had the soul existed, a test tube would be the last place where one would be likely to discover it, and the fallacy of that chemist's argument runs through most Nineteenth Century science. Naturally it found only what its methods were capable of detecting and its faulty logic ran like this: "What my methods cannot investigate is not science; what science cannot investigate is not worth thinking about; what is not worth thinking about does not exist." It convinced the world simply because it dealt so successfully with what it could deal with.

Justice Oliver Wendell Holmes once declared that science teaches us a great deal about things that are not really very important; philosophy a very little about things that are of very great importance. This is indeed a very unfortunate fact, but not so unfortunate as the further fact that we forget the second half of Holmes' statement. Philosophy tends to become "logical positivism" which is only a rationalization of scientific methods and dismisses as "meaningless" whatever questions science cannot seem to answer or promise to answer. Dazzled by science's success, even imaginative literature tends to become sociology and psychology instead of dealing with the intangibles which have, in the past, been its chief concern.

Since man first began to think conceptually he has carried on with his fellows or with himself a dialogue which concerned itself with the great questions arising out of the fact that he had indeed become Man; that he has seemingly unique desires, needs, hopes, and fears. He invented what no other creature seemed capable of, namely Ethics, Aesthetics, and the other branches of metaphysics. He asked: "What is Justice?" "What is Beauty?" "What is The Good Life?" And though he never reached final answers, though he arrived at many different and often incompatible ones, he continued to ask; and it was the asking which made him always recognizable as that very very special animal called a human being.

Today this dialogue which has continued so long is faltering—even among philosophers and artists. We have been insistently taught that since neither philosophy nor art has ever reached any sure conviction or even any general agreement, and since we seem to be no nearer than we were two thousand years ago to answers, then we should stop asking for them. We should, we are told, turn even more exclusively to that *contriving* at which we have been so successful, to that search for means and that neglect of ends which is responsible for the technological wonders of our civilization. We are urged, therefore, to rest content with being, not *Homo sapiens,* or man the thinker, but merely *Homo faber,* or man the maker.

Because I had accepted all this, less happily but hardly less completely than so many of my intellectual contemporaries, I wrote *The Modern Temper*. Because I no longer accepted it, I hoped now to refute myself. Man, I said, is not a mere machine explicable in terms of Newtonian physics and Nineteenth Century chemistry though psychologists, sociologists, and even many writers of imaginative literature have joined the old-fashioned scientists in trying to persuade us that he is. The Minimal Man they disregard is the most important man, and the characteristics which make him such might, however slowly, become more pronounced and more effective than they are if that importance were recognized. But if, on the other hand, the dialogue not only falters but ceases, if the existence of the Minimal Man is forgotten by intellectuals and society is more and more deliberately organized around the concept of man as less than minimal, then he may in the end become what he is taken to be. This may be our last chance. If we do not resolve now to think rather than merely contrive, and to will rather than merely to submit ourselves to "the logic of evolving technology," we may never think again.

The Measure of Man was published in 1954 and given the National Book Award for Non-Fiction for that year. There were some, especially among those who had accepted some specific religious faith, who complained that I did not "go far enough." For instance, a very sympathetic review in the Jesuit *America* remarked that the author could not see why, having gone so far, I could not take what was to him the logical next step into Roman Catholicism. But I had gone as far as I could go and though I have elaborated in other books some of the ideas merely suggested in *The Measure of Man* it is as far as I have been able to go. I doubt that I shall ever be able to go further.

Even this has however carried me a long way from where I was in *The Modern Temper,* and I find that what I am able to believe and suspect about man and the universe is something sufficient to live by. At least I have lived by it for some years now more contentedly than I had been able to live before.

15

▲
▲▲▲

When I had returned from Cornell to settle down in our new house in Tucson and to formulate what I could of my own more modern temper I said to Marcelle: "Well, I don't suppose I shall ever cross the Mississippi again."

What I meant was partly that, at the moment, I felt no compelling desire to do so but even more that I was not sure I would ever be able to afford such a trip. Never previously had I attempted to earn my living exclusively —or even chiefly—by free-lance writing and it did not seem that it would be easy. As it turned out, however, I have crossed the river a good many times during the nine years just past and I found that I could sell for modest sums as much as I was able to write—books, reviews, and essays—to half a dozen or more magazines including most recently—and somewhat to my surprise—the *Satur-*

day Evening Post ("Adventures of the Mind" series) and *Life* Magazine (an introductory essay for its special Nature Issue). I have also been invited more often than I could accept to give individual lectures or series of lectures at various colleges, including an endowed course of five at Stanford. Hiram Haydn, editor of *The American Scholar,* asked me to take over the department which Irwin Edman had conducted brilliantly for a number of years and I accepted gladly, changing the title to "If You Don't Mind My Saying So . . ." This series has continued since the first issue of 1955 and I have found very agreeable the opportunity to write what I happened to think about any subject whatever with the advance assurance that an intelligent audience was at least potential.

Looking back upon these and many other activities it seems that I must have led a very busy life, but I almost never felt (as for many years I had in New York) that I was pressed or harassed. Better health than I had enjoyed for many years had a good deal to do with this. So did the absence of routine interferences. I fell quickly into the habit of going to my desk for a few hours every morning, then spending the afternoon either reading or, very often, exploring the near-by country. Though never extremely gregarious I also soon became one of a little circle of congenial friends and I seemed, all in all, to have happened into what was for me an almost ideal way of life.

Opportunities, great and small, turned up one after another. An important one rose out of the invitation to be one of the original trustees when the Arizona-Sonora Desert Museum was established by the Pack Foundation in 1952. Hence, I had the pleasure of seeing, and to some extent participating in, its growth from small beginnings to its present status as an internationally known institution nearly unique in its aim to exhibit as completely as possible, and in a beautiful natural setting some 15 miles from Tucson in the middle of beautiful desert country, the flora and fauna of that Sonoran Desert which extends from southern Arizona into northern Mexico. When William H. Carr, its founder-director, resigned and was succeeded by William H. Woodin, the latter and his wife Ann became two of our closest friends.

At the time when I wrote the first of my Connecticut "nature books" I had thought of myself as simply a writer of familiar essays who was, for the moment, finding his subjects in country life. I would still not think of pretending to be more than an amateur so far as the biological sciences are concerned. But publishers and reviewers were presently referring to me as "a naturalist" and I have let that pass since the term is a broad one and need not mean more than "one who is deeply interested in the natural world." In one published *vita* I said that the only claim I would make was this: "I probably know more about plants than any other drama critic and more about the theater than any botanist." That, I am afraid, the ill-disposed may call the perfect description of a dilettante.

The most recent of the major opportunities which have unexpectedly presented themselves arose when I happened to meet Mr. Kenneth Bechtel, an important man of affairs in San Francisco. Almost by accident we discovered together Baja California, the primitive Mexican peninsula which stretches eight hundred miles south of the United States border on the Pacific side and in so doing encloses the Gulf of California between the Mexican mainland and its own narrow tongue of land. A ruggedly beautiful but almost roadless area of desert and desert mountains bordered by innumerable but empty beaches, it consists mostly of an extension of the same Sonoran desert which I had explored persistently elsewhere. But it exhibits also many unique features in the flora and fauna, and since February 1958 I have made fifteen separate trips—expeditions some of them might almost be called—mostly in the company of Mr. Bechtel and involving transport by airplane, yacht, landing barges, four-wheel-drive vehicles, and small boats, to say nothing of burros. For a professional writer the result was inevitable: a book called *The Forgotten Peninsula,* published in 1961.

This account of travels in Baja California may or may not be the last of my "nature books" but it is at least the latest, and such books have absorbed more of my time, effort, and attention since 1950 than any other activity.

All of them have been, in varying degrees, travel books and descriptive accounts of unusual natural phenomena somewhat belletristic in tone. They have also circled around, even when they did not directly discuss, the large questions provoked by an effort to understand nature's far from simple plan and man's ambiguous relation to the universe as nature makes and controls it. They have dealt with what we know and do not know as well as with the pleasures to be had in close contact with many of the lesser living creatures. They have also dealt with the problem we face when we realize that man, the most efficient predator, and the only creature capable of upsetting the established order and balance of nature, is rapidly exploiting the whole earth so exclusively for his own benefit that it is easy to see not very far ahead the possibility that he will be almost alone in a world he himself has made. In the background, even when not explicit, has been the conviction that since man has become, for the first time in history, capable of cutting himself off from his deepest roots he should think twice before he does so.

To some this is mere sentimentality at worst, at best a failure to realize that since man is "the highest" of living things he has a right, perhaps even a duty, to multiply his own species to a point where he occupies or uses the whole earth, even though that must mean the elimination of every other plant or animal which does not contribute directly to his support. I have tried to present a rational as well as emotional basis for believing that such convictions are so unwise that they may lead us to destruction, perhaps a physical destruction, perhaps only an intellectual and spiritual one.

Until very recently nature has been part of the context of man's life. What will he become if that context has ceased to exist?

For me it all began, I think, by my recognizing in myself an emotion at first not even partially rationalized. I had simply discovered that in Redding, Connecticut, I found something more than merely a relief from the pressures of city life; that there was something very positive in a consoling, indeed a quasi-mystical sense, of being a part of something larger than myself or my society. I took pleasure in knowing that living things, in various forms both like and unlike me, were sharing the world with me. Sentimental though many would call it, I found myself thrilled by even the recurring phenomena of the seasons, so that in the last chapter of *The Twelve Seasons* I stated a conviction, new to me, though it has been stated many times in one way or another by those who found it true for them:

> From another year which I hope will be based in the country—if not, alas, spent continuously there—I promise myself many advantages. But none of them is more obvious or more inclusive than the privilege of being permitted to be continuously aware that I am indeed alive—for that is a fact which the city makes most people forget, and one which

can be fully appreciated only by those whose own souls feel the ebb and flow of vital tides, who build their mansion on an inlet of the sea, not on some landlocked harbor which nowhere communicates with any deeper and vaster body. Only those within whose consciousness the suns rise and set, the leaves burgeon and wither, can be said to be aware of what living is.

Such a conviction had set me to looking more closely both inside and outside myself as I walked the mild Connecticut countryside and hoped that I might be able someday to say that, like Thoreau, I had traveled extensively in Redding—which was just as rich in its own way as Concord. It had set me also to reading technical books of biology and natural history as well as the great nature writers of the past. One result was that when I came to write the second of the Connecticut nature books, *The Best of Two Worlds,* I was able to expand a remark made in the first to a spring peeper ("we are all in this together") into an essay, half rational, half mystical, which I called "The Colloid and the Crystal" and which has, I think, been more often included in anthologies than any of the other chapters in either of these two books.

I had happened to see one winter morning my Christmas Cactus in full bloom just in front of a windowpane completely covered with a great frost flower formed during the night. Nothing, I said to myself, could be more beautiful in its own way than that frost flower which seems, moreover, to imitate the pattern of fronds and leaves. But it is not an imitation because it is far older, and for all the superficial similarity of form no two things could be more different. To the physicist and the chemist one is a crystal, the other a colloid or jelly. And in those two simple words is implied the greatest of mysteries, since the crystal never lives while protoplasm, still confessedly not understood by even the most advanced biochemist, is the jellylike basis of all life.

What, I asked, is the most important difference between them? Is it not that the frost flower has been precisely what it is for longer than the mind can conceive and will go on being precisely that wherever and for as long as there is moisture and a temperature that drops below the freezing point? It obeys laws, always in the same way. It cannot change, it cannot resist.

> Life is rebellious and anarchical, always testing the supposed immutability of the rules which the non-living changelessly accepts. Because the snowflake goes on doing as it was told, its story up to the end of time was finished when it first assumed the form which it has kept ever since. But the story of every living thing is still in the telling. It may hope and it may try. Moreover, though it may succeed or fail, it will certainly change. No form of frost flower ever became extinct. Such, if you like, is its glory. But such also is the fact that makes it alien. It may melt but it cannot die.
>
> Like the star, the snowflake seems to declare the glory of God, while the promise of the amoeba, given only perhaps to itself, seems contemptible. But its jelly holds, nevertheless, not only its promise but ours also, while the snowflake represents some achievement which we cannot possibly share. After the passage of billions of years, one can see and be aware of the other, but the relationship can never be reciprocal. Even after these billions of years no aggregate of colloids can be as beautiful as the crystal always was, but it can know, as the crystal cannot, what Beauty is.

Any pantheistic religion must have some sense of the oneness of man with the rest of the universe or at least with the animate part of it, but the Hebrew-Christian tradition is strong against such a sense. God is outside nature, man belongs only to Him, and, as I discovered in my reading, those late renaissance Christians who re-introduced into the modern consciousness a sense of oneness brought it in again by, as it were, a back door. Nature is not God but it is God's creation and, as the Seventeenth Century English biologist, John Ray, argued, it is our duty to admire the "wonders of God's creation" because we are the only part of it capable of appreciating them. For a time these wonders became the chief support of theism against atheism until Darwin, with one book, seemed to brush it away. Thus we were thrown back again upon some kind of pantheism as the only alternative to a concern with the human alone.

Presently I came across a simple statement by the American entomologist, William Morton Wheeler, which seemed to me to sum up so neatly what I had come to feel that I must quote it here even though I have quoted it elsewhere more than once:

> Why animals and plants are as they are we shall never know; of how they came to be what they are, our knowledge will always be extremely fragmentary; but that organisms *are* as they are, that apart from members of our own species they are our only companions in an infinite and unsympathetic waste of electrons, planets, nebulae and stars, is a perennial joy and consolation.

Modern biology has increasingly focused its attention on that "how" of which our knowledge will always be extremely fragmentary; increasingly it has tended also to shrug off the "why" as a mere improbable chemical accident, and to dismiss as mere sentimentalism the perennial joy and consolation. Despite some exceptions, like that of Wheeler himself who was too formidable a technical scientist to be scorned, the joy and consolation have fled for refuge to old-fashioned natural history (as distinguished from biology) and to those "nature writers" of whom I aspired to be one.

We are again hearing more about Conservation than at any time since Theodore Roosevelt made it an issue, but as I have tried to point out, especially in a chapter of *The Voice of the Desert,* there is no adequate motive for any conservation which means more than efficient exploitation except in the feeling that our fellow creatures are indeed a consolation.

That other living things are fellow creatures in ways not always recognized was, I suppose, the chief thesis of the book I called *The Great Chain of Life* (1956). When Darwin became the first to insist without equivocation that man is an animal, most of his contemporaries felt that he had flung an insult into their faces. He had called them "beastly" and he had added another insult to that which the word implied by making the beast a mere machine. But what even some biologists are now beginning to recognize is that the contrast between what is animal and what is human is not so absolute as has sometimes been suppposed. All the so-called "higher" faculties of man have indeed "evolved"; and most of them are shared to some extent by "lower" creatures. As we move from the most primitive to the most complex, what we find them achieving is not merely better means of surviving. After all, some of the most elementary have survived many millions of years longer than some of the more advanced and may quite possibly survive longer than man himself. An insect is a more efficient parent than a cat; its blind instinct works better; and what the bird or the mammal has achieved is not a better chance to survive as a species but a more intense consciousness in which something like love goes along with blind instinct.

"How right was Darwin?" I asked, and I answered: "Only partly." Natural selection, which operates only to perpetuate that which has survival value, can account for much. But it cannot account for the intensification of consciousness. If nature has a tendency, if she "wants" anything, it is not merely to survive. It is to realize more completely the potentialities of protoplasm. Of the "why" we may, as Wheeler said, be always ignorant and of the "how" we may never know more than a very little. But the evolutionist himself has spread before us a story from which it seems to me impossible not to draw the conclusion that there is some drive toward "the higher," not merely toward that which has the best chance of survival.

But if man is the "highest" animal yet to appear, then —it may be asked—is there anything to be gained by preserving indefinitely the links in the chain? Are all other creatures "lower" and therefore to be regarded as merely something which has fulfilled its function? If so, then is the only reason for preserving them that we can use them as objects of curiosity, perhaps learn something useful from them about our own physiology, or even get from them some consolation for what would otherwise be our loneliness amid "an infinite and unsympathetic waste of electrons, nebulae and stars"?

There is, so it seemed to me, also something else. In our rise to our human state we have lost something despite all that we have gained by becoming so largely intellectual, so persistently given to the questions "why" and "for what purpose." We often call our lives "a rat race"; but did any rat ever think of his own existence in such terms?

Is it a merely sentimental delusion, a "pathetic fallacy," to think that one sees in the animal a capacity for Joy which man himself is tending to lose? I do not think it is. We have invented exercise, recreation, pleasure, amusement, and the rest. To "have fun" is a desire often expressed by those who live in this age of anxiety. Most of us have experienced the desire and most of us have at times actually "had fun." But recreation, pleasure, amusement, fun, and all the rest are poor substitutes for Joy; and Joy, so I at least am convinced, has its roots in something from which civilization tends to cut us off.

Are some at least of the animals capable of teaching us this lesson of Joy? Some biologists deny categorically that they feel it. But by no means all and by no means the best. If I listen to a cardinal singing outside my window as I write I am convinced. The gift for real happiness or joy is not always proportionate to intelligence as we understand it, even among the animals. As Professor N. J. Berrill has put it: "To be a bird is to be alive more intensely than any other living creature, man included. Birds have hotter blood, brighter colors, stronger emotions . . . They are not very intelligent . . . but they live in a world that is always the present, mostly full of joy." Similarly Sir Julian Huxley, certainly no mere sentimental "nature lover," wrote after watching in Louisiana the love play of herons who, with loud cries of ecstasy, twine their necks into a lover's knot: "Of this I can only say that it seemed to bring such a pitch of emotion that I could have wished to be a heron that I might experience it."

This does not mean that Sir Julian would desire, any more than I would, to be *permanently* a bird. Perhaps some capacity for joy has been, must be, and should be, sacrificed to other capacities. But some awareness of the world outside of man, some willingness to risk the contemptuous epithet "nature lover" must exist if one is to experience the happiness and solace which some of us find in an awareness of nature, and in our love for those of her manifestations where the sacrifice of some of the capacity for joy in the interest of a capacity to think has not been very insistently demanded.

In the epilogue to *The Great Chain of Life* I wrote:

> Those who have never found for themselves either joy or solace in the teeming busy life which still animates those portions of the earth man has not entirely pre-empted for his own use might best be advised to begin by looking, not for the joy they can *get* but for the joy *that is there*. And perhaps when they have become aware of joy in other creatures they will *get* by sharing it.

Whether or not I shall write any more books after the present one I do not know but of the two just previous to it I have mentioned one only in passing and the other not at all. *Human Nature and the Human Condition* (1959) was in some sense a continuation of *The Measure of Man; The Forgotten Peninsula* was built around an account of the thirteen journeys I had made into Baja California, and *The Grand Canyon* came from the fascination that region exerted.

This might suggest that the latter two are unrelated to the first, but in my own mind at least they are not. One is, to be sure, part travel book, part natural history, and it stresses strongly the contrast between our country and a land where, despite a history of European occupation longer than that of any part of the United States, man has changed very little the natural world which he found there. But it also converges toward a last chapter which contrasts the painfully low "standard of living" endured and sometimes seemingly enjoyed by its few inhabitants, with that "affluent society" just north of the border. The intention was not, I hasten to add, to argue that this existence on the edge of destitution is a Good Life; though I could not but ponder the casual remark made to me by a half-Mexican, half-English son of a ship-jumping sailor who had been born and spent most of his life in a minuscule village on the desert sea coast. "I have two brothers," he said in his rather good broken English, "who live in the United States and are always urging me to come there; but I would rather stay here where I don't have to work."

Part of the intention of the two travel books might have been suggested if I had taken as motto for both a sentence from the first chapter of *Walden:* "I would fain say something, not so much concerning the Chinese and Sandwich Islanders as you who read these pages, . . . something about your condition, especially your outward condition or circumstances in this world, in this town, what it is, whether it is necessary that it be as bad as it is, whether it cannot be improved as well as not."

It happened that I had published all three books before I read *The Affluent Society,* that able and much discussed work by John K. Galbraith. Nevertheless, the three are parallel in some minor respects though it seemed to me that what I had to say about both our own society and that of Baja California was also a critique of Galbraith's thesis. That too much of our affluence is used merely to create more of the same rather than for truly human purposes is something which I very firmly believe. But to me—though apparently not to him—it seems that the deepest malady of our society is not fundamentally economic, or at least not to be cured by the merely economic means Galbraith suggests. At bottom it is our inability to define the Good Life in any terms except those of affluence—no matter how nearly universally that affluence may be spread. Even if *everybody* has bread (and cake besides) it still remains true that it is not by bread and cake alone that a Good Life is lead.

To this Galbraith has, of course, at least an implied answer. Spend enough of our wealth on education and from an educated population a valid concept of the Good Life will emerge. But we already "school"—if we do not educate—more extensively and more expensively than any society before ours; yet I cannot see that the schooling is effective except with a small minority. The high school, even the college, graduate seems still to think that after he has two cars in the garage and in the living room an "entertainment center" consisting of radio (F.M. and A.M.), television, and a phonograph (three speeds and sometimes even four), there is nothing he needs to complete his happiness except another TV set for the bedroom and perhaps a tape recorder.

Moreover this must continue to be so for as long as we equate going to school with getting an education, and cannot define education in any reasonable sense. If we call it "life adjustment" that means nothing unless you ask first "adjustment to what kind of life"—or rather it really means adjustment to precisely the kind of life and the idea of the good life already prevailing. Unless education to some extent maladjusts the educated man to life as it is lead, it can neither improve anything nor even change anything.

Yet we cannot define education because we do not (as has been said so often that the phrase has almost ceased to mean anything) "have any standards." The phrase is actually far from meaningless. It means that we have lost faith in even the possibility of such standards and must continue to be without them so long as we continue to disregard the reality of even that Minimal Man who, by reason, instinct, or some mysterious capacity, can arrive at the simple conclusion that some things are better than others, even though they are not at the moment so considered by most members of a given society.

In place of a genuine standard we have put nothing except majority opinion, or the beliefs and desires of the average man. We take polls and compile statistics. We equate the "normal" with the "average" and remember just enough of the true meaning of the first of these terms ("that by which a thing is to be judged") to conclude that "the average" is indeed "that by which a thing should be judged." Hence men, institutions, and society are judged, not by what they might or ought to be, but simply by what, on the average, they are. What we ought to want, value, and do is simply what the majority *does* want, value, and do.

Another phenomenon which Galbraith does not stress, although it seems to me to be another of the unfortunate consequences of thinking only in terms of general "affluence," is this: Outside our relatively few remaining geographical areas of poverty and outside what he calls the victims of "case poverty," that is to say individuals in prosperous areas who are destitute because of illness, misfortune, or simply lack of average ability, there is another and important class which is so far from affluent as to be often in desperate straits. To see a struggle against the limitations of a desperately "low standard of living" look at the young student or the artist, look at even many of those not young who are engaged in pursuits which create little wealth for anybody and hence pay little to those who engage in them.

The plumber who makes more than the professor is no longer merely a joke. He is one of the characteristic phenomena of our times. It is relatively easy with a minimum of ability and industry to make what is called, even in our affluent society, "a decent living" at most of the semiskilled trades. But it is increasingly difficult for the intellectual or artistic worker to rise to the economic level of the mechanic who repairs the second-hand automobile which the intellectual must have if he is to go back and forth to his place of employment. Leisure as well as sufficiency tends to become the exclusive privilege of the two large "superior classes," namely the executive and the practitioner of some mechanical trade. In fact leisure is coming to be something which belongs to the latter alone since he can stop at the end of his seven-hour day (soon to be further reduced) and hand his task over to some member of another shift, while the executive or the technical expert cannot turn over the work he has been doing to someone else. We may soon have a society in which only "the worker" has leisure or any sort of margin to his life. Even should the latter turn to something more than mere "entertainment" to fill up his leisure—and he doesn't show much disposition to do so—it would still be true that those who could put such spare time to the best uses have the least of it.

It was my thesis in *Human Nature and the Human Condition* that none of the unfortunate aspects of that condition which prevails today can be changed until we again accept some concept of the normal or desirable as distinct from what prevails or from what the majority wants, seems to want, or has been persuaded to think that it wants.

But where, I will be asked, can such a standard be found? We no longer believe in either the revealed Will of God or the Inner Voice. Neither do we believe in that old delusion "right reason." God, even if you admit that he may exist, has made no dependable revelation. The inner voice, so we are told, is merely what social or psychological conditioning has made it. Right reason is merely the current rationalization of the traditions of our particular culture. Nothing is good or bad, desirable or undesirable, except in relation to that culture.

To this I reply that man is not completely without a shape and a tendency of his own; that there is a norm in his persisting efforts and values; in a word, a basic human nature despite the overemphasized extent to which "cultures vary." Actually the history of those cultures themselves shows the extent to which man may succeed or fail as he lives in accord with his nature. What is nearly unique in our society is the almost universal tendency to deny just this; to stop asking "what is man for," "what is he most fitted to do," what is "normal" in the real sense that "normal" behavior is behavior which brings happiness and contentment.

That we are not leading such a "normal" life is sufficiently proved by the fact that though we, more than any other people, seem able to get what we think we want and do what we think we want to do, we nevertheless are conspicuously unhappy, dissatisfied, and anxious. Let us try again to ask what is "normal" by the standards of our own fundamental nature.

Science can tell us how to do more and more things; it cannot tell us what ought to be done. Yet that is no reason for refusing to seek somewhere some basis for an "ought" since without it we become victims of all sorts of uncriticized enterprises.

Difficult as the inquiry into the question "what is normal for man" may be, full of pitfalls as past history shows it, we must make it. And even the most casual consideration of the question seems to me to provide at least a few very general answers.

One is that most men at most times—all happy men I believe—have assumed (as we tend to deny) that Good and Evil, Justice and Injustice, the "higher" and the "lower" are, however difficult to define, realities beyond merely prevailing custom. Human nature thus makes us inveterately and "normally" makers of value judgments. A second constant is that human nature does not incline us to be pure materialists. Men have sought God as the ancient Hebrews did, or, like the Greeks, beauty and wisdom. Below these levels they have sometimes put the highest value on glory, courage, personal prowess, or military success and have believed that comfort as well as security were well sacrificed for them. Even the belief, in some savage societies, that a large collection of human heads is the thing most to be desired testifies to the fact that to believe something more worth having than material wealth is as nearly universal as the belief that some things are good and some bad. A society which, like ours, defines the Good Life as identical with the High Standard of Living is running counter to a fundamental characteristic of the nature of man.

We talk about conquering nature, planning society, even of "intervening in the process of evolution." But we should remember the exclamation of Archimedes, "Give me a fulcrum for my lever and I can move the earth," and what we should note most carefully is the fact that a fulcrum must lie outside the thing itself. We cannot move our world unless there is something outside that world which we believe to be solid and immovable.

Unless we know what ought to be done as well as how to do this or that, we become merely skillful technicians without wisdom—which is precisely what we now are. We do not ride, we are ridden. The machines we have made control us. The ancients had a good motto:

"Quo Urania ducit"—Wherever Wisdom leads. Ours has become instead: "Quo Uranium ducit." That means that we have surrendered our right and our duty as human beings—which is to decide and to choose on the basis of what we are.

As for my thirteen trips into Baja California they were undertaken chiefly as holiday adventures—sometimes easy and luxurious thanks to Kenneth Bechtel's Lodestar and yacht, sometimes rugged enough for an old man; as when, for instance, we drove the eight hundred miles from border to uttermost cape in a four-wheel-drive vehicle, carrying our own water and gasoline and sleeping under the stars. Nine days it took because roads are often so bad that we could seldom average more than ten miles an hour and at times were compelled to proceed much more slowly than that.

It was certainly not as a critic of society that I traveled. I had my eye out primarily for rugged beauty and unfamiliar forms of plant and animal life. Hence the book I wrote puts most of its emphasis upon such things. Nevertheless, one would have to be blind to everything else not to wonder at a "human condition" physically so extraordinarily different from that which prevailed in the land one had just left. No one could call either the few scattered inhabitants of Baja's open country or those who inhabit La Paz, its southern metropolis, "affluent." Here is an economy, not of abundance, but of desperate scarcity, where food and water are hard to come by and manufactured goods so scarce that "use up and make do" are not a philosophy but an inescapable necessity, and most things that cannot serve their original purpose any longer are made to serve some other. No one there is likely to be able to understand what is meant by the necessity for an advertising art to "create needs" or by the dangers of "underconsumption."

That one meets there smiling children and seemingly contented men may seem to prove that theirs is to some degree a good life, but one would have to be a very convinced primitivist to conclude that it is the best life—that these people would not be better off if they had more. Contentment, as it has been occasionally pointed out since the time of Socrates, means "full to a given capacity" and hence a contented pig is not as *happy* as a contented man. However contented the best satisfied average citizen of Baja California may be, his human capacity has not expanded to its limits. He is "deprived" even though he may not know that he is.

Approaching the end of the book it came to seem to me—as it had not when I began—that a fitting conclusion might be some attempt to compare affluence with deprivation and that the affluent society might best be criticized, not as seen by itself, but in violent contrast. And the thing which struck me first when I attempted to do so was that we have come to assume that there is no choice except that between the two extremes; that a civilization must be either an economy of painful scarcity or of ever-increasing abundance up to and beyond superfluity.

Under the system we have created there does, indeed, seem no other choice. Our "prosperity" cannot be stabilized. It depends upon a constant increase without which it falters and begins to decline unless "the pumps are primed." We invent the automobile and then face depression and calamity unless we can somehow dispose of more and more of them. It began as a means of transportation, then became a status symbol, and now—at least so one must assume from the problems discussed by economists—its most essential function is to provide employment for those who make it. Are not the same paradoxes to be found if we examine most of the other "pillars of our economy"? Pondering these and similar questions I found myself wondering whether or not there was indeed no choice except that between the scarcity of primitive simplicity and an ever-increasing complexity and abundance which creates its own problems; which, indeed, creates the suspicion that it cannot go on indefinitely, that some limit must ultimately be reached so that prosperity must collapse because it cannot be increased any further.

Just before I had finished with *The Forgotten Peninsula* it happened that Marcelle and I went to Berkeley, California, where I had accepted a very generous invitation to be for a term in residence at the University as visiting Ford Research Professor—without any specific duties. To my considerable surprise the invitation had come from the Department of Political Science which would give me no explanation except (with a smile of course) that there were a lot of political scientists about and that I would be a change at least—possibly agreeable. Since I am by no means deeply read in sociology, economics, or political science, I posed to several of my *pro tem* colleagues a series of questions. Has any recent writer seriously discussed the possibility that there may be an optimum degree of complexity, technical development, population density, affluence, and abundance; the possibility that in these things there is actually a golden mean? If this possibility has been considered, what conclusions have been drawn? If such an optimum degree could be theoretically defined is it nevertheless impossible for a society which has reached it to remain at, or near, this optimum point?

I drew blanks one after another until one professor replied with a smile that he believed Aristotle was the last person to raise the questions and that I had better consult his *Politics*.

Of course I promptly did so, and if Aristotle did not answer all my questions I found in the *Politics* two simple statements with which most Americans might be persuaded to agree in theory but which few actually believe—if their ambitions and actions are an indication of their belief. One of these statements is that the purpose of a city is to make a Good Life possible; the second that "Most persons think it is necessary for a city to be large, to be happy."

Certainly there are few villages, towns, or cities in the United States, few from New York to the smallest unincorporated community, most of whose inhabitants would not think it shameful to be called anything but "progressive" and who would not wish that their home town should grow. Not everyone, so I have discovered by inquiry, believes that "it is necessary for a city to be large, to be happy" but most of them want theirs to be larger nevertheless, and that, I can only conclude, must mean that they do not accept Aristotle's premise, namely, that the purpose of a city is to make a Good Life possible. What, then, *is* its purpose? Seemingly, just to be big and important and "progressive." Seemingly, in other words, citizens exist for the sake of the city, not the city for the sake of the citizens—just as, so it seems, we have come to assume that industry does not exist for the sake of people but people in order to permit industry to flourish and expand.

Aristotle proposes certain simple criteria for determining what the optimum size of a city was under the conditions which prevailed in ancient Greece. Obviously ours would have to be different. But are no criteria possible?

In my limited reading I have never come across any

attempt to propose criteria of even the most general application. The problems which are created by great size, enormous complexity, and even overabundance are recognized, and methods for extenuating them are discussed. But the assumption seems to be always either that we cannot or that we should not call a halt, that progress which does not see itself as continuing indefinitely along a rising curve must lead to catastrophe. It must be either the City of the Future or Baja—if not something even more "underprivileged" and deprived.

When Carlyle called economics "the dismal science" he did not mean that any consideration of the physical bases of society was necessarily dismal. He meant only that the orthodoxy of his day was dismal because it accepted the theory that a good life was not possible except for a very few and that a system which condemned most to starvation and slavery was best even for them because it alone could protect them from conditions still worse. Shortly after Carlyle's time economics became a relatively cheerful science by insisting that society could produce enough to provide a minimum sufficiency for nearly everybody. But if economics, as seems to be the case, now assumes that we cannot define a Good Life as something more than merely an ever more populous, powerful, rich, and complicated one, then economics has become again a dismal science.

Suppose we did decide that there actually is a point beyond which it is not desirable to go; and suppose we would like to know whether or not we are approaching, perhaps even have passed, it. Could we then in any way "do anything about it"? Or are we so much the victims of "evolving technology" that we can only be carried helplessly along to whatever condition it is preparing for us? But it is hardly worth while even to ask this second question without asking first whether it is possible to formulate a criterion for determining the optimum point.

That would certainly not be easy, especially in terms of detail. But criteria no more precise or less difficult to measure are thought worth proposing in connection with other problems. We have, for instance, already satisfied ourselves that the largest possible number of children per family is not the best number and we have suggested that it be artificially limited. Why should we not consider what seems the analogous contention of Aristotle that cities also may be too populous?

Is it not obvious that the process of mechanization has passed its optimum point when it has ceased to make life more leisurely, less tense, and more comfortable and become instead a burden to maintain—as is proved by the fact that we are more hurried than we were when we could not travel so fast and are nervously, if not physically, more overburdened than before we had so many labor-saving devices? Have we not passed the optimum point when people are urged to go into burdensome debt to buy a new automobile, not because they have need of it, but because if they do not workers will be out of a job and the collapse of the automobile industry will lead to the collapse of the whole economy? And is not this only one example of the way in which we have come to ask first, "What are the needs of industry," "the needs of our economy," even "the needs of science," rather than the needs of human beings? Do we not thus refuse to ask whether industry and science exist for man or whether, as we seem more and more to assume, man exists for them? Isn't the standard of living too high when men are driven to exhaustion trying to raise it still higher? Has not production become too great if consumption has become a problem?

While I was in San Francisco a few months after *The Forgotten Peninsula* was published, I heard an anecdote concerning one of our greatest industrialists and constructors who was invited to give the commencement address at near-by St. Mary's College. He chose as his subject "The City of the Future" which he glowingly described in terms of its communication centers, its rocket ports, and all the other wonders of that science-fiction world which is rapidly becoming a world of fact. When he had finished the Rector arose and began dryly: "Mr. —— has described to you the City of the Future. I would like now to say a few words about The City of God."

I was reminded of this pleasant little incident when I attended the 1961 commencement at the University of New Mexico in order to receive an honorary degree. There I heard the principal address given by a first-class scientist who is also the head of one of the great electronic development companies, which happens to have as one of its principal interests the development of such mysterious devices as those which "store information" and, incidentally, those which can already make rough, usable translations from Russian into English at the rate of (I believe he said) about a thousand words a minute.

The speaker was both highly competent and obviously of great intellectual as well as merely technical gifts. In many respects his attitude and predictions were moderate and he did not, like the speaker at St. Mary's, see the wonders of the future merely in terms of still more freeways, faster planes, and transportation by rockets. Neither did he attribute more than merely mechanical ingenuity to his machines which have "memory" and can translate from the Russian. When I asked later if these so-called "brains" were really analogous (as some say they are) to a human brain or actually no more so than a slide rule is, he said without qualification that they were not at all like a brain, rather more like a collection of slide rules operated semiautomatically. They, he insisted, cannot replace human thinking. Their purpose is to free men from mechanical drudgery or, as Norbert Wiener once said, to make it possible to use human beings for purely human purposes.

Hopeful as these generalities sounded I began to have doubts when he went on to discuss what the benefits would be. The scholar, the scientist, and the lawyer, he said, would no longer be compelled to search for information. All relevant facts would be "stored" in information centers where they would be instantly available. Feed into your machine an appropriately punched card and all you needed to find would be delivered to you almost instantaneously. Therefore every expert would be better informed, decisions could be made more quickly, and everything would move faster. We would be enormously more efficient. But, I kept asking myself, is this what we need *most?* Is the principal defect of our society that things do not happen fast enough, that we are not more efficient in carrying out our tasks?

There are, of course, those who insist again and again that "more facts" and "better communications" would solve our problems. But the store of facts has been enormously increased and communications greatly improved during the decade just past—at least in the ways electronics promise to improve them. Is it more facts more readily available that we need most? Would not a wiser use of them be more helpful? Would the bravest of brave new worlds not be one impossible to describe merely in terms of its more efficient machines? Are we as much better off as we hoped? Would we perhaps be better off if other problems of a different kind had been solved instead? Does not the very success which technology achieves mean that too large a proportion of the energy and brains available is devoted to it? Would it do us as much good to have more facts more readily available to those who make decisions, as it would to have wiser men to make them—even on the basis of what we now know and have available?

The powerful and intelligent visionary to whom I was listening was telling us to expect an ability to do things even greater than the almost terrifying ability we now have. But an increase in this ability would not make us any better able to say which things ought to be done. "Know how" has increased by leaps and bounds; "know why," "know what," "know whether or not," all lag. Some scientists would say they cannot be increased, that they involve demonstrably "meaningless questions" by virtue of the very fact that science cannot answer them. But if that is indeed true then I am tempted to go so far as to say that we might be wise just to call a halt in our search for the power *to do* on a grander and grander scale the things we do not know whether or not we should do at all. The only "ought" we now recognize is that which impels us to do whatever we find that we can do. If we can get to the moon, then we ought to get to the moon. But I, at least, am most interested in the problems which computers cannot solve. And as machines get to be more and more like men, men will, I fear, come to be more and more like machines.

To some no doubt all this will seem only the typical grumbling of the old fogy who probably looked with disfavor on the typewriter and the adding machine. Old fogies shook their heads over the airplane; they thought twenty-five miles per hour in an automobile too fast; and, I suppose, some conservative cave man was sure no good would come of the wheel. By experience I have learned that you cannot criticize anything without having it supposed that you favor some opposite extreme. If you say that automobiles should not be built to go at ninety miles an hour, you are asked scornfully if you want to go back to the horse and buggy, as though nothing between ninety miles an hour and eight were possible.

The first Samuel Butler describes the temperament of a certain contemporary by calling him the kind of man who would go on "Crying 'Fire! Fire!' in the middle of Noah's flood." Such men are very numerous today. It is, indeed, their voices which are most heard and most heeded. In an age already dizzy with speeding up they cry: "Hurry. Hurry. Too slow, too slow." The Golden Mean has been pejoratively rebaptized Middle-of-the-Roadism and few will risk being labeled as proponents of that weak compromise. To me it seems that more of what we already have so much of is at least not what we now need most. It *is* possible to have too much of a good thing. More of some other good things are what we ought to be looking for.

Just glance at the brave new world, not as the satirist Aldous Huxley imagined it, but as its enthusiastic proponents describe it in sincerely enthusiastic terms. A year or two ago such a description was offered almost simultaneously by a writer in one of the "service magazines" addressed to women and by an imposing panel of distinguished scientists. The fundamental similarities between the two are ceetainly not encouraging to those of us who hope to find ultimate happiness in something other than gadgets.

Here is a quotation from an announcement of the magazine article:

Is automation going to fill *your* home with pleasant surprises? Will magic eyes light each room? Will you own a portable piano, cordless electric clocks—and a telephone you can answer without lifting the receiver? Discover how this exciting new development can make your home life *happier*. (These last italics mine.)

The eight distinguished scientists who appeared on a TV program included two Nobel Prizemen and the following are what they promised us: (1) delicious vegetable steaks, (2) mail delivered by satellites, (3) recreational resorts on space platforms, (4) machines which will abolish all physical labor. When all these are available then man will, no doubt, be truly happy.

As I write this I am approaching my sixty-eighth birthday. Does that explain away everything I have said? If it doesn't, if my attitudes are still worth examination, what shall I say of them? Shall I claim that, besides being merely an old man, I am now—as is very fashionable among a large class of intellectuals—"alienated"?

This is a shibboleth or crucial test question of the moment. Every decade, it seems, has one. In the Twenties it was "Are you Liberal?"; in the Thirties, "Are you Socially Conscious?"; in the Forties, "Do you realize that this is One World?" Perhaps the Sixties will invent another but through the Fifties it has been: "Are you Alienated?"

That question I cannot answer even to myself without asking first, "alienated" from what? From the convictions, ambitions, and value judgments of many—perhaps most—of my contemporaries? "Yes." From what are probably the most widely held convictions concerning Man and the assumption that at best he is not quite what I called once before "Minimal." "Yes." But from what I believe man actually is, what human life can be, I am certainly not alienated. And that, I think, sets me apart from at least many of those who call themselves both alienated and existentialist.

Often I wonder if some of these latter are not merely, as I once was, completely "alienated" only because of what some science, much psychology, and most sociology have persuaded them to accept as fact.

Many contemporary poets, critics, and novelists insist that modern man, even when he is not conscious of the fact as a philosophical conviction, is no longer able to identify himself with his country, his age, or, for that matter, with the human race. But that is not to be wondered at if they continue to feel within themselves even dimly that they are indeed human beings and not that parody which the so-called "sciences of man" have tried to make of us.

These are confused and troubled times. Perhaps the world has seldom before been so puzzling and so obviously insecure. But it has in the past been very strikingly both, without—so it seems—producing such an epidemic of all-inclusive alienation. Perhaps what so many now feel alienated from is not man or even every aspect of their society as it is from the picture of both which sociology and psychology offer and which has been increasingly accepted as a true one. If I actually believed that my fellow creatures were nothing but "economic men" subject to pressures, or that they can be adequately described in terms of the "sex satisfactions" they seek, and "the desires for status" by which they are driven, I too would feel completely alienated. If I do not it is because I *am* very much alienated from much contemporary psychology, sociology, and political science. They have attempted to explain me to myself and I reject the explanation.

16

▲
▲▲▲

When Edward Gibbon presented the second volume of his *Decline and Fall* to the Duke of Gloucester, brother to George III, the latter accepted it with the immortal words: "Another damned, thick, square book! Always scribble, scribble, scribble! Eh, Mr. Gibbon?"

This is sufficient to suggest that the upper classes did not always have a high regard for literature even in the Eighteenth Century when it enjoyed a prestige it has never enjoyed since. But that did not prevent a Gibbon from striking such a pose as he did in his autobiography when the time came to describe the completion of his greatest work:

> A sober melancholy was spread over my mind by the idea . . . that whatsoever might be the future fate of my history, the life of the historian must be short and precarious.

Today even the greatest of writers would hesitate to describe his feelings in such portentous terms and a humble one can hardly dare to be dignified at all. Besides, this present writer comes of a long-lived family. I may, like some members of it, reach ninety-nine or even a hundred. I may even write more books. Therefore I do not feel especially grave at the thought of completing this one. An autobiography is not necessarily an obituary.

I look now out of the window across the desert toward the same range of mountains I have seen and admired almost daily during the nine years just past, and I reflect that these nine years have been, in many ways, the pleasantest of my life. I do not, to be sure, think "the best is yet to be" either for me or, in the immediate future, for the fellow citizens of a troubled world. Occasionally, when I learn of some late development of technology and of the use that will be made of it, I am inclined to imitate in reverse Lincoln Steffens' exclamation: "I have been over into the future and it does not work!" But I hope to find things to interest me still and at times even fall into what Bernard Shaw denounced as the most irresponsible of attitudes—that which enables us to say with a complacent sigh, "Oh, well; perhaps it will last out my time."

Since finishing the book on Baja California, I have made two more trips into the region. On one of them we spent six weeks visiting the islands of the Gulf and I plan to go again. But though neither Marcelle nor I have been in Europe since before the Second World War, I am not sure that I shall ever return there. It must have been more worth seeing when we saw it even though there is no doubt a good deal of extravagance in my feeling that it has lost its character to become little more than a tourist center for Americans.

A former student who reviewed one of my recent books

said something about his memory of me in the lecture hall at Columbia and then added that he did not recognize the picture of "a happy farmer" on the dust jacket. Actually I have changed a good deal less than that would suggest, while the Tucson to which I came has changed a great deal more. Ten years ago it was a town rather than a city. Now it is a city in the throes of growth so rapid that new subdivisions are opened almost weekly, and the citizen who goes away for a ten-day vacation is likely to find that three more supermarkets have sprung up during his absence. Those who direct its affairs are not students of Aristotle and they hold it to be a self-evident truth that a city to be happy must not only be large but in the process of getting larger at an ever-increasing rate.

Because I felt a personal obligation to the man who invited me, I talked once at a Rotary Club luncheon on the assigned topic "Tucson as a Place to Write." It was still, I told the audience, a pretty good place. But it was becoming less good day by day. Every time I saw one of the Chamber of Commerce posters which read "Help Tucson Grow," I said to myself, "God forbid." Should they not, I asked, adopt a new motto: "Keep Tucson Small"? Next day the newspaper reported that "most of the audience assumed that Dr. Krutch had his tongue in his cheek." And so, I think, they did.

Only a few months ago the military authorities announced that Tucson had been selected as one of the expendable cities to be ringed with bases of Titan missiles. It was frankly admitted, not only that a direct hit would of course annihilate us all, but also that, due to the prevailing winds, a near miss would blanket us with fallout. A small minority protested that it might be wiser to locate such bases in the still available areas not so dangerously close to any large community. But the protest got nowhere. In great alarm the city fathers begged us to say no more lest the army should, in a huff, decide to confer its blessings elsewhere. Said the mayor: "It will be a fine thing for the community." Said the president of the Chamber of Commerce: "It's something we have been working for—and hoping for—for a long time."

So far as I know the question of patriotism was never raised. No one said, "If some cities have to be expendable, and if Tucson is a logical choice for one of them, then we must, like good soldiers, accept our fate." All the talk was of payrolls and the money that would be spent in our community. In fact, the only sensible remark I heard made during the whole discussion was that of a maverick commentator on the radio. Perhaps, he suggested, the best description of the proposed constructions was this: "A disaster with fringe benefits." And I wonder if that would not fit equally well a number of other triumphs of technology.

Many years ago when Raymond Weaver had gone off on one of his characteristic quests for the esoteric and had taken lessons from Evangeline Adams, then the most sought after astrologer and one consulted by some leading figures in fashion and finance, he cast my horoscope. It guaranteed, so he said, that I would live to a ripe old age but die "a public and spectacular death." I have often wondered just what this portends. Death on the barricades, or perhaps public execution? But could anything be more spectacular than vaporization by a hydrogen bomb? And that has now become a more probable possibility.

Growing cities project their influence (both beneficent and otherwise) into the surrounding countryside, and though there are many open spaces left in Arizona, they are shrinking, and as good roads increase they become more and more resort areas rather than country in which one has the sense of being an explorer. Areas which I first saw at the time of my earliest visits in the Thirties and which were then almost empty as well as accessible only to those willing to make a certain effort are now traversed by paved highways, sometimes disfigured by billboards, and dotted by motels not always innocent of that hideous calamity, the neon sign—a modern ugliness which (it is only a mild consolation to know) was, for once, a French rather than an American invention.

A few years ago I was asked by the editor of the *New York Times* travel section to answer the question, "How much of the Old Southwest glowingly described by Chamber of Commerce pamphlets can a traveler still find?" Quite a good deal, I replied, provided he will take the trouble to look for it off the commonest tourist routes. But if he is planning a visit he had better come soon since the Old Southwest is disappearing rapidly. If, even now, he follows only the routes recommended, he will see cities which look much like those to be found everywhere else in the United States plus the staged "tourist attractions" which are frankly reconstructions for play acting. Disneyland in California is perhaps one of the most significant of recent institutions. Among many other things one may see there, so I am told, a remarkable simulacrum of the Grand Canyon, and the time seems fast approaching when simulacra will be all that is left to remind us of what a vanished world, which some still find interesting, was like. All the plants will be in gardens and greenhouses, all the animals in cages, and all the scenery in stage sets.

Quite recently a sizable minority in the United States has taken a new interest in Conservation and the National Parks. It is also supporting the proposal to create Wilderness Areas which it is hoped may preserve segments of the great continent our ancestors inherited in something near to that pristine condition which is disappearing from the National Parks as more and more "recreational facilities" tend to turn them into what is less a natural area than an amusement park. Here in Tucson a large section of desert and mountain just west of the city is owned in part by the county and in part by the national government. A portion of it has recently been made a National Monument, and just on the edge of the Monument is the Arizona-Sonora Desert Museum of which I have been a trustee since it was first established nine years ago.

Devoted exclusively to the exhibition of living animals and plants of the Sonoran Desert of Arizona and northern Mexico, all either out-of-doors or in simulated natural environments, it has grown enormously during its seven years and drew nearly 200,000 visitors in 1961. I have spent a good deal of time there and various members of the staff, especially the present director, William H. Woodin, and the associate director, Lewis Wayne Walker, have become among my closest friends. Such institutions cannot, of course, furnish even the most observant visitor the equivalent of direct contact with the Southwestern scene and its natural inhabitants. But they supplement such direct contact now and they may be, in the future, all that it is possible to preserve—at least if the population explosion continues. Recently one of those terrifying demographic studies predicted that within a quarter of a century Phoenix and Tucson, now 125 miles apart, will have merged into one continuous community.

Perhaps these last few pages suggest that I am, if not "alienated," at least disgruntled and querulous. But just as the lady in Detroit who had read *The Modern Temper* was astonished to find me looking "less depressed" than she expected, the reader may, I fear, suppose me less happy than I am. I am, I think, rather more satisfied than most with both my past and my present. In much that I disapprove of in contemporary society I have not been compelled to participate very fully, and I have been unusually fortunate in being able to live a good deal of my life as I chose to live it and to be loyal to the values I cherish.

An exasperated reader of my department "If You Don't Mind My Saying So . . ." in *The American Scholar* once wrote to demand that if, as seemed to him unlikely, there were any aspects of America and the Twentieth Century I did approve of, I would let him know what they were.

I was able to say that there were many such things, including even most of the convenient gadgets for which I think we pay too high a price though they are good enough in themselves. I am, for example, inclined to believe that in the long run the human race would have been better off if the airplane (to say nothing of the hydrogen bomb) had not been invented—for the simple reason given in *Rasselas* by the inventor of a flying machine who refuses to give it to the public: "Men should not be able to fly before they have become virtuous." But that did not prevent me from taking advantage of it on some of my explorations in Baja California.

More important to me as an individual is the fact, mentioned just a few paragraphs back, that contemporary America has permitted me an extraordinary amount of freedom to live my own life rather than the life most of my fellow citizens either choose or are compelled to lead.

I am a member of a distant minority. My opinions, tastes, and preoccupations would seem foolish or perverse to the majority, even if it ever took the trouble to inquire what they are. I grow no crops; I produce no goods; I have, indeed, done nothing to increase our prosperity. Even as an entertainer I have never attracted an audience large enough to count for much in a society where the majority is supposed to rule. Judge as that majority judges and I am a parasite who has never done anything for the society which has supported me. Yet it has permitted me to live comfortably by my own modest standards—far more comfortably than those similarly misfitted into other societies of the past or present.

Few of my fellow citizens have spent so large a proportion of their time doing things they chose to do for their own sakes, rather than merely to make a living; and if the financial rewards have not been great as financial rewards are now measured, I have enjoyed a Standard of Living high enough for me, and a margin of leisure around my life far wider than that enjoyed by most of those who earn large incomes. In fact, I have never ceased to be amazed at what society has permitted me to get away with. Why has it not taken me by the scruff of the neck and said, "Root, hog, or die"?

Part of the answer is, I suppose, that a certain careless generosity is characteristic of Americans and part that in our famous economy of abundance the crumbs which fall from the overloaded table are not noticed. No one much minds contributing to the support of a few parasites. Four out of five of the people with whom I came in contact while I was going about my business in New York, or when I go about it now in Tucson, put little, if any, value on the things to which I have devoted my life. Yet few, if any, seem to resent my devoting myself to them. The second Samuel Butler observed that Englishmen contributed to the support of the Vicar because they felt that they were hiring someone to be good for them "vicariously." Many of the men of affairs I meet seem to take much the same attitude toward me. They have no time for literature, philosophy, or the appreciation of nature, but they are glad to have someone else look after these things for them. But most, I think, are just easy going.

This aspect of Twentieth Century America that has proved so helpful to me is, naturally, one of which I approve; and I approve also of something which I take to be a political consequence of the easy-going temperament—namely, what I suppose should be called the "pluralism" embodied in our laws and institutions. I know that many thoughtful people call it "inconsistency" or even "a flagrant illustration of the inner contradictions of capitalism." We cannot, they say, seem to make up our minds whether we believe in free enterprise or a planned economy. We profess to put our faith in majority rule, yet we tolerate a constitution and a supreme court that can frustrate it. If we believe that democratic education is a function of the state, why then, they ask, should we permit the affluent to send their children to private schools and even allow them to contribute to such schools the tax money which might be used by the democratic state to support state schools? And yet, looking back upon my own life, I cannot but conclude that the inner contradictions of capitalism had a good deal to do with making that life possible.

In the cracks and crannies of a rather ramshackle social structure, people like us (if the reader does not mind my use of the plural) manage to find refuge. I don't think our society exactly wants to give the maverick a chance, but as long as that society remains illogical it does so. Life would certainly have been harder for me in either Russia, or, I suspect, in any purely *laissez-faire* society. A muddle presents opportunities of its own. Fulbright awards are fine, but there is always the possibility that the fellow who doesn't quite fit the Fulbright pattern may get a Guggenheim instead. And the artist or scholar has good reason to be glad that the government does not control all the plums.

I am by no means sure that the present muddle (called "a mixed economy") which has proved so favorable to me is not destined to be considerably clarified before long. I suspect that even now young men looking for a crack or a cranny are finding it harder to discover one than it was in my time—unless, that is to say, they find congenial one or another of the now multiplying semibureaucratic jobs in which they carry to the heathen in various underdeveloped countries the gospel of American culture and the American Way of Life.

As of this moment I suffer no nostalgia for the good old days, but should I, like one of my uncles, live to be ninety-nine, I may by then be regretting the good old days of the Fifties and early Sixties.

Am I—have I always been—what is contemptuously called "an escapist"? In 1915 I did not resolve to serve my community but ran away to New York where I thought things were already more congenial with my taste. In 1950 I fled from the city to Arizona for the same reason. And if Progress confers upon Tucson too many more "disasters with fringe benefits" I may abandon it also to the fate it has chosen.

So far as my thinking is concerned it has often been addressed to what seemed to be eternal problems in their contemporary form. I have also spent at least as much time mulling over the thoughts which come down to us as voices from the past—with especial attention to Samuel Johnson and Henry Thoreau, both of whom seem to many eccentric, peripheral, not really relevant. Yet different as they are they have in common the fact that both—the one an optimist and the other fundamentally pessimistic—believed in making the best of things without waiting for Utopia and living as well as they could in this world. That also is, by one definition, "escapism."

I cannot say that I have been continuously as happy as Thoreau said he nearly always was. I cannot say that "I have heard no bad news"; that "I love my fate to the very core and rind"; or that "I was born in the most favorite spot on earth, and just in the nick of time too"—though the "nick of time" part I am more inclined to subscribe to. Should I be asked on my deathbed whether I have made my peace with God, I am not sure that I will be able to answer quite as confidently as he, "I am not aware that we had ever quarrelled," but like Thoreau, I have sought joy and I have sometimes found it. "Rarely, rarely, comest thou, Spirit of Delight!" But when it does come, there is no other human experience equal to it. On the other hand, I have sometimes all but acquiesced in the gloomiest of Johnson's generalizations: "Human life is everywhere a state, in which much is to be endured and little to be enjoyed"; occasionally even in the most chilling of all: "The natural progress of the human mind is not from pleasure to pleasure but from hope to hope."

Though I am not, I hope, indifferent to the fate of my fellows or the future of mankind, I am not primarily what is called today "socially oriented," and I do not believe it always wrong to seek one's own salvation where one can find it. Johnson and Thoreau agreed that, as the latter put it, God did not send me into the world without some spending money, and I am ready to interpret and then defend what many would regard as among Thoreau's most outrageous sayings: "I came into this world, not chiefly to make this a good place to live, but to live in it, be it good or bad."

Had he not included the qualifying phrase "not chiefly," *Walden* itself would be an inconsistency since one of its purposes was certainly to make this a better place to live in. But to me the fact that his pronouncement has a positive as well as a negative side is also very important. Though it announces his intention not to be chiefly a reformer, it announces also his determination to *live in* rather than to denounce as unlivable the world in which he found himself. It is the little stress put upon this second part of a program which alienates me from so many of our contemporary critics of society even when I agree with many of their censures. They complain, whine, and bewail the fact that "conditions" or "the system" has made it impossible for them to enjoy even the palliatives which Johnson admitted to be possible. At best they spend their lives in protest; at worst, like some of the beatniks, they wallow in self-destructive vices while proclaiming the queer conviction that by biting off the nose to spite the face they somehow revenge themselves against society.

In my most recent previous book I had occasion to mention a popular ballad sung for me by a twelve-year-old in a remote village of Baja California. Its many verses added up to this: "I gave you my true love. You rejected it, so now there is nothing for me to do except get drunk." This seems to me to represent in its most primitive (but not very different) form the beatnik "revenge against society." Both are, moreover, merely developments of the Byronic version of romanticism; and they are the end of the road taken when the Eighteenth Century ideal of good sense was exchanged for Sturm and Drang. "Let us cultivate our garden," said Voltaire. "Let us explore our wilderness," said those who sought adventure. And exploring our wilderness is what, for at least a hundred years, we have been most insistently devoting ourselves to.

In my youth I was inclined to side with Nietzsche: "Only he who has chaos within can give birth to a dancing star." Now I sometimes wonder whether dancing stars are what we have managed to generate. Perhaps, after all, "The Gods approve the depth and not the tumult of the soul." Or is this merely what one comes to believe when one has ceased to be young?

In any case I must say this: If I have ever seemed to chime in with those who, though they are fortunate themselves, merely whine that the world they find is not good enough to live in, I much regret the fact. All postponements are potentially dangerous and to postpone life itself is the most stupendous of follies. One can no more live in the future than one can live in some good old day of the past. One must live now or not at all; and not to live at all is the greatest of mistakes. At the very worst one can say with Johnson: "He who sees before him to his third dinner, has a long prospect." I find that kind of courage admirable, and I think it wiser to eat one's three dinners than to refuse them on the ground that the times are out of joint and one's appetite taken away.

I think that life has treated me better than most and for that I am more disposed to be grateful than I am to feel guilty. I have occasionally known joy and few, I suspect, know it more than occasionally. But, as I said on the very first page of these confessions, I have had an interesting life in the special sense that I myself have usually been interested in it. This, I think, is what I have most wanted —certainly more than I wanted wealth, or power, or great position—though I do not scorn the modest popularity my books have achieved. If I do not quite "love my life to the very core and rind," I am even less inclined to bewail it. Neither am I eager to take my leave of a world where there will be, I hope, a good deal to be enjoyed as well as to be endured.

INDEX

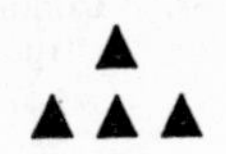